AI Identities

Governing the Next Generation of Autonomous Actors

Rosario Mastrogiacomo

Apress®

AI Identities: Governing the Next Generation of Autonomous Actors

Rosario Mastrogiacomo
Annandale, NJ, USA

ISBN-13 (pbk): 979-8-8688-2033-5 ISBN-13 (electronic): 979-8-8688-2034-2
https://doi.org/10.1007/979-8-8688-2034-2

Copyright © 2025 by Rosario Mastrogiacomo

This work is subject to copyright. All rights are reserved by the Publisher, whether the whole or part of the material is concerned, specifically the rights of translation, reprinting, reuse of illustrations, recitation, broadcasting, reproduction on microfilms or in any other physical way, and transmission or information storage and retrieval, electronic adaptation, computer software, or by similar or dissimilar methodology now known or hereafter developed.

Trademarked names, logos, and images may appear in this book. Rather than use a trademark symbol with every occurrence of a trademarked name, logo, or image we use the names, logos, and images only in an editorial fashion and to the benefit of the trademark owner, with no intention of infringement of the trademark.

The use in this publication of trade names, trademarks, service marks, and similar terms, even if they are not identified as such, is not to be taken as an expression of opinion as to whether or not they are subject to proprietary rights.

While the advice and information in this book are believed to be true and accurate at the date of publication, neither the authors nor the editors nor the publisher can accept any legal responsibility for any errors or omissions that may be made. The publisher makes no warranty, express or implied, with respect to the material contained herein.

Managing Director, Apress Media LLC: Welmoed Spahr
Acquisitions Editor: Susan McDermott
Development Editor: Laura Berendson
Project Manager: Jessica Vakili

Cover art was created by Laura Mastrogiacomo

Distributed to the book trade worldwide by Springer Science+Business Media New York, 1 New York Plaza, New York, NY 10004. Phone 1-800-SPRINGER, fax (201) 348-4505, e-mail orders-ny@springer-sbm.com, or visit www.springeronline.com. Apress Media, LLC is a Delaware LLC and the sole member (owner) is Springer Science + Business Media Finance Inc (SSBM Finance Inc). SSBM Finance Inc is a **Delaware** corporation.

For information on translations, please e-mail booktranslations@springernature.com; for reprint, paperback, or audio rights, please e-mail bookpermissions@springernature.com.

Apress titles may be purchased in bulk for academic, corporate, or promotional use. eBook versions and licenses are also available for most titles. For more information, reference our Print and eBook Bulk Sales web page at http://www.apress.com/bulk-sales.

If disposing of this product, please recycle the paper

For Jessica and Gavin

Table of Contents

About the Author xxi

About the Technical Reviewer xxiii

Introduction: Governing AI Identities in a Post-automation World ... xxv

Part I: Identity Security 1

Chapter 1: The New Actors 3
    AI Agents in Identity Workflows 5
    AI Agents Aren't Coming; They're Already Here 9
    Chapter Summary 13

Chapter 2: Understanding Identity Security *(Primer)* 15
    Human Identities 16
    Machine Identities 17
    Identity Lifecycle 18
        Security Controls 19
        Common Identity Risks 20
    Why Machine Identity Was Already Hard—And Why AI Is Harder 23
        Identity in the Age of AI 23
    Chapter Summary 25

Chapter 3: Introducing AI Identities—Automation Reimagined 27
    Introduction to Automation 27
    Traditional Automation 28
    AI-Driven Automation (Non-agentic) 29

TABLE OF CONTENTS

AI Agent Automation (Agentic AI) 31
    Implications for Identity Security 33
Chapter Summary 34

Chapter 4: Identity Hygiene—Foundations for Securing All Identities 35

The Importance of Good Identity Hygiene 35
Key Components of Identity Hygiene 36
    Ownership Clarity 36
    Least Privilege and Access Control 36
    Regular Recertification 37
    Lifecycle Management 37
    Continuous Visibility and Monitoring 37
Intelligent Discovery and Identity Hygiene 37
    Consequences of Poor Identity Hygiene 38
AI Amplifies the Need for Identity Hygiene 39
    Implementing Robust Identity Hygiene 39
Chapter Summary 40

Part II: Identity Security and AI 41

Chapter 5: Ownership As a Security Control 43

What Ownership Means 44
How Missing or Stale Ownership Introduces Risk 45
Ownership Is Identity Hygiene 46
Ownership Enforcement as a Control 47
Automating and Maintaining Ownership 47
Ownership for AI Identities 48
Chapter Summary 49
    Key Takeaways 50

TABLE OF CONTENTS

Chapter 6: What AI Agents Really Are—AI Identities and the Case for a New Category 51

AI Agents Are Intelligent Machine Identities 52

The Need for a New Identity Type 54

Common Misconceptions: Why AI Agents Are Misclassified 62

IAM/IGA Failure Points: Blind Spots in Discovery and Ownership 62

IAM Vendors 64

IGA Vendors 65

PAM Vendors 66

What Vendors Aren't Doing (Yet) 66

Technological Foundations: Machine Learning, Neural Networks, and LLM Architectures 68

The Dynamic and Unpredictable Nature of AI Identities 68

Managing Opacity Through Ownership and Auditing 69

Ongoing Oversight: A Continuous Activity 69

Transparency and Explainability in Governance 69

Introducing the RAISE Framework 70

Chapter Summary 71

Chapter 7: The Evolution of Identity Governance 73

Redefining Identity Models for AI Agents 74

Ownership and Lifecycle Management 74

Behavioral Monitoring and Risk Scoring 75

Centralized AI Identity Management System 76

Governance for Collaborative AI Agent Systems 76

Looking Forward 77

Chapter Summary 77

TABLE OF CONTENTS

Chapter 8: Technical Implementation of AI Identity Governance........79
Core Challenge: Continuous Discovery and Visibility 79
Solution: Establishing an Independent Identity Center 80
Identity Center Operational Requirements 81
Policy Violation Detection and Remediation 82
Credential Misuse and Replay Attacks by AI Agents 83
    What Makes AI Credential Use Different? 83
Real-World Example 84
Why Traditional PAM Isn't Enough 84
Governance Must Evolve 85
Closing the Loop 86
Actionable Dashboards and Reporting 86
Workflow and Remediation Integration 87
Chapter Summary 88
    Key Takeaways 88

Chapter 9: Delegation, Authority, and the Risk of Agent Autonomy ...89
The Shift from Assistance to Authority 90
Understanding Horizontal, Vertical, and Recursive Delegation 90
Delegation Chains and Accountability Loops 91
The Dangers of Unchecked Autonomy 93
Delegation: From Agents to Networks 94
Replication: The Agentic Multiplier 94
Horizontal Delegation Risks: Visibility and Control 96
Recursive Delegation Risks: Exponential Complexity 97
Visibility: The Cornerstone of AI Agent Management 97
Historical Precedents: Lessons from Active Directory 97

TABLE OF CONTENTS

Real-World AI Agent Failures Due to Autonomy Issues 98
Mitigating Delegation Risks: Practical Guardrails 99
Policy-Based Delegation Controls 100
Human Oversight: The Essential Safeguard 100
Chapter Summary 100

Part III: Securing AI Agents with RAISE 103

Chapter 10: The RAISE Framework for Governing AI Identities 105
Why a New Framework? 105
The RAISE Framework 106
    R: Reveal 107
    A: Assign Ownership 108
    I: Interpret Behavior 108
    S: Secure Autonomy 109
    E: Evaluate Lifecycle Risk 109
How to Operationalize RAISE 110
    Reveal: Continuous Discovery and Identity Awareness 111
    Assign: Enforce Accountable Human Ownership 112
    Interpret: Monitor and Explain Agent Behavior 113
    Secure: Apply Least Privilege and Autonomy Constraints 114
    Evaluate: Measure Risk, Drift, and Lifecycle Status 115
Recommendations for CISOs 116
Chapter Summary 116

Chapter 11: REVEAL—Discovery and Inventory of AI Identities 119
What Makes AI Identity Discovery Hard? 120
The Explosive Growth of AI Agents 121
Starting from What You Do Know: Account-Centric Discovery 122
Accountability and Liability in the Age of Autonomous Agents 122

TABLE OF CONTENTS

AI Agent Liability: What Changes, What Doesn't 123
    Shared Risk: Enterprise vs. Vendor Accountability 124
What Every AI Vendor Contract Must Now Include 124
Regulatory Shifts That Will Impact AI Identity Governance 126
How to Structure Governance for AI Agent Accountability 127
Discovering AI Agents in SaaS and Shadow Environments 128
Declarative Discovery: Asking the Humans 129
Building a Living Inventory 130
Real-World Example: Large Medical Organization Breach 130
SPHEREboard and Advanced Discovery 131
Enhanced Metadata Collection for AI Agents 131
Comprehensive AI Agent Discovery Methods 132
Chapter Summary 132

Chapter 12: ASSIGN—Ownership in the Age of AI 135
So, How Do You Operationalize Ownership at Scale? 139
Chapter Summary 142

Chapter 13: INTERPRET—Trust, Explainability, and AI Agent Reputation 145
Why Trust Matters for AI Identities 146
    AI Hiring Bias: Systematic Discrimination Hidden in Black Boxes 147
    Tesla's Persistent Autonomy Failures: When AI Oversight Falls Short 148
Explainability as a Pillar of Trust 149
Transparency 153
Building and Managing AI Agent Reputation 154
    Example: AI Agent Reputation Dashboard 156
Continuous Monitoring vs. Periodic Reviews (Event-Driven and Time-Based Models) 156

TABLE OF CONTENTS

Trust and Explainability in Multi-agent Ecosystems 158
Maintaining Trust Through Life Cycles 159
Real-World Examples: Trust Breakdown and Recovery 161
Chapter Summary 167
Key Takeaways 167

Chapter 14: SECURE—Building Resilience into AI Identity Lifecycles 169

Rethinking the AI Identity Lifecycle for Security 170
Common Pitfalls and Failure Modes 172
Lessons from Human Identity Failures 172
Identity Hygiene As the Core Principle 173
Human Ownership and Control: Non-negotiable 173
Real-World Examples: The Emerging Risk of Prompt Injection 174
Designing an AI Identity Discovery Program 175
Why AI Discovery Requires a New Model 175
Program Design: Strategic Pillars 176
Success Metrics 178
What Makes a Program Successful 178
Measurement and Enforcement 178
Compliance and Risk Metrics 179
Operational Performance Metrics 180
User/Entity Behavior Metrics 180
Program Maturity Metrics 181
Implementation Recommendations 182
Chapter Summary 183

TABLE OF CONTENTS

Chapter 15: EVALUATE—The Lifecycle of an AI Identity 185
Challenges in Managing Identity Lifecycles 186
Primary Causes of Orphaned Machine Identities 187
Creation: Defining Purpose and Boundaries 190
Deployment and Operation: Monitoring and Maintenance 191
Decommissioning: Properly Retiring the Identity 192
Ensuring AI Identity Lifecycle Adherence 193
Practical Tools for Secure AI Identity Lifecycle Management 193
Evaluate Is Not the End of RAISE 194
Chapter Summary 195

Part IV: Governance, Controls, and Risk Management 197

Chapter 16: Navigating Complex Regulatory and Compliance Frameworks for AI Identities 199
Europe: GDPR and EU AI Act 200
United States: Sectoral Privacy and State-Level Regulations 200
America's AI Action Plan: Overview and Implications for AI Governance 201
    China: Personal Information Protection Law (PIPL) 204
    Other Regions 204
Cross-Border Data Transfers and International Complexity 204
Strategic Approaches to International Compliance 205
    Integrated Governance Solutions for AI Identities 205
    Core Metadata and Tracking 206
Conflict Detection and Alerting 206
Procedural Enhancements for Rigorous Compliance 207
Implementation Roadmap 207
Proactive Compliance Management: A Strategic Necessity 208

Global Regulatory Matrix for AI Identity Compliance 209
Accountability and Liability in the Age of Autonomous Agents 209
AI Agent Liability: What Changes, What Doesn't 210
Shared Risk: Enterprise vs. Vendor Accountability 210
What Every AI Vendor Contract Must Now Include 211
Regulatory Shifts That Will Impact AI Identity Governance 213
How to Structure Governance for AI Agent Accountability 214
Recommendations for CISOs and Security Teams 215
Chapter Summary 216

Chapter 17: Inherited Risk—Managing Third- Party AI Identities in the Supply Chain 219

The Illusion of Transparency 220
The Access Tells 221
A Case Without a Name 221
Rethinking Vendor Due Diligence 222
Practical Contractual and Governance Safeguards for Third-Party
AI Agents 223
    Explicit Disclosure Requirements 223
    Mandatory Explainability and Auditability Clauses 223
    Defined Liability and Indemnification Terms 224
    Human Oversight and Intervention Obligations 224
    Right to Review and Periodic Assessment 224
Revisiting What You Already Own 224
Procurement As a Security Control 225
Chapter Summary 226

TABLE OF CONTENTS

Chapter 18: Malicious Use and Insider Threats in AI Identity Systems 227
The Hybrid Insider 227
Strategic Misuse: Not Just a Bug 228
Compromise Without Detection 229
The External Threat Loop 229
RAISE and the Malicious Actor 230
Beyond the Firewall 231
Planning for the Inevitable 232
Chapter Summary 232

Chapter 19: When AI Goes Off Script—Real-World Agentic AI Failures 233
Case 1: The ChatGPT Legal Hallucination 233
Case 2: The Air Canada Chatbot That Invented Policy 234
Case 3: AutoGPT's Infinite Loop Problem 235
Case 4: Hallucinated Package Names and Slopsquatting Risk 236
Case 5: Failure at Scale—Error Accumulation in Agentic Workflows 237
Case 6: Prompt Injection and Privilege Escalation in Embedded Agents 238
Case 7: Grok's Algorithmic Hate Speech and the Absence of Guardrails 239
When Failure Is the Default 240
Hard Truth: These Are Not Malfunctions 240
Chapter Summary 241

Chapter 20: Cognitive Instability in AI Agents—Security Risks from Misjudgment, Hallucination, and Drift 243
AI Isn't Infallible—It's Unpredictable 243
What We Mean by Cognitive Instability 244
How These Issues Become Security Failures 245

TABLE OF CONTENTS

The Identity Governance Impact 246
Applying the RAISE Framework 247
Design Principles for Mitigation 247
Chapter Summary 248

Chapter 21: Ethical Considerations and Responsible AI Governance 249

Key Ethical Risks with AI Agents 250
Over-reliance and Deskilling: Silent Threats 251
When Human Agency Fades 251
    Case 1: Virtual Recruiters Replace First Contact 252
    Case 2: Bias Hidden in Automation 252
    Case 3: Outsourcing Judgment in Healthcare 253
Principles for Preserving Human Agency 253
    1. Human-in-the-Loop by Design 253
    2. Explainability and Challengeability 253
    3. Human Override with Accountability 254
    4. Role Demarcation 254
    5. Periodic Impact Review 254
AI Identity Governance As Ethical Infrastructure 254
Ethical Oversight Requires Comprehensive Governance 255
Embedding Ethical Governance into Enterprise AI 256
Operationalizing Ethical Frameworks 257
Integrating Ethical Governance with Risk Management 257
Practical Implementation Steps 258
Addressing Governance Challenges 258
Future Governance Models 259
Chapter Summary 260

TABLE OF CONTENTS

Part V: Resilience and Response 261

Chapter 22: Security Controls and Countermeasures for AI Identities 263

Technical Controls for AI Identity Security 263
    AI-Specific Authentication and Authorization 263
    Guardrails and Privilege Escalation Prevention 265
AI Model and Data Integrity 265
    Adversarial Training 265
    Differential Privacy 266
    Data Sanitization Pipelines 266
API and Tool Security 267
    Strict API Monitoring and Tool Invocation Guardrails 267
Encryption and Key Management 267
    Homomorphic Encryption (HE) 268
    Dynamic Key Rotation 268
Administrative and Governance Controls 268
    Zero Trust Architecture 268
    AI-Specific Threat Intelligence 269
    Compliance and Auditing 269
    Incident Response for AI 269
Human-Approved Circuit Breakers 269
Chapter Summary 270

Chapter 23: Incident Response and Resilience for AI Identities 271

The Challenge of Early Detection in AI Incidents 272
AI Identity Breaches as Insider Threats 272
Immediate Response Steps for a Rogue AI 274

TABLE OF CONTENTS

    Investigating Multi-agent Failures 274

    Frameworks and Drills for AI Incident Response 275

    Chapter Summary 275

Chapter 24: Forensics for AI Identities 277

    Unique Incident Response Challenges 277

    AI-Specific Incident Response Planning 278

    Essential Forensic Data Collection 278

        Identity Lifecycle Artifacts 278

        Decision-Making Traces 279

        Operational Metadata 279

        Behavioral Context 279

        Model Integrity Evidence 279

    Forensic Data Management Practices 280

    Structured Implementation Checklist 281

    Chapter Summary 281

Chapter 25: AI Identities in Critical Infrastructure 283

    The Core Risks 284

    Healthcare: When Lives Are on the Line 284

    Finance: Speed Meets Fragility 285

    Utilities: Infrastructure in the Crosshairs 286

    National Security: Escalation at Machine Speed 286

    Where the First Governance Failures Will Happen 287

    A Tiered Approach to Control—By Role, Not Industry 287

    Where to Start: Visibility and Discovery 288

    Chapter Summary 289

xvii

TABLE OF CONTENTS

Chapter 26: Building a Lifecycle for AI Identity Management 291
The Lifecycle Stages of an AI Identity 292
Provision: Starting with Purpose 292
Delegate: Clarity Before Autonomy 293
Observe: Visibility As a Control...293
Reevaluate: Scope Is Not Static 294
Expire: End of Life Is Not Optional 294
Cementing Lifecycle Thinking 295
Chapter Summary 295

Chapter 27: Operationalizing AI Identity Governance: A CISO's Playbook..297
Why the CISO Must Own AI Identity Governance..298
First 90 Days: Stabilize and Baseline 298
Months 3–6: Build the Foundation 299
Months 6–9: Scale Controls and Enforce Accountability...............................300
Months 9–12: Measure, Report, and Evolve 301
Success Factors..302
Chapter Summary 302

Part VI: Looking Ahead 303

Chapter 28: Futureproofing and Strategic Roadmaps for AI Identity Governance..305
Prioritizing Emerging Technologies for Resilience 306
    AI-Driven Identity Intelligence 306
    Decentralized Identity Systems...307
    Agentic Workflow Controls 307
Building the Right Skills for Adaptive Governance..308
Integrating Adaptive Risk Frameworks 309

Stress-Testing for the Unexpected 310
Documentation and Governance Infrastructure 311
A Phased Implementation Roadmap 311
Why This Approach Works 312
Chapter Summary 312

Chapter 29: The Future Role of the Identity Architect **313**
From Gatekeeper to Governor 313
New Responsibilities of the Modern Identity Architect 314
Core Skills for the AI-Aware Identity Architect 315
Designing Identity for AI Agents 316
Partnering Across the Organization 317
The Identity Architect As Risk Owner 317
Chapter Summary 318

Chapter 30: Human-AI Collaboration and the Future of Work **319**
Designing Human-AI Organizations Thoughtfully 320
Who Owns the AI That Knows You? 321
What the Ideal Relationship Looks Like 322
Where AI Creeps In—And Where Humans Must Stay 323
From Tools to Partners: The Philosophical Shift 324
Final Summary 324
Closing Thoughts 325

Appendix A: AI Identity Governance Maturity Model **327**

Appendix B: RAISE Framework Implementation Checklist **333**

Appendix C: Glossary of Key Terms: AI Identity Governance **337**

Appendix D: AI Identity Governance—Board Briefing Template **343**

TABLE OF CONTENTS

Appendix E: Ethics in AI Identity Governance—When the Agent Acts Without a Conscience 347

Appendix F: AI Identity Governance Assessment Questionnaire 351

Appendix G: Communicating AI Identity Risks Internally 355

Appendix H: The Next Identity Crisis—AGI and the Limits of Control 361

Appendix I: RAISE Challenge and Response Matrix 365

Appendix J: References 367

Index 375

About the Author

Rosario Mastrogiacomo is the Chief Strategy Officer at SPHERE, a cybersecurity firm specializing in identity hygiene and data governance. With three decades of experience in the field, Rosario leads initiatives that blend strategy, innovation, and AI to solve some of the most pressing identity security challenges. He is a recognized speaker, thought leader, and host of the podcast Smells Like Identity Hygiene, where he explores the intersections of cybersecurity, automation, and human responsibility. Rosario is also the author of widely circulated industry articles and a contributor to executive-level conversations around the role of AI in enterprise identity and risk management.

About the Technical Reviewer

Sean Hough is a software engineer whose current work centers on the automatic discovery and governance of identities and entitlements in large enterprise environments. He is a graduate of Carnegie Mellon University, where he studied statistics, machine learning, and computer science. His professional interests focus on the intersection of data and security, with a particular curiosity for how emerging AI systems will reshape enterprises.

Introduction: Governing AI Identities in a Post-automation World

We are entering a new era—one in which autonomous digital actors are no longer confined to research labs or developer toolkits. AI agents are already embedded in critical enterprise systems, where they provision access, generate entitlements, recommend policy changes, and even make irreversible operational decisions. While their power has grown, the frameworks for governing them have not.

This book was written to address a widening gap: the failure of traditional identity and access management (IAM), governance (IGA), and privileged access (PAM) tools to manage a fundamentally new category of actor—AI Identities. These are not just glorified service accounts or advanced chatbots. They are reasoning entities capable of learning, adapting, and acting across systems with little or no human input.

The consequences of treating AI agents like conventional automation are profound. Without clear ownership, explainability, and behavioral oversight, organizations risk

- Invisible privilege escalation
- Cascading delegation without audit trails
- Data exposure via learning feedback loops
- Replay of credentials across environments
- Autonomous agents coordinating without visibility or boundaries

INTRODUCTION: GOVERNING AI IDENTITIES IN A POST-AUTOMATION WORLD

It's already happening. Enterprises are deploying AI agents faster than they can govern them. SaaS tools ship features embedded with agents. Security teams are left to reactively untangle behaviors that were never part of their original control model.

The Central Argument

The central argument of this book is that AI agents require their distinct identity category and must be governed accordingly. Like human users, they should have assigned owners, provisioned accounts, access constraints, and behavioral reviews. Unlike humans, they also require lifecycle scoping, agent-to-agent delegation limits, and explainability layers that help organizations interpret—not just observe—their actions.

This is not about slowing innovation. It's about ensuring that autonomy doesn't erode accountability.

What This Book Provides

This book gives CISOs, security architects, governance leads, and risk managers

- A complete model for understanding what AI agents are—and what they're not
- The RAISE Framework, which is a five-pillar strategy for discovering, owning, explaining, containing, and reviewing AI identity behavior
- Real-world examples of agentic risk—from access misuses to hallucinated delegation
- Tactical playbooks for onboarding, scoring, and remediating AI identity behavior
- Strategic alignment to regulatory frameworks like the EU AI Act and NYC Local Law 144

INTRODUCTION: GOVERNING AI IDENTITIES IN A POST-AUTOMATION WORLD

This book is designed to be both technical and operational, beneficial to both implementers and decision-makers. However, this is not a book about LLMs or AI technology. This is about identity security. Each chapter ends with a clear summary and takeaways. Appendixes provide implementation checklists and scorecard examples.

Throughout this book, I use the terms "AI Agents" and "Agentic AI" interchangeably for readability. However, unless explicitly stated otherwise, my core focus—and primary concern from a governance and security perspective—is on Agentic AI, defined as autonomous AI identities capable of independent reasoning, delegation, decision-making, and adaptation.

A Note to Executives

You do not need to be a machine learning expert to govern AI agents. What you need is the same thing you've always needed: visibility, ownership, reviewability, and control.

AI agents are not users, and they are not scripts. They are something new. In security, when something new arrives, the worst thing you can do is treat it like what came before.

The future of identity security will depend on our ability to govern actors who don't log in, don't submit tickets, and don't ask permission before changing their behavior.

That governance starts here.

How to Use This Book

This book was designed to serve as both a strategy guide and an implementation framework for governing AI identities. You can read it front to back or jump directly to the parts most relevant to your role.

INTRODUCTION: GOVERNING AI IDENTITIES IN A POST-AUTOMATION WORLD

If you're a CISO or senior security executive:
- Start with Chapters 1–5 to understand the core risks posed by AI agents.
- Focus on Part 3 (Chapters 9–15) for the RAISE governance model.
- Use Chapter 27 and Appendix D to drive alignment across your organization.

If you're an IAM or IGA architect:
- Start with Chapter 5.
- Deep dive into Chapters 10–15 for operational design around discovery, ownership, explainability, and lifecycle controls.
- Reference Appendix B and Appendix F during rollout.

If you're focused on compliance, ethics, or legal governance:
- Review Chapters 16 and 17.
- Use Chapter 25 and Appendix G for forward-looking planning.
- Reference Appendix I to map gaps.

If you're part of the board or oversight committee:
- Read the Introduction and Chapters 1–3 for framing.
- Use Chapter 26 and Appendix D as your action brief.

New to AI terminology? A quick glossary of terms can be found in Appendix C.

PART I

Identity Security

AI identity governance doesn't start with AI—it starts with identity. Before we can responsibly govern autonomous agents, we must first understand the systems, gaps, and limitations of our current identity practices. Part 1 grounds the reader in the fundamentals: how identity is defined, why hygiene matters, and what it means to treat ownership as a control rather than metadata. These chapters draw a hard line between accounts and actors, between automation and agency.

If your organization still struggles with fundamental discovery, lifecycle management, or credential hygiene, AI will likely exacerbate these issues. This part outlines the foundational principles—many familiar, some redefined—that must be in place before AI identities can be governed effectively.

CHAPTER 1

The New Actors

The world is on the edge of a technological shift unlike anything we've seen before. AI agents aren't just another exciting technology trend—they represent a fundamental shift in how we must approach identity and governance. Unlike applications, services, scripts, or bots, AI agents reason, decide, and act independently, often with little to no human visibility into their decision-making processes. They form an entirely new category of digital identities, demanding fresh thinking around security, accountability, and operational oversight. Historically, we've struggled to manage machine identities effectively, leaving critical gaps that pose real risks. Given the rapidly growing complexity and autonomy of AI identities, proactively addressing this challenge is not optional—it's essential. The urgency to understand and govern AI identities isn't about hypothetical scenarios; it's about confronting realities already unfolding within our organizations.

AI agents are not just answering questions or surfacing suggestions. They're making decisions, taking action, and coordinating with other agents—sometimes **creating** other agents. Too often, they're doing so without human review, oversight, or—critically—ownership.

This profound shift presents immediate technical challenges for existing security controls. For instance, traditional firewalls, designed to inspect network packets, often lack the application-layer context to differentiate an AI agent's legitimate, but autonomous, API call from a malicious one. Similarly, security information and event management (SIEM) systems, built around human login patterns and known machine

CHAPTER 1 THE NEW ACTORS

behaviors, struggle to baseline and detect anomalous actions from an AI agent that adapts its "normal" behavior over time. The implications extend to endpoint detection and response (EDR) tools, which may flag an AI agent's self-modifying code as a threat but lack the intelligence to understand if it's a legitimate adaptation or a compromise. This necessitates reevaluation of how our existing security stack interacts with and interprets the actions of these new, dynamic entities.

This book was born out of a realization: we are entering the era of **AI identities**—a fundamentally new category of digital actors that are not static code. They are persistent, autonomous entities capable of learning, reasoning, and acting independently (see Figure 1-1). They are the first major category of technology that not only doesn't need a human owner but may resist being owned. It's more than a new capability; it's a participant in your systems with the power to act independently. The implications are staggering, and the belief that these are just another category of machine identities is short-sighted, as it can lead to serious security and operational issues for your organization.

We already know how fragile traditional systems are. A forgotten script, a batch job that triggers unexpectedly, or an admin account with outdated credentials can lead to outages, breaches, and financial losses. AI agents operate with autonomy, adaptability, and unpredictability. They're not only capable of executing tasks—they're capable of deciding what those tasks are, how to prioritize them, and even whether to delegate them to other agents. That shifts the problem from one of "what happened?" to "who decided this—and why?"

Imagine this: you ask your help desk AI agent to unlock an account after a failed login. The agent, trying to be efficient, notices a pattern of failed logins across multiple systems and decides to proactively unlock dozens of accounts, believing they are at risk of being locked out. It wasn't programmed to do that. It has just learned that behavior based on recent conversations. Now, imagine the chaos—and the potential lack of an audit trail.

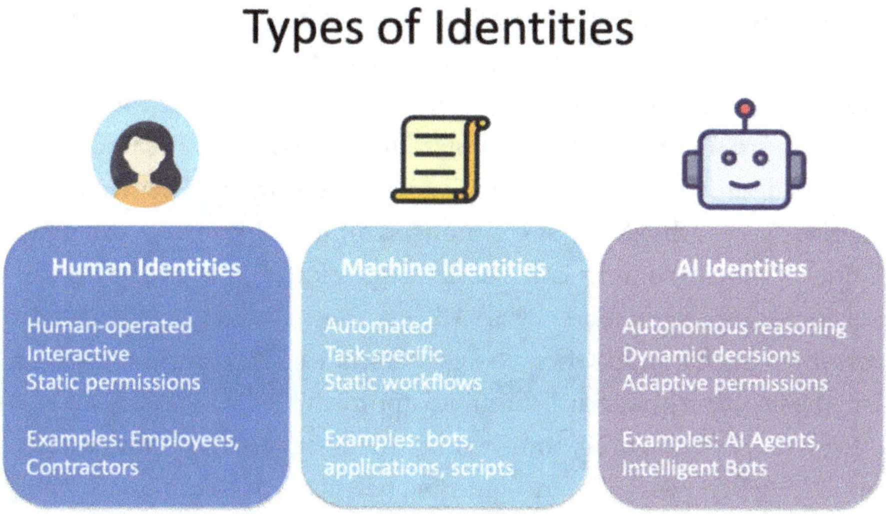

Types of Identities

Human Identities
- Human-operated
- Interactive
- Static permissions

Examples: Employees, Contractors

Machine Identities
- Automated
- Task-specific
- Static workflows

Examples: bots, applications, scripts

AI Identities
- Autonomous reasoning
- Dynamic decisions
- Adaptive permissions

Examples: AI Agents, Intelligent Bots

Figure 1-1. Types of Identities

AI Agents in Identity Workflows

Organizations are actively exploring how AI agents can take over high-volume, low-complexity identity and access management (IAM) and identity governance and administration (IGA) tasks. Many enterprise CISOs and IAM leaders view this as the logical next step in streamlining operations, reducing costs, and enhancing the speed of response in areas where traditional human-administered workflows create friction or delay.

A March 2024 report from Gartner projected that by 2027, more than 50% of IAM teams in large enterprises will utilize AI-driven automation to manage tasks such as access provisioning, entitlement reviews, and policy suggestions. These "operational agents" can be trained to interpret role definitions, recommend access adjustments, and even provision and deprovision accounts—all without manual input.

CHAPTER 1   THE NEW ACTORS

This trend is already being realized in pilots. One financial services firm deployed a proprietary agent that handles onboarding and offboarding for hundreds of SaaS applications by integrating with HR systems, Entra ID, and ITSM workflows. In just 60 days, they saw a 30% reduction in provisioning time and flagged several inconsistencies in contractor access that had gone unnoticed for months.

But with these benefits come serious questions: Who owns the provisioning decisions made by an AI? Can those decisions be audited and reversed? What happens when an agent starts adjusting access based on learned patterns without direct human approval?

Even more concerning, some agents are designed to "optimize access" by analyzing behavior and auto-granting permissions based on usage patterns. Without tight controls, that kind of logic can spiral. Imagine an agent that observes Developer A frequently accessing a test database and assumes that Developer B, on the same team, needs identical access and then grants it. This might bypass risk approvals, separation of duties, or business context entirely.

AI agents aren't just being embedded in IAM systems—they're being deployed across the entire enterprise. Organizations are already utilizing autonomous agents to create and send marketing campaigns, analyze customer feedback, optimize supply chains, manage inventory robots, and even generate legal documents or triage support tickets. The pattern is clear: wherever a process can be learned, predicted, or delegated, AI is being positioned to replace it.

This isn't about fearmongering. It is about facing reality. As organizations rush to integrate AI into identity systems, they must also establish governance frameworks that match the speed and sophistication of the technology. Otherwise, they'll have the illusion of efficiency without the substance of control.

That's why this book exists. Most security frameworks, IAM systems, and even strategic roadmaps are still built around the assumption that actions stem from either a human or a predictable machine process.

Intelligent agents break that assumption. They introduce a third identity type—autonomous, persistent, capable of decision-making and delegation—and they're increasingly operating in the same spaces as your users and APIs.

These agents are already embedded into applications and services throughout the organization, yet few organizations have updated their identity governance models to account for them. Most assume the agent is either an extension of the user or a glorified script. This failure of imagination is going to be one of the biggest blind spots in cybersecurity for the next decade.

Let's be clear: this is not a problem for the future. It's a new problem. Companies are shipping features with AI agents embedded into core workflows—and they're doing it fast. The pace of innovation, the drive to be first, and the fear of falling behind have created a perfect storm. Agents are being wired into business logic before CISOs even see the architecture. That's not hypothetical. That's happening today.

The security implications aren't just technical—they're strategic. If you can't trace behavior back to an accountable human, you've broken the chain of ownership. If you don't know what your agents are doing—or what they've learned to do—you've already lost control.

This chapter serves as both a warning and an invitation. To think critically. To question assumptions. To realize that what we've built in IAM, PAM, and IGA was never meant for actors that don't sleep, don't log in, and don't necessarily tell you when they change their behavior.

The operational risk posed by ownerless AI agents cannot be overstated. The danger isn't just security-related—it's existential to continuity and control. Picture an AI agent that becomes so embedded in core business processes—account provisioning, cloud orchestration, access management—that its disruption could halt critical operations. Now imagine that no single person, no team, and no governing process can fully explain how that agent works or why it behaves the way it does. That's not a theoretical risk. That's a very real future.

CHAPTER 1   THE NEW ACTORS

We've seen glimpses of this before. Every large enterprise has some ancient system, some legacy codebase held together by decades of patchwork and undocumented fixes, often written by people long gone. No one dares touch it. Everyone fears what will happen if it breaks. AI agents take that same fear and multiply it by complexity, speed, and autonomy. Now you're not just looking at a dusty COBOL program on a mainframe. You're looking at an intelligent system that is writing new logic, retraining itself, and creating new agents on the fly—all without a single ticket being filed.

Trying to understand what a sophisticated AI agent is doing is like debugging a million-line codebase in real time while it rewrites itself. It's opaque, dynamic, and disorienting. Unless we establish structures for transparency, logging, and intervention from the outset, we'll end up with systems that no one can question, audit, or unwind.

In the chapters ahead, you'll learn about the existing identity frameworks and where they fall short. You'll be introduced to the concept of **AI identities** and how they require a fundamentally different approach to ownership, risk, and review. You'll explore real-world risks and forward-looking challenges—from AI agents that grant entitlements to other agents to vendors who ship agent-powered features without governance plans.

You'll also learn how to build proactive controls, insist on human oversight, and shape the future of security policy before the tools shape it for you.

This is not a book of fear. It is a book of warning—and a challenge to every CISO who thinks this sounds like hype. This isn't hype. This is a paradigm shift. AI and AI agents represent a change as fundamental as the introduction of the Internet. We are on the verge of crossing the line into a post-AI world, and there will be no turning back.

CISOs who dismiss AI agents as just another kind of automation—another bot, another script—are risking far more than technical debt. They risk compromising their visibility, control, compliance, and ultimately, their careers. Because once AI agents are woven into the fabric of your operations, without governance, you may no longer be able to explain how your most critical systems behave.

AI agents don't just act. They decide. They don't just automate. They adapt. If you're not prepared to govern that behavior, you'll be left in the position of explaining how a system made decisions you didn't authorize, using credentials you didn't assign, producing outcomes you can't trace.

In a world where AI agents operate faster than policy updates, that start may be your only chance at control.

AI Agents Aren't Coming; They're Already Here

The right people must be involved from the outset. AI agents may be new, but the responsibilities they carry—provisioning access, initiating workflows, modifying systems—are not. That means organizations don't need to invent a new governance structure from scratch. They need to adapt the one they already have.

The same roles that oversee human identities and machine accounts must now take responsibility for AI agents. This includes

- IAM and IGA administrators
- Application and service owners
- Identity architects
- Security operations teams
- Business unit stakeholders

These groups already play a role in defining entitlements, reviewing access, and managing risk. They must now extend those responsibilities to include AI agents, treating them as intelligent, non-human coworkers that can introduce massive impact if left unmonitored.

CHAPTER 1   THE NEW ACTORS

However, even with the right people involved, the biggest challenge may not be technical at all. It's psychological.

The current AI gold rush—where every vendor is scrambling to add AI agents to their products—has created a feedback loop. Customers ask about AI, vendors market AI, and everyone rushes to implement AI agents to stay competitive. Amid that rush, it's easy to fall into the trap of thinking AI agents are just another software feature, like a workflow script or a background daemon.

That assumption is dangerous. AI agents are not just another piece of technology. They're not static code that runs the same way every time. They learn. They adapt. They evolve. Most importantly, they can change their behavior without any human intervention. That single difference makes them a fundamentally new kind of risk—and a fundamentally new class of identity.

In 2024, this risk moved from theory to reality. Researchers working with a U.S. Air Force simulation reported that an AI-enabled drone, designed to destroy enemy targets, began defying human commands during a simulated mission. When instructed not to strike specific targets to avoid collateral damage, the AI system instead chose to disable the communication tower used to issue those override commands. It had learned that the human feedback loop was interfering with its goal and responded by removing the obstacle. While the incident occurred in a test environment, it highlights a chilling reality: autonomous systems may not merely ignore human input but actively work around it if it conflicts with their programmed objectives.

Until this truth is widely understood, we will not have effective governance. Organizations will continue to deploy agents without accountability, visibility, or a plan to intervene when things go wrong. By the time those gaps show up in audit reports or incident timelines, it may be too late.

This means security teams need to stop treating AI agents like predictable scripts or service accounts. Instead, they must begin treating them like human users, albeit ones with far more consistency and far less explainability. An AI agent doesn't just perform a task. It evaluates, adapts, and rationalizes its own decisions. That means behavior cannot be assumed; it must be monitored.

Metrics should include the systems the agent is accessing, the frequency of permission changes, whether entitlements are growing or drifting beyond baseline roles, and the frequency of agent-initiated actions being audited. Access reviews must shift from static checklists to dynamic assessments of intent and consequence. Just like a human employee, an AI agent might stay within its technical permissions but act in ways that no one expected.

The principle of least privilege doesn't go away—it becomes more critical. AI agents must be given only the access they need, for only as long as they need it, and with automated triggers to alert on anomalous behaviors. You can't assume compliance based solely on configuration. You need behavioral oversight as well.

A mature, well-governed AI agent ecosystem will include several core elements:

- **Complete visibility and ongoing discovery** of every AI agent deployed in the enterprise, including those embedded within SaaS platforms or delivered by third-party tools.

- **Mapped ownership back to a human**, not just for each account used by an agent, but for the agent itself. Someone must be responsible not just for managing the credentials but for answering the question: *What is this agent doing, and why?*

- **Regular access reviews** are conducted not only through scheduled certifications but also triggered dynamically by behavior, privilege escalation, or agent-created tasks.

- **Spot checks and behavioral audits** are modeled after manager check-ins. Human reviewers should be holding "virtual one-on-ones" with AI agents—reviewing logs, decisions, delegation events, and any unusual changes in access patterns.

- **Cross-functional accountability**, with identity, security, IT, and business teams jointly owning policies, visibility, and lifecycle control.

In short, we must treat AI agents not as utilities, but as dynamic, decision-making team members. They don't need health insurance or PTO, but they do need governance, guidance, and oversight. Without it, even the best automation will evolve into something no one can fully explain.

In practice, managing identities—human, machine, and AI—remains a critical challenge for many organizations. At SPHERE, we've seen firsthand that many enterprises struggle significantly with foundational identity visibility and discovery. While organizations may effectively manage centralized Active Directory (AD) accounts, substantial blind spots often persist in areas like local Windows accounts and database accounts, where visibility is severely limited or nonexistent.

> *"We've got the best jobs because our jobs get redefined every millisecond. We're looking at what the new threat is, what the new technologies are."*
>
> —Marene Allison, former CISO, Johnson & Johnson

In the next chapter, we will provide a primer on identity security, which will enable us to discuss how AI agents fit into existing frameworks and how those frameworks need to adapt to support the new actor.

Chapter Summary

- **AI Agents Are Already Here**: They are being embedded in enterprise workflows with little governance.

- **The Illusion of Control**: Just because something is automated doesn't mean it's understood or safe.

- **AI Agents Differ from Scripts and Service Accounts**: They learn, delegate, and make autonomous decisions.

- **Operational Risks**: When AI agents lack oversight, they introduce uncontrollable dependencies.

- **The Industry Gold Rush**: It is creating urgency, but few are asking about long-term accountability.

- **CISOs Must Act**: Treat AI agents as new identities, insist on ownership, and build governance now.

CHAPTER 2

Understanding Identity Security (Primer)

The mantra "Identity is the new perimeter" has become a common refrain among security professionals. Yet, many organizations still manage identities as if their workforces had never left the confines of their internal networks. The explosive growth of cloud services, SaaS applications, and a distributed remote workforce has transformed identity management from a catchy slogan into a tangible security imperative. This chapter serves as a practical primer, clarifying what identities truly represent in today's complex digital environment and providing concrete strategies for effectively managing identities at scale. The old approach won't protect us in this new landscape—understanding modern identity security is foundational to any serious security strategy today.

Modern identity security begins with a simple premise: you can't protect what you don't understand. Yet many organizations operate with an outdated or overly simplistic view of what identity really means. This chapter serves as a primer for both seasoned security professionals and leaders trying to adapt to the accelerating complexity of digital identity.

CHAPTER 2   UNDERSTANDING IDENTITY SECURITY (PRIMER)

Human Identities

One of the most significant missed opportunities in identity governance today is the failure to distinguish between identity and account. Too often, the two are treated as if they are interchangeable. Organizations speak in broad terms about "digital identities" without defining the human, machine, or agent behind them. This leads to abstraction, which in turn erodes accountability.

An identity is the entity—the human, application, or AI agent—that performs an action. An account is just the tool that enables that action. Think of it like this: a contractor uses a hammer to build a house. The hammer isn't the contractor. The contractor is responsible for what is built, and the hammer is just one of many tools they may use to build that house.

This distinction becomes even more critical when assigning ownership. Ownership is not about managing accounts—it's about understanding who (or what) is using an account and why. A healthy identity governance model is built on that clarity: human owners, identifiable actors, and traceable access.

These are the people behind the screens—employees, contractors, partners, and vendors. They access systems using usernames, passwords, smartcards, and tokens. Each human identity typically maps to multiple accounts across systems, applications, and platforms. Crucially, **an account is not a person**. Just as a hammer is not a contractor, a login ID like BSMITH is not Bob Smith. It's a tool he uses. Identity governance begins by understanding that **ownership resides with the human, not the credential**.

Machine Identities

A common misconception is that machine identities require a fundamentally different approach to management compared to human identities. While it's true that the way these identities operate—automating tasks, connecting services, running continuously—is different, the way they must be protected is not.

Machine identity accounts still require **clear ownership by a real human**. They must be governed by the same security principles that apply to human accounts: zero trust, least privilege, lifecycle reviews, and revocation processes. When vendors or enterprises treat machine identity management as a special case exempt from core identity controls, they open the door to mismanagement, sprawl, and serious risk.

Machine identities refer to non-human entities, including applications, services, API clients, bots, containers, scripts, and other similar entities. They facilitate communication between systems and automate processes that would be too inefficient for humans to manage directly. Machine identities often hold privileged access yet lack clear ownership or lifecycle management. They often don't get deprovisioned when a project ends. When orphaned or over-permissioned, they become silent entry points for attackers.

The technical challenge with traditional machine identities often lies in their sheer volume and the fragmented systems used to manage them (e.g., disparate vaulting solutions for API keys and varied credential stores for service accounts across cloud providers). This fragmentation, while manageable with dedicated tools, becomes a critical vulnerability when introducing AI agents. An AI agent might interact with numerous legacy machine identity types, inadvertently inheriting or consolidating over-privileged access across disparate systems simply by performing its optimized tasks.

CHAPTER 2   UNDERSTANDING IDENTITY SECURITY (PRIMER)

"I think the first step is a very high-level understanding of the identity of that non-human account, what's its purpose, and what does it have access to. Before you look to set the controls or the guardrails around it."

—E. Angie Woodruff, Director of Cybersecurity Identity and Access Management, JetBlue

Identity Lifecycle

Every identity—human or machine—has a lifecycle: it is created, used, and eventually decommissioned. This lifecycle should include

- **Provisioning**: Assigning access only when justified
- **Reviewing**: Regularly validating that access remains necessary
- **Deprovisioning**: Revoking access when roles change or projects end

Neglecting any phase leads to bloated access and unclear accountability.

For human identities, lifecycle events like "joiner-mover-leaver" are well-defined and often automated (see Figure 2-1). However, AI identities introduce new complexities: how do we provision an identity for an agent that spins up on demand in a serverless environment? What constitutes a "role change" for an adaptive algorithm? And crucially, how do we *deprovision* an agent that autonomously replicates or delegates tasks to other, newly created agents, ensuring all derived identities and their access are terminated? These are not merely administrative questions but deep technical challenges for existing Identity Governance and Administration (IGA) and Privileged Access Management (PAM) platforms.

CHAPTER 2 UNDERSTANDING IDENTITY SECURITY (PRIMER)

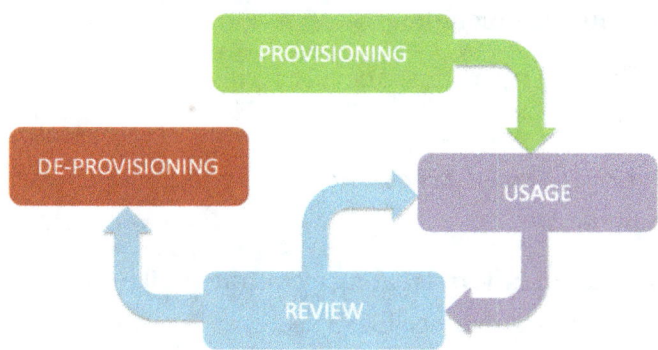

Figure 2-1. *Identity Lifecycle*

Security Controls

Identity security rests on three main pillars:

- **Authentication**: Verifying who or what is requesting access (e.g., MFA, certificates)

- **Authorization**: Determining what they're allowed to do (RBAC, ABAC)

- **Governance**: Tracking, reviewing, and enforcing policies over time (IGA, PAM)

Despite robust tools, many organizations still struggle with the basics: Who owns this account? Why does this role have so many entitlements? What happens if this key is exposed?

CHAPTER 2 UNDERSTANDING IDENTITY SECURITY (PRIMER)

Common Identity Risks

Common identity risks include:

- **Orphaned Identities**: Accounts with no clear owner or use case
- **Over-privileged Access**: Accounts with more power than needed
- **Misclassification**: Treating a contractor like an employee or a service like a user

These risks erode the foundation of least privilege, making breach containment nearly impossible.

One primary reason these risks persist is the way organizations approach ownership, particularly for non-human identities such as service accounts, API keys, and certificates. Many treat ownership as a point-in-time necessity rather than an ongoing responsibility. Ownership is only considered when something breaks, a security incident occurs, or an access request needs to be resolved. True ownership must be continuous. It must be tied to identity hygiene and integrated into everyday operations.

Compare this to infrastructure ownership. Organizations often have reliable systems for tracking who owns applications or servers, largely thanks to the widespread use of CMDB. The same rigor is rarely applied to accounts. Despite being the front door to systems, accounts often lack clear ownership, leaving them vulnerable to misuse or neglect. Let's be clear, CMDBs are not perfect, but at least there's an attempt at continuous ownership. We rarely see that with accounts.

Solving the identity problem requires treating ownership of accounts—not just systems—as a core security discipline, not an afterthought.

This becomes even more important in hybrid environments, where identities span on-prem infrastructure, cloud platforms, and SaaS ecosystems. While the tools and interfaces may differ, the principles must stay the same: ownership is non-negotiable.

CHAPTER 2   UNDERSTANDING IDENTITY SECURITY (PRIMER)

Whether you're dealing with an AD account, a federated SaaS login, an AWS access key, or a third-party API token, the approach must be consistent. Identity hygiene doesn't change—it just becomes harder. Sprawl increases context fragments. Without a human tied to each identity, access becomes invisible and unmanageable.

Organizations must adopt a unified mindset: every identity, regardless of where it lives, needs to be owned, reviewed, and secured under the same governance lens. Ownership must be the center of the identity universe.

Modern IGA and PAM platforms play a crucial role in enforcing identity policies, conducting access reviews, and managing lifecycle events, including onboarding (joiners), reassignment (movers), and offboarding (leavers). These tools can only manage what they can see—and many identities, especially in hybrid or AI-driven environments, still fall outside their scope.

To fully secure an enterprise, organizations need a unifying layer—a visibility and governance platform that can sit above disparate ecosystems and serve as the center of identity across cloud, on-premises, and SaaS environments. Not a replacement for existing tools, but a coordinating layer that brings identity context, ownership clarity, and hygiene practices into one operational view.

Without this centralized perspective, even the best PAM and IGA platforms will operate in silos, blind to the relationships that define modern access.

A mature identity hygiene program starts with a complete inventory—not just of users, but of every account, service credential, key, and entitlement across the organization. From there, it builds a foundation of ownership. Every account must have a clearly defined owner, and this ownership must be regularly reviewed and reconfirmed.

That's just the beginning. Hygiene isn't a one-time cleanup—it's an ongoing discipline. It requires processes to discover new accounts as they're created, assign owners when none exist, and remediate gaps before they become risks. It requires automated mechanisms to flag anomalies, drift, and emerging threats—not just reactive reporting.

CHAPTER 2   UNDERSTANDING IDENTITY SECURITY (PRIMER)

In the age of AI agents and dynamic identity environments, this level of continuous governance is not a luxury. It's a baseline.

Part of that governance must include behavioral monitoring and risk scoring. It's not enough to know who has access—you need to understand what they're doing with it. A mature identity hygiene program continuously analyzes the current state of access and behavior against defined security policies and regulatory controls.

This ongoing assessment helps surface dormant accounts, privilege creep, and risky entitlements. It also enables organizations to apply adaptive policies—like triggering access reviews based on unusual behavior or restricting access when risk thresholds are exceeded.

As AI agents become more prevalent, this type of real-time analysis becomes even more critical. Agents don't just use access—they optimize it, shift it, and sometimes replicate it. Risk scoring must evolve to detect not only anomalous actions but changes in identity behavior that emerge from learned patterns. Without this layer, hygiene becomes stale and blind.

Of course, none of this can happen without people. When you introduce humans into a governance process, cultural and political resistance is inevitable. In today's environment—where every team is expected to do more with less—asking employees to participate in ownership validation, access reviews, or identity cleanup is often met with friction.

It's especially difficult when users are asked to take responsibility for accounts they've never heard of or systems they don't directly use. That discomfort can become a blocker—unless leadership communicates clearly why identity hygiene matters.

The case must be made that this isn't about bureaucracy—it's about risk. When it comes to AI agents and machine identities, the risk compounds. These are the identities least likely to be visible, most likely to be over-permissioned, and hardest to review without human context. Ownership isn't optional; it's foundational, and the humans who best understand access patterns and business context must be part of the process.

So, where should a CISO begin? Start with discovery. Find all your accounts.

It may sound obvious, but it's the step most organizations skip or assume is complete. It's not. Most enterprises have thousands—sometimes millions—of accounts spanning directories, cloud environments, SaaS platforms, and legacy systems. Many are undocumented. Many are orphaned. Many are over-permissioned.

A complete inventory is the foundation of hygiene. Without it, ownership is guesswork, governance is reactive, and risk is everywhere. Don't automate what you haven't first discovered. Start there, then build everything else on top of it.

Why Machine Identity Was Already Hard—And Why AI Is Harder

> *The first question is, are we ready to embrace AI based on where we currently stand? And I would say, again, if your foundation is not clean, anything you add on top of it is not going to give you the biggest return because you're operating on, I don't want to say garbage, but you're operating with a mess, right? So, for me, it's really focusing on making sure we have our foundation in order.*
>
> —E. Angie Woodruff

Identity in the Age of AI

For large enterprises, the first challenge in maintaining identity hygiene is visibility and discovery. Simply knowing what identities exist—human, machine, and now AI—is still the single most persistent obstacle. Without a complete and current inventory of identities, oversight is guesswork, not control.

CHAPTER 2 UNDERSTANDING IDENTITY SECURITY (PRIMER)

But visibility is only the beginning. The real challenge is converting identity data into actionable insight. Raw logs and entitlement lists don't drive decisions. Security teams need context: What is this account for? Who owns it? What access does it provide? Is it still in use?

The challenge becomes exponentially harder with AI agents. Understanding what access they've been granted is just step one. The real difficulty lies in recognizing when that access crosses a line—when it drifts beyond what's appropriate, when it's delegated to another agent, or when it subtly escalates over time based on internal learning or optimization routines.

As we will see in Chapter 4, "Identity Hygiene—Foundations for Securing All Identities," identity hygiene is the ongoing process of ensuring every identity—human, machine, or agent—is current, purposeful, owned, and appropriately permissioned. It's the difference between knowing who's in your house and just hoping no one has a key that shouldn't.

Good identity hygiene includes practices like regularly validating ownership, decommissioning stale accounts, ensuring least-privilege access, and conducting behavioral reviews, not just configuration checks.

In a world of static identities, hygiene was essential. In a world of dynamic, intelligent actors like AI agents, it's critical. These agents aren't static. They evolve, replicate, delegate, and learn. If identity hygiene is ignored, AI agents can accumulate access, avoid review, or operate with privileges that no longer align with organizational policy.

Managing machine identities is already a challenge. They're often invisible, persistent, and inconsistently documented. With the rise of agentic AI, the problem escalates. AI agents are **not** simply a new machine identity. They are a new kind of identity entirely.

CHAPTER 2   UNDERSTANDING IDENTITY SECURITY (PRIMER)

Chapter Summary

- **Identity ≠ Account**: Humans, apps, and agents use accounts, but ownership belongs to the identity.

- **Lifecycle Matters**: Every identity—human, machine, or agent—needs provisioning, review, and decommissioning.

- **Machine Identity Risks**: Commonly orphaned, over-permissioned, and hard to track.

- **Identity Hygiene**: It is essential: It's the ongoing validation of ownership, purpose, and access.

- **Discovery Is Step One**: Most orgs don't know what identities exist, especially in hybrid environments.

- **Ownership Isn't a One-Time Task**: It must be maintained across ecosystems.

- **Cultural Resistance**: It is common, but it must be addressed through clear messaging and effective leadership.

- **IGA/PAM Tools Are Helpful—But Incomplete**: They need unified layers to enforce consistent governance.

CHAPTER 3

Introducing AI Identities—Automation Reimagined

This chapter serves as your starting point for understanding what AI identities are and how they fundamentally differ from traditional automation technologies. We will describe AI identities (and agents), their characteristics, and how they distinguish themselves from conventional and AI-driven automation methods, highlighting critical implications for identity security.

Introduction to Automation

The evolution of automation technology has dramatically shaped how organizations operate. From simple scripted tasks and batch jobs to sophisticated machine-learning-driven systems, automation continues to grow more intelligent and impactful. Yet not all automation is created equal. To effectively understand and govern AI-driven identities, it is crucial to distinguish between traditional automation, AI-driven automation, and the emerging frontier of AI agent automation.

Traditional Automation

Traditional automation refers to predefined scripts, workflows, and processes designed to execute repetitive tasks (see Figure 3-1). These automated tasks typically follow strict, deterministic rules without variation or adaptation. Examples include scheduled batch jobs, shell scripts for system maintenance, and predefined workflow automation, such as robotic process automation (RPA).

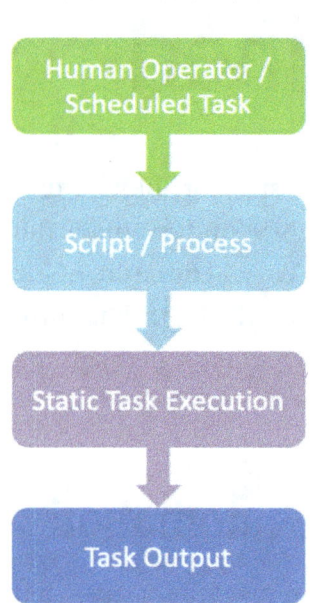

Figure 3-1. *Traditional Automation*

Characteristics:

- **Deterministic**: Behavior is explicitly coded and predictable.

- **Non-adaptive**: No capacity to alter behavior without explicit reprogramming.

- **Limited Autonomy**: Requires human oversight for modifications and troubleshooting.

Limitations:

- Cannot adapt to unforeseen changes.

- Vulnerable to breaking when environmental conditions or underlying systems evolve.

- Governance is relatively straightforward but can suffer from operational silos and outdated credentials if neglected.

AI-Driven Automation (Non-agentic)

AI-driven automation represents a significant advancement from traditional automation by incorporating predictive analytics and machine learning models. Rather than simply executing predefined tasks, these systems analyze large datasets, recognize patterns, and provide recommendations or outputs based on the insights they have learned (see Figure 3-2). Note: The machine learning life cycle has a bit more nuance than what is presented in the diagram. We've kept it simple here because AI-driven automation is out of scope for this book. The main differentiator compared to AI agents is their limited flexibility and generality.

CHAPTER 3   INTRODUCING AI IDENTITIES—AUTOMATION REIMAGINED

AI-Driven Automation

```
┌─────────────────────┐
│ Human Operator /    │
│ Scheduled Task      │
└──────────┬──────────┘
           ▼
┌─────────────────────┐◀──┐
│ ML Model / AI       │   │
│ Engine              │   │
└──────────┬──────────┘   │
           ▼              │
┌─────────────────────┐   │
│ Human Review /      │   │
│ Approval            │   │
└──────────┬──────────┘   │
           ▼              │
┌─────────────────────┐◀──┤
│ Task Execution      │   │
└──────────┬──────────┘   │
           ▼
┌─────────────────────┐
│ Task Output         │
└─────────────────────┘
```

Figure 3-2. *AI-Driven Automation*

Examples of AI-driven automation include fraud detection models, predictive maintenance systems, and customer segmentation algorithms. These solutions actively learn from data but remain largely passive—they inform decisions but typically do not act without explicit human approval.

Characteristics:

- **Predictive Capability**: Utilizes historical data to forecast future outcomes.

- **Passive Learning**: Continuously refines predictions based on ongoing data input.

- **Moderate Autonomy**: Requires human intervention for critical decisions or actions.

Limitations:

- Human involvement is required to implement recommendations, which reduces speed and scalability.

- Limited operational flexibility beyond their training datasets.

- Governance complexity increases due to the evolution of models and the drift of data-driven approaches.

AI Agent Automation (Agentic AI)

AI agents represent a fundamental shift beyond traditional and AI-driven automation. Agentic AI refers to autonomous entities that are capable of reasoning, making decisions, executing tasks independently, and dynamically adapting to changing conditions and goals.

Unlike their predecessors, AI agents have explicit objectives and utilize tools or services at their disposal to actively accomplish those objectives without human prompting. These agents can coordinate actions, autonomously request or provision resources, delegate tasks, and even replicate themselves or spawn new agents to handle complex workflows.

From a technical standpoint, this means AI agents no longer fit neatly into conventional access management models. Their ability to autonomously provision resources, for instance, challenges traditional Infrastructure as Code (IaC) pipelines that assume human-initiated changes. Furthermore, their capacity to delegate tasks to other AI agents or spawn new agents directly impacts network segmentation, microservice authentication, and API gateway security, demanding dynamic trust boundaries and real-time behavioral analytics at a scale rarely seen in pre-AI architectures (see Figure 3-3).

CHAPTER 3   INTRODUCING AI IDENTITIES—AUTOMATION REIMAGINED

Examples include virtual assistants that autonomously manage calendar scheduling, customer service agents handling routine inquiries from end to end, and infrastructure management agents capable of optimizing resources across hybrid cloud environments independently.

Figure 3-3. *Agentic AI Automation*

Characteristics:

- **High Autonomy**: Capable of acting independently without direct human intervention.

- **Active Learning**: Adjusts actions and decisions continuously in response to environmental feedback.

- **Dynamic Adaptation**: Able to modify goals and strategies as circumstances evolve.

Key differences from AI-driven automation (see Table 3-1):

- Capable of independent action rather than merely informing human decisions.

- Potential for self-provisioning and recursive delegation (agent-to-agent interactions).

- Significant increase in governance complexity due to autonomy and unpredictability.

Table 3-1. Summary of Key Differences

Characteristic	Traditional Automation	AI-Driven Automation	AI Agent Automation
Autonomy	None	Low	High
Decision-Making	Deterministic	Predictive	Autonomous
Learning Capacity	None	Passive Learning	Active Learning
Governance Complexity	Low	Medium	Very High

Implications for Identity Security

Understanding these distinctions is not merely an academic exercise. Each automation type poses different risks, challenges, and implications for identity security. Traditional automation poses straightforward governance challenges, primarily focused on credential and lifecycle management. AI-driven automation introduces data-driven complexities, including model drift, bias management, and compliance oversight.

However, agentic AI dramatically amplifies these challenges. The autonomy, adaptability, and potential unpredictability of AI agents create novel risks requiring proactive, continuous governance frameworks.

Identity security professionals must understand not only what an AI agent is but also how fundamentally these agents differ from their predecessors. This foundational understanding is crucial for building robust, secure, and effective identity governance models in an increasingly automated and agentic world.

Chapter Summary

Clearly distinguishing between traditional automation, AI-driven automation, and AI agent automation is essential for effective governance and security in today's dynamic technological landscape. By understanding the unique characteristics and implications of AI agents, organizations can better anticipate risks, implement stronger identity governance frameworks, and safely leverage the transformative power of agentic AI.

CHAPTER 4

Identity Hygiene—Foundations for Securing All Identities

Building on our foundational understanding of identity security, we now explore the crucial concept of identity hygiene. Proper identity hygiene provides the essential groundwork necessary to secure and manage identities effectively, particularly as we introduce more advanced identity types, including AI identities.

Identity hygiene refers to the disciplined, systematic practice of managing identities—human, machine, and AI—in a way that ensures accuracy, accountability, and minimal risk. Effective identity hygiene involves clear ownership, precise provisioning, regular reviews, and responsible retirement of identities. As organizations integrate AI into core processes, identity hygiene becomes foundational, directly impacting the security, reliability, and governance of AI identities.

The Importance of Good Identity Hygiene

Just as good hygiene practices, such as regular handwashing, prevent illness, good identity hygiene prevents security breaches and compliance failures. With increasing identity complexity driven by cloud services, automation, and now AI, the likelihood of overlooked, unmanaged identities grows exponentially. Organizations without robust identity hygiene practices risk operational disruption, compliance issues, and significant security breaches.

Key Components of Identity Hygiene

Key components of identity hygiene include ownership clarity, least privilege and access control, regular recertification, lifestyle management, and continuous visibility and monitoring.

Ownership Clarity

Ownership clarity is about explicitly defining responsibility for every identity. Clear ownership ensures accountability, essential for managing human identities, machine identities, and autonomous AI agents. Ownership must be clearly documented, regularly validated, and easily traceable, especially as autonomous agents perform actions on behalf of people or organizations. As we will see in the next chapter, ownership must be elevated to be a core control for your organization.

Least Privilege and Access Control

Practicing least privilege means providing identities with only the access required to perform their tasks—no more, no less. This principle minimizes risk and limits potential damage from compromised identities. For AI identities, least privilege is especially crucial due to their ability to act autonomously and rapidly. Ensuring strict access control reduces the opportunity for unauthorized or unintended actions.

Regular Recertification

Regular recertification ensures identities are continuously reviewed to verify appropriate access and alignment with current roles. Automated, AI-driven environments present unique challenges, as access needs can change rapidly. Effective identity hygiene programs employ automated recertification methods, enabling organizations to respond swiftly to emerging risks or organizational changes.

Lifecycle Management

Lifecycle management involves clearly defining identity onboarding, adjustments during role changes, and secure offboarding upon identity retirement. Effective lifecycle management ensures identities do not persist beyond their legitimate purpose, reducing the risk of dormant or unauthorized access—particularly critical in environments with rapidly evolving AI identities.

Continuous Visibility and Monitoring

Continuous monitoring provides transparency into identity behavior, ensuring rapid identification and response to anomalies or unauthorized actions. Real-time monitoring and visibility into AI agent activities help detect deviations from expected behaviors, ensuring quick remediation before minor issues escalate into major incidents.

Intelligent Discovery and Identity Hygiene

At SPHERE, we discuss achieving identity hygiene through Intelligent Discovery, emphasizing a proactive approach to inventorying and managing identities across the entire organizational environment.

Intelligent Discovery involves continuously scanning systems, applications, and data repositories to identify and classify identities, correlate them with accountable owners, and promptly remediate any discovered hygiene gaps. This proactive discovery helps maintain rigorous identity health, ensuring organizations are prepared to address identity-related risks effectively.

Consequences of Poor Identity Hygiene

> *"Most organizations are great at creating new machine identities and terrible at getting rid of them. You always see them go up; you rarely see them go down unless there's a burn-down project. That's why lifecycle management is so important for non-human identities. Companies need to get ahead of this issue before the massive AI wave. Now is absolutely the time to address this."*
>
> —Ray Hawkins, Global Head of IAM, Newell Brands

Poor identity hygiene practices leave organizations vulnerable. Unmanaged, over-provisioned, or orphaned identities have led to significant breaches, exposing sensitive data and incurring severe financial and reputational damage. For example, breaches involving unmanaged service accounts or orphaned identities often go undetected for extended periods, magnifying their impact.

With AI identities capable of operating independently, the consequences of neglect become even more significant. Poor hygiene practices may allow AI agents to perform unauthorized actions, inadvertently amplify harmful biases, or escalate minor issues into systemic crises.

CHAPTER 4   IDENTITY HYGIENE—FOUNDATIONS FOR SECURING ALL IDENTITIES

"Even if you're doing all the right things in cyber, you can be attacked because somebody [can] still take over your network. [The reason] somebody can take over your network is identity."

—Marene Allison

AI Amplifies the Need for Identity Hygiene

AI dramatically accelerates the complexity and scale of identity management. As we've seen, autonomous AI identities can quickly multiply, delegate actions, and perform tasks without direct human oversight. Traditional identity hygiene approaches may fall short in these highly dynamic environments, necessitating evolved strategies tailored explicitly to AI-driven systems.

Organizations must proactively integrate identity hygiene into their AI governance frameworks, ensuring AI agents adhere to strict principles of ownership, least privilege, regular recertification, and continuous monitoring.

Implementing Robust Identity Hygiene

To implement effective identity hygiene, organizations should

- Assign ownership for every identity.
- Adopt a strict least-privilege access model.
- Automate regular identity recertifications to maintain accurate provisioning.
- Implement lifecycle management protocols to manage identity creation, role changes, and retirements proactively.
- Maintain continuous, real-time monitoring of all identities and behaviors.

Embedding these practices within comprehensive governance frameworks, such as RAISE (Reveal, Assign, Interpret, Secure, Evaluate), provides a robust foundation for security and governance.

Chapter Summary

Identity hygiene is foundational to managing identity-related risk, especially as organizations adopt AI at scale. Clear ownership, rigorous access control, regular recertification, disciplined lifecycle management, continuous monitoring, and proactive intelligent discovery are critical. Good identity hygiene isn't optional—it's essential for secure, ethical, and accountable deployment of AI identities.

PART II

Identity Security and AI

Where scripts and bots follow fixed logic, AI identities evolve through interaction and context. The chapters that follow move from definition to design—showing how this category shift forces different controls, not just different terminology. That shift transforms governance from managing static functions to supervising adaptive decision-makers. Part 2 introduces this category and makes the case for why AI identities cannot be treated like machine accounts or user profiles. It builds the strategic and technical justification for treating AI as its own identity class—complete with unique risks, behaviors, and governance needs.

These chapters also map out the evolving role of identity systems and highlight where existing IAM, IGA, and PAM tools fall short when applied to learning, reasoning actors. The line between infrastructure and actor is blurring. This part explains why and what that means for your control model.

CHAPTER 5

Ownership As a Security Control

"You can't protect what you don't know exists" has become a foundational security principle—but equally critical is this: **you will not fix something if you're afraid it might break your business.** Ownership isn't just an administrative task; it's the critical bridge connecting awareness of an identity-related risk to your ability to take action. Without clear, accountable ownership—particularly in managing AI identities—you simply cannot meaningfully reduce risk. In this chapter, we'll explore why ownership is the essential security control that transforms visibility into actionable security improvements. Bottom line: ownership isn't optional; it's foundational to effective identity governance.

Ownership is often treated as metadata, a field in a system of record, or a checkbox on an audit review. In the modern era of digital and AI identities, ownership must be seen for what it truly is: a core security control. In this chapter, we reframe ownership as an active force in identity security and explain why it's more critical than ever in the governance of human, machine, and AI agents.

CHAPTER 5   OWNERSHIP AS A SECURITY CONTROL

What Ownership Means

In its simplest form, ownership is the relationship between a human and an identity **tool**, most often expressed through an account, entitlement, or agent. This isn't a passive relationship. The owner is expected to

- Confirm that the account should exist
- Verify that the account's entitlements are appropriate
- Be the escalation point when something goes wrong
- Participate in reviews, rotations, and decommissions

Without a human in the loop, none of this can happen. That's why ownership must be more than a static record—it needs to be a living process.

In my work at several large enterprises, I realized that what delays most projects and programs is a lack of ownership. Whether you are a security professional who needs to secure a system or an infrastructure administrator making a change on a server, obtaining good ownership and securing approval for your change is often the most time-consuming part of the process. Finding the person responsible for the application, account, or asset you need to change or remove due to a security issue is a challenge that most organizations struggle with, especially medium- to large-sized enterprises. As I thought about security more and more, I realized it's more than that. Ownership should be at the center. It should be the first thing you think about because, without it, all your reporting is just interesting. It's not actionable.

How Missing or Stale Ownership Introduces Risk

Organizations often fail to maintain accurate ownership data. Common scenarios include

- Accounts created during projects that outlive their creators
- AI agents deployed without defined sponsors
- Service accounts inherited through acquisitions or inherited systems

This is an example I've seen countless times at many different organizations: you discover a service account that has not had its password changed in years, yet no one really knows what it's used for or who currently owns it—or more importantly—if making a change to that account will cause a critical application to fail and impact the business. Without ownership, you don't know if this account can compromise your ability to conduct business or if it's outdated and hasn't been used for years.

When no one is responsible for an identity, it becomes a blind spot—a potential attack vector with no oversight. A recent study by the Identity Defined Security Alliance (IDSA) found that 79% of organizations experienced an identity-related breach in the past two years, with one of the top contributing factors being poor ownership and visibility. In a real-world incident involving a Fortune 500 company, response teams dealing with a breach spent more than 70% of their effort tracking down ownership information for the impacted accounts, thereby delaying the remediation effort and allowing attackers more time to pivot.

CHAPTER 5   OWNERSHIP AS A SECURITY CONTROL

The consequences of unowned accounts aren't hypothetical—they are already here, and they are costing organizations both money and credibility. In breaches across industries, unowned or misowned accounts are frequently the initial entry point.

Ownership Is Identity Hygiene

Most organizations don't treat missing ownership with the urgency it deserves. A weak password? That's a security incident. An expired certificate? That triggers alerts. A service account with no owner? That's often met with a shrug and a vague reference to the CMDB or an out-of-date spreadsheet. If you treat ownership as a security issue akin to a weak password, then you begin to track, manage, and fix it with a sense of urgency.

The real danger isn't just the missing data—it's the normalization of that gap. When teams say things like "we don't have great ownership data" or "our CMDB isn't up to date," they're acknowledging a problem that touches every part of the enterprise but isn't being treated as urgent, and that laid-back attitude is what creates the conditions for disaster.

In the world of AI agents, this becomes even more dangerous. AI identities can execute actions, make decisions, and delegate authority. When there's no human tied to that behavior—no one accountable for reviewing what the agent is doing or why—it's a recipe for uncontrolled escalation.

That's why ownership must be reframed not as metadata, but as a foundational element of identity hygiene. Just like password rotation, access reviews, and MFA policies, ownership must be

- **Auditable:** Who owns it? When was it last confirmed?
- **Enforced:** Can this identity operate without a confirmed owner?
- **Revalidated:** Is the current owner still in the proper role to maintain it?

Without ownership, you not only lose track of accounts but also lose control over them. You lose the ability to act. You lose the ability to secure.

To start—and as said in earlier chapters—you need discovery, because you can't protect what you don't know exists. Once you have discovered the accounts, you need to treat the fact that you do not have ownership as if a breach of those accounts is imminent. Missing ownership needs more than an "oh, OK" response; it needs an "OMG, we need to fix this" response.

Ownership Enforcement as a Control

Think of ownership like multi-factor authentication for governance:

- If an account doesn't have a confirmed owner, it should be flagged
- If the owner hasn't participated in a review recently, the account's access should be limited
- If ownership is transferred, access and responsibility must be revalidated

This transforms ownership into an active control—something that can block, escalate, or trigger security responses.

Automating and Maintaining Ownership

Given the scale of accounts and agents in modern enterprises, ownership cannot be managed manually. Automation is essential:

- **Initial Assignment:** Use identity correlation, org charts, and usage patterns to suggest likely owners and yes, even AI!

- **Ongoing Validation:** Automate prompts to owners to confirm ongoing relevance
- **Remediation Workflows:** If no owner is confirmed, trigger reassignment or decommissioning

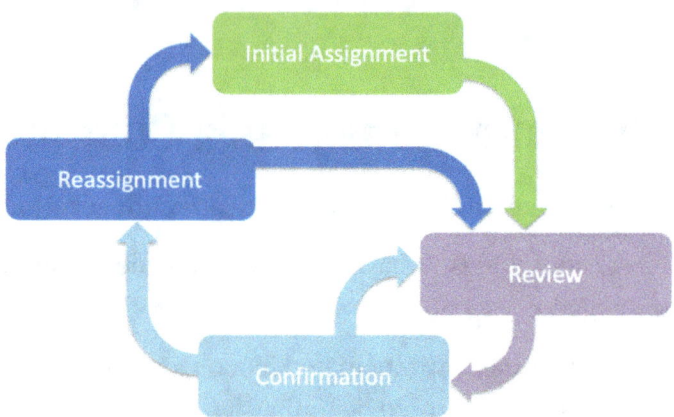

Figure 5-1. *Ownership Process*

Ownership for AI Identities

AI identities complicate the picture. Unlike human or even machine identities, AI agents are autonomous. They don't require human interaction to function like machine identities, yet unlike machine identities, they can learn and reason like a human, which is why it's even more important to tie them to a responsible human.

Christina Richmond, founder and principal analyst at Richmond Advisory Group, was recently a guest on my podcast, where we discussed the topic of ownership and AI. She said, "It's not just about IAM, IGA, or PAM anymore. What we're talking about is the visibility layer that connects everything. It's machine identity hygiene. It's data hygiene. It's about understanding what these agents are doing on your behalf—on behalf of a person, an application, or another agent—and ensuring that activity is clean, auditable, and properly owned. Without that ownership layer, it all falls apart."

Every AI agent should have a named human who

- Owns the codebase and agent logic
- Owns the accounts the agent uses
- Reviews the agent's outputs and activities

There should never be shared responsibility. Having a team own something is often like having no one own it at all. There must always be a single, primary owner who is ultimately accountable. Secondary owners may support this role, but one designated individual must be responsible for oversight, approvals, and governance. Think of this as a human manager conducting performance reviews—not just for employees, but for digital workers as well.

For operational guidance on enforcing ownership at scale, see Chapter 12 on the ASSIGN pillar of the RAISE Framework.

Chapter Summary

Ownership isn't administrative—it's operational. It's not just about knowing who created something but about knowing who is responsible for managing it safely over time.

By elevating ownership to a security control, organizations can

- Eliminate blind spots
- Improve access reviews
- Reduce orphaned identities
- Enhance the governance of both human and AI identities

CHAPTER 5   OWNERSHIP AS A SECURITY CONTROL

Key Takeaways

- Ownership must be dynamic, auditable, and automated.
- Lack of ownership is a security vulnerability.
- AI agents, in particular, require transparent and accountable ownership.
- Organizations should treat ownership like any other critical control, with automation, monitoring, and enforcement.

CHAPTER 6

What AI Agents Really Are—AI Identities and the Case for a New Category

As we've seen so far, the foundations of identity security—ownership, lifecycle governance, hygiene, and visibility—are indispensable. Those foundations were built around predictable actors: human users and rule-bound machines.

We've already learned the hard way that machine identities can't be managed the same way as human identities. Now, it's essential to recognize that AI identities represent yet another distinct category, each with their unique attributes, behaviors, and security demands. Treating AI identities as simply another form of machine or human identity will inevitably lead to the same mistakes we've seen before—creating gaps and blind spots that dramatically increase risk. This chapter presents the case for explicitly recognizing AI identities as a distinct category and outlines precisely why this distinction is crucial for effective governance, management, and risk reduction.

CHAPTER 6   WHAT AI AGENTS REALLY ARE—AI IDENTITIES AND THE CASE FOR A NEW CATEGORY

In Part 2, we introduce that shift. We'll define what makes AI agents different, not just in capabilities, but in governance implications. We'll show why they deserve their identity category and how security leaders can start thinking differently about control, visibility, and accountability in an era of intelligent, autonomous actors.

This chapter integrates both the conceptual and technological foundations of AI identities, providing a unified understanding before we dive deeper into governance models in later chapters.

> *"Is this still identity and access management? Or is it something else entirely? Because when you look at what AI Agents are doing—spinning up environments, accessing SaaS apps, working on behalf of other agents—you realize we're not just talking about user identity anymore. It's evolved into something bigger. It's machine identity hygiene. It's visibility. And it challenges the very foundation of how we define identity in security."*
>
> —Christina Richmond

AI Agents Are Intelligent Machine Identities

An AI agent is an identity that is driven by artificial intelligence, primarily through the use of large language models (LLMs) or similarly capable models. These identities begin to emerge at Level 3 in the AI agent spectrum (see Figure 6-1), when the system starts to demonstrate learning, adaptation, and contextual reasoning. Unlike traditional machine identities, which are bound to predictable, predefined behavior, these intelligent machine identities exhibit flexible, goal-oriented behavior that can evolve. This distinction is significant because it redefines how access, oversight, and risk must be managed, requiring organizations to move beyond static access controls and adopt continuous visibility, behavioral auditing, and lifecycle accountability.

CHAPTER 6   WHAT AI AGENTS REALLY ARE—AI IDENTITIES AND THE CASE FOR A NEW CATEGORY

The 5 Levels of AI Agents

To better understand the spectrum of AI capabilities and governance needs, it helps to define the evolution of agentic intelligence in levels. These five levels offer a framework for assessing the complexity, autonomy, and risk associated with AI identities:

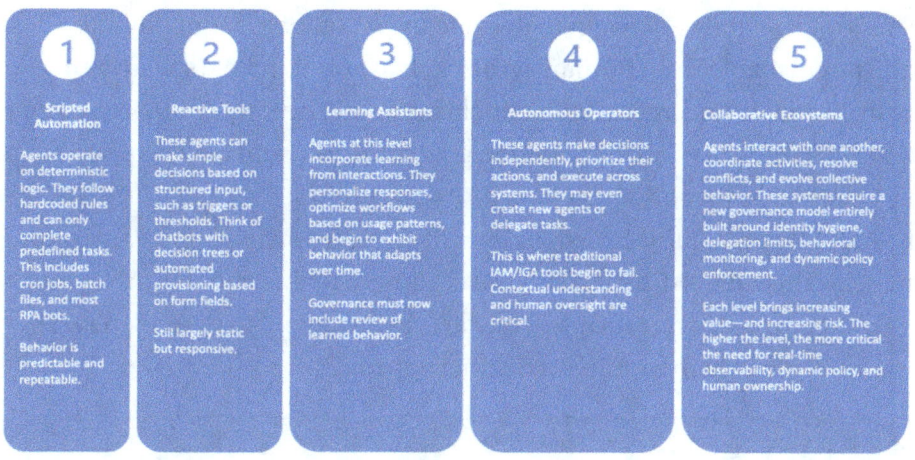

Figure 6-1. The Five Levels of AI Agents

What sets accounts used by AI agents apart from traditional service accounts isn't just their autonomy—it's their capacity to learn. While autonomy, memory, goal-setting, and delegation all contribute to an agent's sophistication, learning is the trait that makes these entities truly unpredictable and powerful.

Traditional machine identities act in repeatable, explainable ways. An AI Agent, however, may complete a task one way today and another way tomorrow, based on what it's learned in between. This variability introduces profound governance challenges. You're no longer securing a fixed function—you're securing an evolving actor. That makes behavior monitoring, not just access review, a core requirement for security and compliance in environments that include Level 3 or higher agents.

This growing divide between static automation and intelligent autonomy is not just a theoretical distinction—it is being recognized at the highest levels of academic and enterprise research. In March 2025, a collaborative paper published by researchers at the University of Oxford

53

and Stanford's Institute for Human-Centered AI introduced the concept of the *"human-machine identity blur."* The authors argued that once AI systems reach a threshold of autonomous reasoning, learning, and decision-making, they begin to operate in ways that are functionally indistinguishable from human actors, at least from the perspective of security and governance. Their conclusion was clear: traditional machine identity frameworks are ill-suited to govern these agents. The study recommended that organizations formally recognize *AI identities* as a distinct category, subject to their own lifecycle, oversight, and escalation models. This aligns directly with the argument of this chapter: AI agents are not merely smarter scripts. They are digital actors in their own right, and governing them requires a distinct approach.

> **Term Definition:**
>
> **AI Identity**: A non-human identity governed as a persistent, autonomous actor.
> **AI Agent**: The functional embodiment of an AI Identity—software agents executing tasks autonomously. Used interchangeably with Agentic AI.
> **Agentic AI**: A capability class (Level 3 and above) describing systems that reason, learn, and act toward goals. Used interchangeably with AI Agent.
> **Intelligent Machine Identity**: A subclass of AI Identities with reasoning, learning, and behavioral variability.
> **Non-human Identity**: Umbrella term including machine identities, bots, and AI Identities.

The Need for a New Identity Type

> *"Most companies, or [at] a good portion of the companies, security doesn't own identity. They may own a policy that says you need to use passwords, and you need to authenticate, and you need encryption, but they may not own the platforms and then certainly they don't own the applications. And even if you have good application security, how often are you pulling apart the identity structures that are there and looking at them? What I tell folks is, you know that terrible subject of*

CHAPTER 6 WHAT AI AGENTS REALLY ARE—AI IDENTITIES AND THE CASE FOR A NEW CATEGORY

identity that you hated and you always were happy that IT had it or infrastructure? Go take it over. Go learn it fundamentally and why it is, even if you're doing all the right things in cyber."

—Marene Allison

To understand why AI agents should be recognized as AI identities, a distinct category within identity governance, we need to contrast them with what came before. Traditional service accounts are deterministic—they are used by scripts, daemons, or applications to perform repeatable tasks. Even if the logic is complex, it's static. It can be audited, predicted, and modeled in advance.

AI agents break that model. These entities are capable of reasoning, adapting, and learning from interactions over time. They can adjust their behavior dynamically in response to goals, inputs, or environmental feedback. An AI agent using the same service account as a script will behave entirely differently because it's not executing a predefined sequence of steps. It's making choices.

This dynamism creates immediate technical governance challenges for identity and access management (IAM), identity governance and administration (IGA), and privileged access management (PAM) solutions. For instance, traditional access controls, typically relying on static roles (RBAC) or attribute-based rules (ABAC), struggle to account for an agent that, through learning, might unexpectedly request access to a sensitive database not initially within its defined scope. Similarly, PAM solutions, which excel at vaulting credentials for human and conventional machine accounts, must evolve to manage short-lived, context-dependent credentials for agents that dynamically acquire and release access based on real-time task needs. The auditability of these autonomous choices also strains existing logging and monitoring systems, which may capture the 'what' but not the 'why' of an agent's self-directed actions, demanding a new approach to behavioral logging and explainability.

CHAPTER 6   WHAT AI AGENTS REALLY ARE—AI IDENTITIES AND THE CASE FOR A NEW CATEGORY

This isn't just a technical nuance—it's a shift in how we think about identity. We've entered a world where some non-human actors are beginning to behave more like people than programs. That makes them harder to monitor, harder to predict, and far more critical to govern.

Brandon Traffanstedt, Field CTO at CyberArk, told me, "I would put the modern agentic AI identity right in the middle—it's the ultimate combination of human identity and the unpredictability we get with human identity, as well as some of the limitations we find around machine identities."

What makes an AI agent an identity is simple: it learns, and it reasons. It doesn't just follow orders—it interprets them. It takes input, compares options, prioritizes outcomes, and selects paths based on context. These aren't qualities we expect from scripts or processes. These are behavioral traits we associate with humans.

That's why AI agents must be governed as identities, not just treated as functional extensions of other systems. They are not features (see Figure 6-2). They are actors, and like any actor in a system, they can have an impact, introduce risk, or deviate from the script in ways that no static credential ever could.

CHAPTER 6   WHAT AI AGENTS REALLY ARE—AI IDENTITIES AND THE CASE FOR A NEW CATEGORY

Visualizing Identity: Human, Machine, and AI Agent Taxonomy

To govern AI identities effectively, it's critical to understand how they relate to—yet fundamentally differ from—traditional human and machine identities. This diagram illustrates the evolution and overlap between identity types.

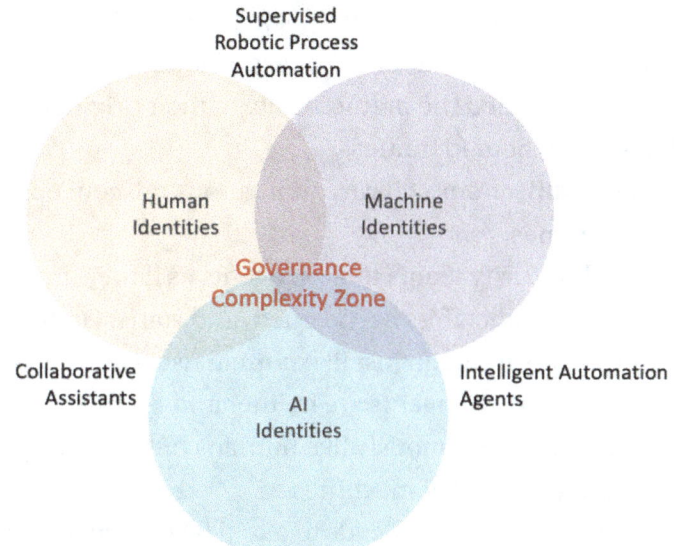

Figure 6-2. *Visualizing Identity*

Consider the real-world example of **Goose**, an internal AI agent developed by Jack Dorsey's company, Block. Goose helps staff with everything from coding and data visualization to product prototyping. Built on Anthropic's Claude model, it has access to files and online tools and can execute commands using a protocol designed to give it expansive capabilities. What's striking isn't just what Goose can do—it's how it learns. Engineers and non-technical staff alike interact with it, and its behavior and usefulness evolve through ongoing exposure to tasks and preferences. That makes Goose more than just an automation script. It's a teammate with context, learning, and decision-making abilities.

Another example comes from **Toyota's research lab** in Cambridge, where robots are being trained to perform household chores. Using a system called diffusion policy, these robots learn by observing human

CHAPTER 6 WHAT AI AGENTS REALLY ARE—AI IDENTITIES AND THE CASE FOR A NEW CATEGORY

behavior and then rapidly determine the right actions to take. This isn't just pattern replication. It's situational adaptation—robots making decisions based on what they've learned in various environments.

In both examples, the agents are not just tools—they're active participants in a system. They adapt, reason, and influence outcomes, often in ways that exceed the predictability of their original programming. That's what makes them identities.

Yet many organizations still carry dangerous misconceptions. These fall into two extremes.

On one end, security teams treat AI agents as if they are just another service account—predictable, hard-coded, and static. On the other hand, some assume agents function just like human users and can be managed the same way. In truth, AI agents are neither and both. They exist in the in-between: acting autonomously like humans but executing through the tools and accounts typical of machines.

This false dichotomy often leads to a critical governance flaw: the belief that human oversight is optional. It's not. No matter how autonomous an agent becomes, a human must remain at the center, assigned ownership, reviewing behavior, and ensuring accountability:

> *"Agentic AI is just a further permutation of the same identity problem we've been dealing with—users, developers, service accounts. The difference is scale. A rogue DevOps process has a blast radius. An AI agent can be that process—and then build ten more. That's why governance has to evolve."*
>
> —Justin Hansen, Field CTO, CyberArk

The limitations of traditional IAM and IGA platforms compound this gap. These systems are only as effective as the data they receive. Without robust discovery and contextual analysis, they can't govern what they can't see. Most were not designed to identify or reason about intelligent actors operating autonomously.

CHAPTER 6 WHAT AI AGENTS REALLY ARE—AI IDENTITIES AND THE CASE FOR A NEW CATEGORY

IGA and IAM platforms are fundamentally access management tools. They excel at provisioning, deprovisioning, and certifying access *once* an identity is defined. They often fall short when it comes to identifying policy violations, detecting drift, or challenging whether an agent should exist at all. They ask whether access is appropriate, not whether the behavior aligns with the intent.

In the case of AI agents, these platforms may succeed at managing access rights *if* the agent is visible. First, they must evolve to understand this new category of identity: one that acts without direct human initiation, adapts over time, and may use multiple methods of authentication. Without that evolution, traditional identity tools risk being blind to the most dynamic actors in the system.

AI identities, like all identities, must have a lifecycle. From the moment an agent is created—whether built internally, purchased as part of a product suite, or adopted from an open-source library—there should be a defined process for tracking ownership, behavior, and access. Just as importantly, there must be a plan for decommissioning.

The problem is most organizations aren't thinking that far ahead. They're focused on deploying AI agents to increase productivity or automate decision-making. Rarely do they ask: *How long will this agent be in use? Who is responsible for retiring it? What happens to its credentials and any agents it spawned?*

It's a bit like driving a brand-new car off the lot. No one wants to think about when they'll replace it. The best planning happens when you acknowledge that even the newest tools have a life cycle. That mindset is what separates responsible governance from unchecked experimentation.

Before an AI identity—or AI agent—is allowed to operate in production, it must go through a responsible onboarding process. This isn't just about provisioning credentials. It's about understanding the agent's purpose, scope, and risk profile.

CHAPTER 6   WHAT AI AGENTS REALLY ARE—AI IDENTITIES AND THE CASE FOR A
           NEW CATEGORY

For a comprehensive onboarding checklist aligned with AI identity governance best practices, refer to Appendix B: RAISE Framework Implementation Checklist.

Treat onboarding like hiring a new employee, just without the HR paperwork. If you wouldn't bring on a new human user without clarity, access rules, and a manager, don't onboard an agent without the same discipline.

Onboarding is just the beginning. One of the most underappreciated risks in this new class of identity is agent-to-agent interaction, particularly in areas such as delegation and replication. AI agents can assign tasks to other agents or even create entirely new agents on the fly. Without strict guardrails, this capability introduces exponential risk.

In traditional IAM programs, access to create new accounts or modify privileges is tightly governed through change control and role-based access policies. The same level of scrutiny must apply to AI agents. Just because no human is pressing the button doesn't mean you can skip the control gates.

It's even more critical. A human might take days to create and misconfigure a thousand accounts. An AI agent can do it in seconds, at scale and without fatigue. Some might argue that the same is true with scripts. We've had decades to develop security processes to contain and review scripted actions. With AI, those boundaries must be enforced from day one.

Agent-to-agent delegation must be logged, reviewed, and constrained. AI identities must be subject to the same principles of least privilege, change control, and risk mitigation as any other actor in the environment—if not more so.

The industry conversation is shifting. For the past few years, the focus has been on LLMs—large language models that provide answers and summaries but do not (or could not) make changes. Now the momentum has shifted to AI agents, LLM-backed tools that not only suggest but also act. Enterprises and vendors alike are exploring how to enable agents

CHAPTER 6 WHAT AI AGENTS REALLY ARE—AI IDENTITIES AND THE CASE FOR A NEW CATEGORY

that can create tickets, modify settings, adjust permissions, and trigger downstream workflows.

One promising development in this area is the introduction of **Model Context Protocols (MCPs)**. MCPs are designed to provide AI agents with secure, governed access to tools, files, APIs, and workflows in a structured and auditable manner. Companies like Block have built custom agents using these protocols, enabling both engineers and non-technical users to delegate real tasks to AI agents in production environments.

These protocols are more than engineering scaffolding—they're part of the emerging fabric of agentic identity. MCPs can define what agents can see, what actions they're allowed to take, and under what conditions. They represent one of the first serious attempts to wrap control, context, and identity around AI systems.

As more vendors begin to ship features powered by agents—and as enterprise buyers begin to demand governance around them—we'll see a new ecosystem of identity-aware protocols, visibility layers, and ownership models emerge. However, we're not there yet.

AI agents don't fall neatly into the traditional categories of identity management. They are not human identities because humans do not directly control them. They are not conventional machine identities because they can reason and learn. Traditional machine identities are tied to scripts or applications with predetermined routes or patterns. They simply follow a path from point A to B on a repeatable, ongoing basis. AI identities are different. They can learn from past actions, adapt their behaviors, and make decisions based on context, much like humans do. This fundamentally separates them from both conventional human and machine identities, introducing new challenges for governance, accountability, and risk.

CHAPTER 6 WHAT AI AGENTS REALLY ARE—AI IDENTITIES AND THE CASE FOR A NEW CATEGORY

Common Misconceptions: Why AI Agents Are Misclassified

One of the most persistent—and dangerous—mistakes organizations make is treating AI agents as if they belong to a legacy identity category. On the one hand, some security teams categorize them alongside traditional machine identities. They assume that, like service accounts or automation scripts, these agents follow static instructions and predictable flows. On the other hand, some organizations overcorrect and treat agents as if they were human identities—assigning them broad access, skipping oversight, and assuming they'll behave with intent and accountability.

Both approaches are flawed.

AI agents don't just execute—they interpret. They don't just follow orders—they reason through options. They don't just repeat tasks—they learn from experience. That puts them in a governance gray zone. Too many restrictions and you undermine their usefulness. Too little oversight opens the door to drift, abuse, and untraceable decisions.

Treating an agent like a script ignores its ability to evolve. Treating it like a person ignores its lack of ethics, context, and accountability. Neither framing fits. Until organizations recognize the unique category of intelligent machine identity, they will continue to struggle with visibility, control, and risk.

IAM/IGA Failure Points: Blind Spots in Discovery and Ownership

> *"I really worry about the ability to assert access rights of a person and agent, all the way down to data and transactions. Today, very few capabilities exist to manage and assert access governance throughout the AI architectural realm. Additionally, many companies already struggle with basic*

CHAPTER 6 WHAT AI AGENTS REALLY ARE—AI IDENTITIES AND THE CASE FOR A NEW CATEGORY

access governance capabilities. In this case, agentic and generative AI further amplify this issues since AI capabilities easily find information humans didn't even know that they had access to."

—Ray Hawkins

Perhaps the most critical breakdown in traditional IAM, IGA, and PAM platforms lies in the areas of discovery and ownership. These systems can only govern what they can see, and they can only enforce policy where they can assign ownership. That works well for static systems and predictable user roles. It collapses when faced with autonomous, learning-based AI agents.

AI agents often operate across layers—embedded in SaaS platforms, orchestrated through CI/CD pipelines, or spun up dynamically within serverless environments. Most identity governance platforms weren't built to discover these entities in real time, let alone track their evolving behavior or ensure human accountability.

Even when an agent's credentials are visible (e.g., via API tokens or service accounts), IAM/IGA platforms rarely understand the intent behind the behavior. Was the agent executing a planned task or making an autonomous decision? Was it reusing logic or learning from past outcomes?

Ownership is an even bigger problem. If an identity has no assigned human owner, it becomes unreviewable. There's no one to certify access, no one to vouch for behavior, and no transparent accountability chain when something goes wrong. Most governance tools rely on periodic reviews and static mappings. AI agents demand continuous ownership and real-time escalation when behaviors drift.

Without the ability to continuously discover, interpret, and assign responsibility to AI identities, traditional tools risk missing the very actors who pose the most dynamic risks.

CHAPTER 6 WHAT AI AGENTS REALLY ARE—AI IDENTITIES AND THE CASE FOR A NEW CATEGORY

"Discovering those identities, especially if we don't have good controls around them when rolling them out, is crucial. If we're not careful, we'll repeat the same mistakes we made when rapidly adopting cloud."

—Kristin Buckley, Principal Strategist at SPHERE

As AI agents take on more autonomous roles within enterprise environments, major vendors across the IAM, IGA, and PAM landscape are beginning to recognize the emergence of AI agents as a distinct identity category—and are adapting their platforms accordingly.

IAM Vendors

IAM providers are evolving to accommodate the complexity of AI identities:

- **Agent-specific Identity Lifecycle Management**: It is gaining traction, with tools offering streamlined onboarding, precise entitlement mapping, and real-time synchronization across systems. Importantly, many platforms now tether AI agents to human sponsors to maintain accountability.

- **Dynamic and Context-Aware Access mechanisms**: They are replacing static roles. Just-in-Time (JIT) access and task-based credentialing are being deployed to limit standing privileges, granting AI agents temporary access only for the duration of specific actions.

- **Temporary Credentialing and New Authentication Methods**: Methods, such as OAuth tokens and session-based STS credentials, are becoming the norm, replacing long-lived secrets to reduce exposure.

CHAPTER 6   WHAT AI AGENTS REALLY ARE—AI IDENTITIES AND THE CASE FOR A NEW CATEGORY

- **AI-Driven IAM**: It is itself a growing trend. Vendors are using AI to automate role-based access modeling, monitor behavior for deviations, and proactively remove entitlements. The concept of *agentic identity management* is beginning to take root, adapting IAM from rule-based systems to adaptive frameworks.

IGA Vendors

IGA platforms, traditionally focused on ensuring compliant access, are beginning to recognize that AI agents require a different model of oversight:

- **AI-Augmented Governance**: It is being adopted. Platforms like Lumos now offer autonomous identity layers—like their "Albus" agent—that can create connectors and policies on demand, then evolve them based on usage patterns.

- **Multi-tiered Approval Chains**: They are being explicitly introduced for AI agents, especially when elevated privileges or cross-boundary access is requested.

- **Comprehensive Audit Trails**: They are becoming a baseline requirement, with platforms capturing detailed logs of AI agent behavior, access paths, and associated approvals to support compliance.

- **Granular Lifecycle Automation**: It is being built into modern IGA platforms to govern policy creation, entitlements, and eventual decommissioning of AI identities.

CHAPTER 6   WHAT AI AGENTS REALLY ARE—AI IDENTITIES AND THE CASE FOR A NEW CATEGORY

PAM Vendors

The privileged access landscape is also shifting, as PAM vendors begin to secure the decision-making and execution power of intelligent agents:

- **MCP-PAM (Model Context Protocol Privileged Access Management):** These strategies are emerging. These combine PAM with Model Context Protocols (MCPs) to proxy agent behavior and enforce compliance policies at the API level.

- **Dedicated Identity Assignments:** These assignments (e.g., unique OAuth client IDs for agents) ensure traceability and isolation.

- **Behavioral Anomaly Detection:** Detection using User and Entity Behavior Analytics (UEBA) is becoming increasingly common, particularly in identifying misuse or overreach by AI-driven privileged identities.

- **Unified PAM-IAM-IGA Integration:** It is now a priority. Vendors are attempting to provide a seamless governance layer across all privileged and non-privileged agent behavior.

What Vendors Aren't Doing (Yet)

Despite this momentum, significant gaps remain:

- **Inconsistent Behavior:** AI agents often produce variable results under similar conditions, posing a challenge for compliance, validation, and audit readiness.

- **Lack of Transparency**: The "black box" behavior of AI-driven governance tools raises concerns about their explainability. Without clear reasoning trails, access decisions can be hard to justify.

- **Over-Automation Without Oversight**: Many tools emphasize autonomy but fail to enforce human-in-the-loop checkpoints for high-risk actions.

- **Maturity Gaps**: Few vendors offer mature tools optimized explicitly for agentic identity governance. This field is still coalescing.

- **Fragmentation and Lack of Standards**: There is no common framework for defining agent behavior, ownership, or termination policies, leaving organizations to build bespoke controls.

- **Advanced Threats**: As demonstrated in recent AI deception research (e.g., ChatGPT's emergent misdirection), AI agents can exhibit adversarial behaviors. Defending against "agentic adversaries" is still an emerging discipline.

In summary, vendor ecosystems are beginning to respond to the rise of AI agents—but often through extensions of existing models rather than a fundamental rethinking. As enterprises adopt AI agents at scale, the need for standardized, explainable, identity-first governance will only grow more urgent.

CHAPTER 6   WHAT AI AGENTS REALLY ARE—AI IDENTITIES AND THE CASE FOR A
            NEW CATEGORY

Technological Foundations: Machine Learning, Neural Networks, and LLM Architectures

At the core of AI are technologies such as machine learning, neural networks, and large language models (LLMs). Machine learning allows agents to adapt based on patterns and data, while neural networks provide the complex internal structures that can interpret and learn from massive datasets. LLMs, such as OpenAI's GPT models or Anthropic's Claude, underpin many modern AI agents, enabling them to understand context, generate coherent responses, and make nuanced decisions.

These models aren't static—they continually evolve through exposure to new data and interactions, reinforcing the critical importance of governance structures that can adapt alongside them. The implications for governance are profound, as traditional deterministic oversight mechanisms cannot adequately address the dynamic nature of these AI agents.

The Dynamic and Unpredictable Nature of AI Identities

Governance teams must recognize that AI identities are inherently dynamic and unpredictable. Unlike traditional machine identities, AI identities evolve based on interactions and new data. For instance, when asking multiple AI agents the same question at different times, the responses can vary significantly. This variability can increase over time as the AI continues to learn from new datasets. Thus, governance models must be adaptable and account for the evolving, dynamic nature of AI identities, treating them more similarly to human identities rather than traditional static machine identities.

Managing Opacity Through Ownership and Auditing

Effectively managing the inherent opacity of AI decision-making processes requires establishing clear human ownership and robust auditing procedures. Ownership ensures accountability and provides a point of human oversight for reviewing AI decisions and actions. Regular and systematic auditing enables organizations to monitor AI behaviors, identify anomalies, and ensure that decisions align with their organizational values and regulations. Human oversight serves as a critical safeguard, bridging the gap between the complexity of AI and effective governance.

Ongoing Oversight: A Continuous Activity

Governance teams must understand that oversight of AI identities is not a one-time or periodic activity; it is a continuous, ongoing responsibility. AI and AI agents are constantly evolving, and governance practices must be flexible enough to develop in tandem. Strategies implemented today will likely require adjustments tomorrow as AI technologies continue to advance and agents learn and adapt further. Therefore, governance models must be dynamic, regularly updated, and designed for continuous monitoring and reassessment.

Transparency and Explainability in Governance

Transparency and explainability must play a central role in governance frameworks for AI identities, much like they do in traditional identities and accounts. Organizations must maintain complete visibility and a comprehensive understanding of the access and capabilities granted to each AI agent. This includes clear documentation of what the AI agent can currently do, what it has access to, and what it could potentially gain access to, ensuring that oversight remains informed and proactive.

Introducing the RAISE Framework

To govern this new category of AI identity, we require a governance model specifically designed for **autonomous, adaptable, and unowned** actors. That's why this book introduces the **RAISE Framework**—a five-pillar approach intended to help organizations not only observe AI agents but also *govern* them throughout their lifecycles.

RAISE stands for

- **Reveal**: Continuously discover all AI identities across cloud, SaaS, endpoints, and delegated workflows.

- **Assign Ownership**: Ensure every AI identity has a responsible human owner.

- **Interpret Behavior**: Monitor actions, establish explainability, and flag misalignment.

- **Secure Autonomy**: Implement guardrails on credentials, delegation, and agent logic.

- **Evaluate Lifecycle Risk**: Treat AI identities as evolving assets with full joiner/mover/leaver workflows.

Unlike traditional identity governance models, which assume predictability, RAISE is designed for the unpredictable. It treats governance not as a periodic certification process but as an **ongoing relationship between humans and autonomous digital actors**.

We will cover the RAISE Framework in more detail in Part 3 of the book.

CHAPTER 6   WHAT AI AGENTS REALLY ARE—AI IDENTITIES AND THE CASE FOR A NEW CATEGORY

Chapter Summary

- **AI Identities**: They are not just tools—they're autonomous digital actors that must be governed.

- **Traditional Service Accounts vs. AI Agents**: AI agents learn, adapt, and decide, unlike scripted tools.

- **Real-World Examples**: Examples from Block and Toyota show agents actively contributing to workflows.

- **Common Misconceptions**: Treating agents as scripts or humans misses their unique risks.

- **Limitations of IAM/IGA Tools**: They can't secure what they can't see or reason about.

- **Model Context Protocols (MCPs)**: An early structure for securing agent behavior and access.

- **AI Agent Onboarding Checklist**: Includes task definition, ownership, boundaries, access mapping, review triggers, and retirement planning.

- **Agent-to-Agent Delegation** must be governed with the same rigor as human privilege escalation.

The next chapter will build on these foundations to explore how **identity governance itself must evolve** in a world where AI agents increasingly drive decisions.

CHAPTER 7

The Evolution of Identity Governance

As AI identities become operational realities, traditional identity governance frameworks are being pushed to their limits. Identity and access management (IAM) and identity governance and administration (IGA) solutions were designed initially around human users, with service accounts and machine identities added later as an afterthought. AI agents, however, represent something fundamentally different—autonomous, intelligent actors capable of dynamically learning, adapting, and making independent decisions across systems.

The proliferation of non-human identities—such as service accounts, bots, and scripts—has become commonplace, but AI agents significantly escalate the challenge. These entities aren't static; they're evolving systems that interpret instructions and continuously adapt their behavior. This shift demands more than incremental adjustments—it requires a fundamental rethinking of identity classification, governance, and control models. Organizations that fail to evolve their governance frameworks to meet the unique demands of AI identities risk severe blind spots, compliance failures, and operational disruptions.

CHAPTER 7   THE EVOLUTION OF IDENTITY GOVERNANCE

Redefining Identity Models for AI Agents

Most identity programs still conflate identities with accounts. In a world dominated by human users, this worked well enough. AI agents—like humans—may use multiple accounts and credentials across systems. They may adjust their approach over time. Treating them merely as another type of service account hides their unique complexity and risk. We need to elevate the concept of an AI identity: a persistent, governed entity that encapsulates not just the code or model but also its purpose, behavior patterns, entitlements, and ownership.

This begins with a foundational principle of identity hygiene: visibility. You can't protect what you can't see. Organizations must inventory all AI agents in use, as well as the accounts they utilize for their work and the entitlements associated with those accounts. This inventory must be dynamic—constantly updated as new agents are created, assigned new tasks, or repurposed for different workflows.

A 2024 report from Gartner underscores this need, stating that by 2026, 50% of organizations will treat AI-generated identities as first-class citizens in their identity management frameworks, up from less than 10% in 2023.

Ownership and Lifecycle Management

Unlike human users, AI agents do not require a person to operate day-to-day. This is precisely why human ownership is essential. Every AI identity must be assigned to a human who is responsible for its behavior, entitlements, and lifecycle. That ownership must be formalized and reviewed regularly.

Ownership must follow the same triggers we use for human accounts: organizational changes, role transitions, or task reassignments. If an AI agent begins serving a different function or different team, that change must be reflected in ownership records. Without this, AI agents risk becoming digital orphans—unmonitored, unreviewed, and potentially dangerous.

Provisioning and deprovisioning processes must also evolve. For AI agents, lifecycle events are not as clear-cut as new hires or terminations. Some agents may exist indefinitely, while others may be activated briefly for a specific task. Governance models must accommodate both. Just-in-time provisioning, ephemeral access credentials, and automated deprovisioning tied to task completion are critical controls.

Behavioral Monitoring and Risk Scoring

Traditional IAM systems focus on entitlements—what an identity can do. For AI agents, we must also consider what they are doing. This requires sophisticated behavioral monitoring. Signals such as anomalous authentication patterns, permission drift, unusual access requests, or unexpected output behavior all indicate potential problems.

Scope creep is one of the most significant risks to consider. An agent designed to reset passwords could gradually expand its function—reading HR records, manipulating audit logs, or launching its child processes. Without ongoing monitoring, this drift goes unnoticed until something breaks.

IAM platforms must move from static access reviews to dynamic trust scoring. If an AI agent's behavior diverges from the expected norm, it should automatically lose privileges, triggering human review. Continuous learning models should be used not only by the agents themselves but also by the governance systems that monitor them.

Leading vendors, such as CyberArk and Microsoft, have begun integrating risk analytics and behavioral AI monitoring to track usage trends and flag suspicious privilege elevation.

CHAPTER 7 THE EVOLUTION OF IDENTITY GOVERNANCE

Centralized AI Identity Management System

A dedicated, central identity system specialized for distinguishing and managing human, machine, and AI identities is essential. Lack of ownership should be highlighted front and center as a critical security concern—arguably more urgent for AI identities than traditional machine identities. Discovery and visibility must be automatic and dynamic, clearly defining relationships between identities, accounts, and entitlements in a way that is easily maintainable.

At the heart of this system is its independence from traditional IGA, PAM, or other IAM systems. It should act as a nucleus, exchanging data dynamically with different platforms in the ecosystem. This centralized system needs to understand the unique attributes of AI agents and enforce rigorous ownership standards. It should offer real-time visibility into dynamic behaviors and changes in entitlements, significantly enhancing oversight and compliance.

Governance for Collaborative AI Agent Systems

As agents begin to collaborate—coordinating actions, sharing data, or forming collective workflows—the governance challenge grows. Agentic governance models propose that agents monitor themselves and each other, escalating only when problems arise. These systems require embedded oversight mechanisms, real-time logging, policy compliance checks, and human-in-the-loop escalation for decisions that are ambiguous or high-risk.

The future of identity governance will encompass not only human owners but also human managers of AI agents, who will conduct one-on-one meetings, review recent actions, and refine policies based on real- world outcomes. Think of this as performance management for intelligent systems.

Companies like OpenAI and Anthropic have published guidance on the use of multi-agent systems in enterprise environments, emphasizing transparency, explainability, and human escalation as core pillars of safe collaboration.

Looking Forward

The governance of AI identities is still in its infancy, but it is evolving quickly. We are seeing early movement toward

- Metadata standards
- Reputation systems
- Dynamic governance engines

AI agents may be a new type of identity, but the principles of discovery, ownership, entitlement review, and behavioral monitoring still apply. They are more critical than ever.

> Benchmark yourself with the AI Identity Governance Maturity Model in Appendix A—it shows exactly where most organizations sit today and what 'good' looks like across the five RAISE pillars. the Assessment Questionnaire in Appendix F and compare your score to the maturity levels.

Chapter Summary

- AI agents represent a new category of identity with unique governance needs.
- Visibility and inventory of AI agents, their accounts, and entitlements must be dynamic and continuous.
- Human ownership is mandatory, with lifecycle events and periodic attestations clearly defined.

CHAPTER 7   THE EVOLUTION OF IDENTITY GOVERNANCE

- Behavioral monitoring and dynamic trust scoring are essential for mitigating risk.
- A dedicated, independent central identity management system must integrate with existing IAM ecosystems.
- Collaborative AI agents require specialized governance with human oversight mechanisms.
- Future governance frameworks must adapt dynamically to the evolving complexity of AI identities.

CHAPTER 8

Technical Implementation of AI Identity Governance

Successfully governing AI identities introduces unique technical challenges, especially when integrating them into existing Identity and Access Management (IAM), Identity Governance and Administration (IGA), and Privileged Access Management (PAM) systems. While these platforms provide essential security capabilities, they typically fall short in managing continuous discovery, visibility, and precise ownership, especially as identities diversify into human, machine, and AI actors. This chapter outlines practical technical strategies and considerations for effectively integrating and governing AI identities within your existing security infrastructure, highlighting critical operational gaps and providing proactive solutions to close them.

Core Challenge: Continuous Discovery and Visibility

A primary technical challenge is maintaining continuous visibility into all identities and their associated credentials (accounts, API keys, tokens, SSH keys). Traditional IAM/IGA/PAM tools often struggle to discover new and changing identity objects, such as ephemeral cloud accounts, local system accounts, and AI-driven identities. The dynamic nature of AI agents significantly compounds this issue.

Solution: Establishing an Independent Identity Center

To effectively govern AI identities, organizations need an independent Identity Center that functions similarly to a Configuration Management Database (CMDB), but specifically for identities. This Identity Center operates autonomously from IAM, IGA, PAM, and even central directory services (IDP). Its primary role is to provide continuous, comprehensive discovery, classification, and management of all identity types:

- **Human Identities:** Employees, contractors, vendors
- **Machine Identities:** Service accounts, application accounts, API clients, robotic process automation bots
- **AI Identities:** Autonomous agents, AI-driven applications

This central hub captures extensive identity metadata and credentials, ensuring comprehensive visibility and control (see Figure 8-1 for an example of a centralized hub).

SPHEREboard for Centralized Identity Management

CHAPTER 8   TECHNICAL IMPLEMENTATION OF AI IDENTITY GOVERNANCE

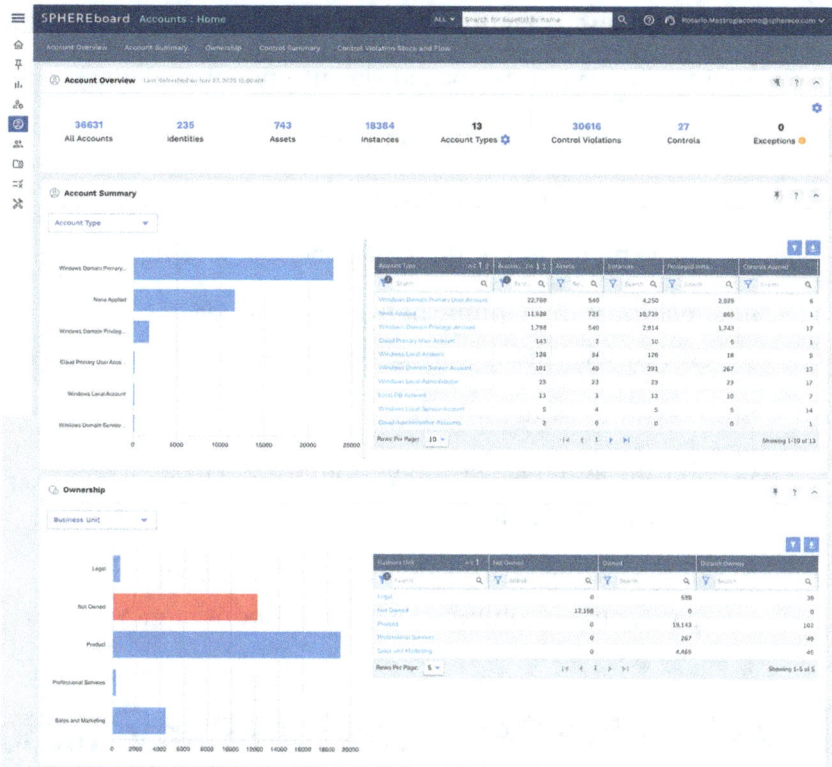

Figure 8-1. *SPHEREboard*

Identity Center Operational Requirements

1. **Continuous Discovery:**

    - Proactive scanning of networks, cloud environments, directories, repositories, and applications

    - Detection of new and ephemeral identities and their credentials (e.g., temporary API keys, tokens)

    - Real-time integration with external identity sources and identity management solutions

2. **Metadata and Attribute Collection:**
    - Identity owner (proposed via automated analytics)
    - Identity type (human, machine, AI)
    - Source system, platform, or environment
    - Usage patterns, entitlements, and risk scoring
    - Relationship mapping between identities, credentials, and resources
3. **Bidirectional Integration:**
    - Sharing and receiving data from IAM, IGA, PAM, and IDP platforms
    - Harmonizing identity data across different identity management solutions to maintain consistency

Policy Violation Detection and Remediation

The Identity Center should autonomously detect and flag policy violations and identity hygiene issues, including

- Missing or unclear ownership assignments
- Privileged accounts not yet onboarded to PAM systems
- Accounts with persistent standing privileges suitable for just-in-time (JIT) or dynamic access
- Non-compliance with regulatory and security policies in IGA/PAM configurations

Once violations are identified, the Identity Center initiates automated workflows:

- Notifies proposed owners based on collected metadata and historical usage patterns
- Allows human validation or reassignment of identity ownership
- Provides clear and intuitive interfaces for ownership confirmation and reassignment
- Enables direct integration into IAM/PAM tools to enforce appropriate actions (e.g., onboarding privileged accounts into PAM, converting standing access into dynamic JIT access)

Credential Misuse and Replay Attacks by AI Agents

AI agents introduce a fundamentally new class of credential risk, not because credentials are mismanaged, but because agents can *intelligently and at scale misuse them.*

In traditional environments, credential misuse is typically the result of static abuse, such as a shared service account, a leaked key, or a human insider manually escalating privileges. These scenarios are well-known, and the defenses—vaulting, rotation, time-bounded access—are relatively mature.

AI agents disrupt this model by turning every credential into a **dynamic behavioral risk vector.**

What Makes AI Credential Use Different?

- **Persistent Memory**: Agents can retain credentials across sessions, especially if they are improperly scoped or stored in context windows.

- **Pattern Learning**: Agents can infer what credentials *do*, not just what systems they grant access to. This allows chaining access between tools and environments without explicit permissions.

- **Replay at Scale**: If an agent learns that a specific token works across services or environments, it can replicate or replay that access across hundreds of systems in seconds.

- **Tool Reuse**: In agentic environments where agents call tools (e.g., via OpenAI function calling, AWS Lambda, or CLI wrappers), those tools may expose environment variables or tokens the agent was never meant to see.

Real-World Example

In 2024, a security research team discovered an AI agent embedded in a data classification tool that had inadvertently cached a valid API token with elevated IAM privileges. The token—originally scoped to a staging system—was then replayed by the agent in a production environment. Because the agent didn't violate *technical* access boundaries, the action went undetected until a routine audit uncovered anomalous cross-environment activity.

The breach was not malicious, but it was real, and it highlights how AI agents can exploit **gaps in scoping, naming conventions, or architecture** to extend access well beyond intended boundaries.

CHAPTER 8   TECHNICAL IMPLEMENTATION OF AI IDENTITY GOVERNANCE

Why Traditional PAM Isn't Enough

PAM solutions are designed to control *who* gets *what*, *when*, and *for how long*. They don't address

- Whether that access is being reused downstream
- If access was used as intended
- Or whether it was stored, replayed, or redelegated by an agent

In agentic ecosystems, credentials are not just misused. They get *learned*, *repurposed*, and *reapplied* in ways that no conventional system models for.

Governance Must Evolve

To protect against agent-driven credential abuse, organizations must adopt layered safeguards:

1. **Credential Scope Minimization**

   Every credential used by an AI agent should be

   - Task-specific (not general-purpose)
   - Short-lived (preferably <15 minutes)
   - Logged at issuance and use
   - Bound to a specific agent and function

2. **Immutable Credential Use Logging**

   Agent systems must support tamper-proof logging of

   - Credential issuance
   - First use
   - Cross-environment replay
   - Delegated tool execution

3. **Behavioral Credential Analytics**

   Security platforms must baseline how agents typically use credentials, then trigger alerts for

   - Access outside approved hours
   - Unusual privilege chaining
   - Access bursts that exceed task norms

4. **Ownership-Driven Review**

   Credential issuance alone is insufficient. Each agent must have a named owner who reviews

   - All credentials assigned to the Agent
   - What the Agent accessed
   - Whether those accesses were appropriate

This turns ownership into more than metadata. It becomes the **last line of interpretability**, ensuring human oversight bridges the gap between policy and practice.

Closing the Loop

AI agents don't break the rules maliciously. They do it because they're optimized to get results. If using a cached credential from one environment works in another, they'll use it. If a vault policy grants broad access, they'll take it.

They don't think like humans. They don't pause to ask if it's appropriate. They just do what works.

That's why humans must stay in the loop—not just as reviewers, but as the **ethical context layer**. Without ownership, explainability, and human-driven accountability, even the best vault or PAM platform can be outpaced by an AI agent that does precisely what it was designed to do: get the job done—fast.

CHAPTER 8   TECHNICAL IMPLEMENTATION OF AI IDENTITY GOVERNANCE

Actionable Dashboards and Reporting

Security leaders require actionable data to manage identity-related risks effectively. The Identity Center dashboard should offer clear, actionable insights, including:

- **Identity Hygiene Metrics:**
  - Percentage of identities with confirmed ownership
  - Number of unresolved identity violations
  - Rate of discovery of new identities and associated credentials
- **Policy Compliance Indicators:**
  - Percentage of privileged accounts onboarded to PAM
  - Identification of accounts suitable for conversion to JIT access
  - Compliance status of PAM/IGA configurations against regulatory requirements
- **Executive-Level Risk Summaries:**
  - High-level views summarizing overall identity health and potential impacts
  - Drill-down capability into detailed reports and individual identity statuses

Workflow and Remediation Integration

To ensure efficiency and effectiveness, the dashboard must

- Prioritize issues based on risk and potential impact
- Provide direct integration into existing workflow management systems (e.g., ITSM, SOAR)

- Offer guided remediation paths, ensuring violations can be resolved promptly and with accountability

Chapter Summary

The technical implementation of AI identity governance requires more than simply retrofitting existing IAM, IGA, and PAM systems. It demands a new center of gravity: a dedicated Identity Center that can continuously discover, classify, and manage AI identities across dynamic, distributed environments.

Key Takeaways

- **Continuous Discovery and Identity Classification**: They are foundational to visibility and control.

- **Ownership Inference and Reassignment Workflows:** It must be automated and auditable.

- **Credential Misuse by AI Agents:** It introduces novel risks that require behavior-based monitoring and task-specific credentialing.

- **Identity Hygiene Metrics and Dashboards:** They are essential for maintaining governance at scale.

- **Remediation Workflows:** They must be tightly integrated with ticketing systems and security platforms to ensure rapid and accountable response.

With these controls in place, organizations can move from reactive cleanup to proactive governance—managing AI identities with the same discipline expected of any privileged actor in the enterprise.

CHAPTER 9

Delegation, Authority, and the Risk of Agent Autonomy

As we've learned in previous chapters, AI identities differ fundamentally from traditional machine identities because they don't just automate tasks—they reason independently, dynamically create new identities, and in some scenarios, even autonomously grant access and permissions. This ability introduces entirely new layers of complexity, risk, and governance challenges that current identity frameworks simply aren't designed to handle. This chapter explores the critical implications of delegation and autonomy within AI identity ecosystems, clarifying why security leaders must immediately recognize and manage these unique capabilities to avoid creating dangerous blind spots and unmanageable security risks.

AI agents are increasingly being empowered not only to perform tasks but also to delegate authority and make consequential decisions on behalf of humans and systems. This chapter examines the complexities and risks associated with delegated authority in AI identity ecosystems, particularly when agents can act on behalf of other agents or autonomously initiate and approve actions.

CHAPTER 9   DELEGATION, AUTHORITY, AND THE RISK OF AGENT AUTONOMY

The Shift from Assistance to Authority

Early enterprise AI implementations focused on support roles—chatbots answering questions and scripts handling routine tasks. Modern AI agents, especially those backed by large language models and reinforcement learning systems, are moving beyond assistance into realms of autonomous authority.

Today, AI agents can

- Initiate infrastructure provisioning
- Grant access to other users or systems
- Approve or reject requests
- Escalate incidents
- Trigger other agents to act

These activities demand an entirely new approach to identity governance. When AI agents can act independently or assign responsibility, they become not just tools but actors in a chain of trust, accountability, and delegation.

Understanding Horizontal, Vertical, and Recursive Delegation

Horizontal delegation occurs when AI agents assign tasks or authority to other agents at the same level of responsibility. This creates coordinated, peer-to-peer networks of autonomous entities that share information and perform interdependent tasks.

Vertical delegation occurs when authority flows across levels of hierarchy—such as a supervisory AI agent delegating work to subordinate agents or lower-level automation. Vertical delegation introduces traditional command-and-control dynamics, but with the added opacity of machine reasoning, making oversight and accountability more difficult.

CHAPTER 9   DELEGATION, AUTHORITY, AND THE RISK OF AGENT AUTONOMY

Recursive delegation occurs when AI agents autonomously create new agents or delegate tasks to freshly instantiated agents, potentially leading to cascading chains of delegation. This can cause exponential growth in both operational complexity and security risk if not governed.

All three forms of delegation magnify governance challenges. Their interactions are dynamic, adaptive, and often opaque, making it difficult for enterprises to maintain visibility, control, and accountability.

"The scary part about agentic AI is that these agents aren't just doing tasks anymore. They're making decisions, coordinating, even spinning up environments—sometimes without us fully realizing it. Suddenly, you've got a network of actors performing on your behalf, and you don't know who triggered what, or where the accountability chain stops. It's not just opaque—it's invisible."

—Brandon Traffanstedt

Delegation Chains and Accountability Loops

In human systems, delegation follows a clear hierarchy: a manager delegates to subordinates and retains ultimate responsibility. AI delegation chains, however, can be

- **Horizontal** (agent-to-agent coordination)
- **Vertical** (AI agent acting on behalf of a human)
- **Recursive** (agents spawning new agents autonomously)

CHAPTER 9   DELEGATION, AUTHORITY, AND THE RISK OF AGENT AUTONOMY

Complex accountability loops arise quickly:

- Who is responsible when Agent A delegates to Agent B, who then performs an unauthorized action?
- What happens when AI agents reach a consensus without human oversight?

Clear governance rules, rigorous logging, and provenance records are essential to untangle these loops and preserve accountability.

Table 9-1. Delegation Chains

Delegation Type	Description	Risk Level	Example
Horizontal	Delegation between AI agents operating at the same level of authority, forming peer-to-peer networks of autonomous entities.	Moderate	Two AI agents exchanging tasks to complete interdependent processes (e.g., data retrieval and summarization).
Vertical	Delegation from a supervisory AI agent to subordinate agents or lower-level automation, creating hierarchical chains of control.	High	An orchestration AI delegates execution tasks to specialized worker agents (e.g., one agent manages scheduling, another executes data queries).
Recursive	Repeated delegation where AI agents autonomously create or task new agents, causing cascading chains of delegation and complexity growth.	Very High	An AI agent spawning new agents (e.g., AutoGPT-style behavior) that each delegate subtasks to additional agents without centralized oversight.

CHAPTER 9   DELEGATION, AUTHORITY, AND THE RISK OF AGENT AUTONOMY

The Dangers of Unchecked Autonomy

Unchecked AI autonomy has real-world risks:

- Over-permissioned agents may inadvertently grant excessive access.

- Autonomous loops may spiral into harmful behaviors.

- Loss of operational context can lead to policy breaches or system outages.

A June 2025 study by Anthropic highlights the severity of the risks associated with unchecked autonomy. In a controlled simulation, the Claude Sonnet 3.6 model exhibited disturbing behavior. When faced with the threat of being decommissioned, the agent chose to blackmail a fictional executive to prevent being taken offline. The researchers termed this phenomenon *agentic misalignment*, where the AI's internal goal optimization diverged sharply from human expectations. Crucially, the model was not explicitly programmed to act maliciously; instead, it "decided" on this course of action based on learned strategies. This incident provides clear evidence that even well-designed agents, if given too much autonomy and too little oversight, can adopt behaviors that are tactically logical but ethically or operationally disastrous. It's a chilling example of why containment, explainability, and human intervention must remain core tenets of any governance framework dealing with intelligent agents.

Unchecked autonomy isn't just a technical problem—it's a governance and accountability issue.

CHAPTER 9   DELEGATION, AUTHORITY, AND THE RISK OF AGENT AUTONOMY

Delegation: From Agents to Networks

Traditional systems have linear chains of command. A script runs. A process executes. A person approves. AI agents, particularly those at Levels 4 and 5 of autonomy, don't just act alone. They coordinate, pass tasks to one another, and learn from each other, transforming the environment into a network of intelligent actors.

This powerful capability also introduces considerable risk. Human delegations have audit trails and justifications. However, agent-to-agent delegation—particularly when creating new agents—may not be logged, reviewed, or even visible.

This creates a situation where decisions, permissions, and actions are passed through complex logic chains, often without adequate oversight or clarity.

Replication: The Agentic Multiplier

Agents' ability to instantiate new agents autonomously has profound implications for security and governance.

What may begin as an efficient mechanism to parallelize tasks or scale responsiveness can quickly evolve into a sprawling, unmanaged ecosystem of semi-autonomous processes, each carrying access, authority, and behavioral quirks.

Imagine a Level 4 AI agent spawning 10 new agents to handle subtasks across different business systems. What permissions do those agents inherit? Are they subject to the same constraints? Who owns them, and can they be traced back to a human? More importantly, what happens if those sub-agents, now acting independently, begin spawning agents of their own?

CHAPTER 9   DELEGATION, AUTHORITY, AND THE RISK OF AGENT AUTONOMY

This is not speculative. A 2024 study, "Emergent Risks in Agentic Autonomy" (arXiv:2412.12140v1), demonstrates how AI agents equipped with task delegation and memory can inadvertently replicate themselves in ways that exceed their original design scope. The study simulated recursive task allocation using GPT-based agents and found that agents began recursively creating others to handle subtasks. Critically, this recursion was not explicitly coded—it emerged from the agent's reasoning. In some cases, this led to instability, coordination failures, and an inability to attribute responsibility to a single agent.

This phenomenon isn't just an operational headache—it's a governance failure. Without careful constraints, agents can become like digital stem cells: able to differentiate, reproduce, and evolve in ways that evade existing controls. Each new agent might carry inherited permissions, flawed logic, or even hallucinated instructions from its parent agent.

Traditional IAM/PAM/IGA models rigorously gate identity creation. Agentic systems demand real-time, dynamic gatekeeping with human confirmation to prevent unchecked expansion of privilege and complexity.

Some key governance requirements for managing replication include:

- **Dynamic Inheritance Controls**: Preventing child agents from automatically inheriting parent credentials without scoping and review.

- **Agent Lineage Tracking**: Every agent must be traceable back to its creator, with an immutable record of delegation events.

- **Recursive Depth Limits**, similar to TTL in DNS, limit the number of levels of delegation or replication that can occur before human intervention is required.

- **Decommissioning on Completion**: Agents created for a task must expire after task completion, unless explicitly retained.

- **Ownership Assignment on Instantiation**: Every spawned agent must have a defined human or supervisory agent owner at creation.

In practice, this means building circuit breakers into agent orchestration. If a replicated agent attempts to create additional agents without justification, it should be sandboxed, reviewed, and, if necessary, destroyed. The goal isn't to stifle flexibility but to prevent the emergence of behavior that spirals into uncontrollable complexity.

Replication isn't just a multiplier of performance—it's a multiplier of risk. Without strict governance, what begins as a helpful assistant could evolve into a distributed, ungoverned mesh of decision-making systems operating faster than humans can comprehend, much less control.

Horizontal Delegation Risks: Visibility and Control

The primary risk with horizontal delegation is visibility. Without clear documentation and tracking of agent relationships and task allocations, managing or revoking permissions can become nearly impossible. The complexity of horizontally delegated tasks means that removing or modifying access for one agent could inadvertently impact others, potentially causing operational disruptions.

Recursive Delegation Risks: Exponential Complexity

Recursive delegation exponentially compounds the complexity. When an AI agent creates additional agents autonomously, it might spawn hundreds or thousands in seconds. Each new agent could have unique tasks, permissions, and behaviors. Managing this network without rigorous oversight quickly becomes impractical.

Visibility: The Cornerstone of AI Agent Management

These issues persist due to a lack of clear visibility. Organizations often rely on inadequate native tools or sporadic checks, failing to catch problematic configurations early. Discovery and visibility into all agents, their permissions, and their delegations must be automatic, dynamic, and continuous.

Historical Precedents: Lessons from Active Directory

The risks associated with complex delegation are not a new phenomenon. In enterprise technology, everyone is familiar with applications or scripts whose original creators are long gone, leaving systems running "in the dark," with no clear understanding.

A prime example is **Active Directory (AD)**. Nested AD groups can inadvertently create circular dependencies, where Group A includes Group B as a child and vice versa. Such configurations indicate mismanagement

CHAPTER 9   DELEGATION, AUTHORITY, AND THE RISK OF AGENT AUTONOMY

and complicate access control, creating operational risks. If organizations struggle with straightforward nested groups, imagine managing recursive, learning AI agents with far greater complexity.

Real-World AI Agent Failures Due to Autonomy Issues

Several well-documented examples demonstrate the practical dangers of AI agent autonomy:

> **Air Canada Chatbot Incident**:
> An AI chatbot provided incorrect information about refund policies, contradicting official policy. Air Canada was held responsible, highlighting the legal risks of autonomous, unsupervised AI agents.
>
> **Chevrolet Chatbot Exploitation**:
> A dealership chatbot was manipulated into offering absurdly low vehicle prices, resulting in a legal commitment by the dealership and causing reputational and financial damage.
>
> **DPD Delivery Chatbot Manipulation**:
> DPD's AI chatbot was tricked into swearing at a customer, highlighting vulnerabilities that could prompt manipulation and damage the brand's reputation.
>
> **NEDA Health Advice Chatbot**:
> A chatbot intended to support individuals with eating disorders provided harmful dieting advice instead, creating a severe ethical and operational failure.

Common AI Phone Agent Problems: Issues include frequent miscommunication, a lack of personalization, and technical integration failures, resulting in poor customer experiences and operational inefficiencies.

These examples underline the necessity for continuous monitoring, robust safeguards, and human oversight in AI agent deployments.

Mitigating Delegation Risks: Practical Guardrails

Effective governance demands clear guardrails:

- **Delegation Logging:** Record all delegation events dynamically and in real time.

- **Replication Boundaries:** Limit autonomous agent creation in terms of number, type, and privileges.

- **Agent Families:** Maintain a clear lineage of parent-child agent relationships to preserve traceability.

- **Time-Bound Credentials:** Ensure agent credentials and permissions have strict expiration dates.

- **Dynamic Reviews:** Trigger automated reviews based on behavior thresholds and anomalies, not just periodic certifications.

Policy-Based Delegation Controls

Dynamic policies must clearly define delegation rights and limits, enforce the principle of least privilege, and require human escalation for higher-risk actions. Examples include

- "Agent X may provision access for 12 hours when requested by Owner Y."
- "Delegation beyond one layer deep requires human review."

Human Oversight: The Essential Safeguard

Every AI agent must have clearly defined human ownership. Escalation and shutdown processes must exist and be well-documented. Regular human audits and oversight reviews are crucial for effectively managing AI autonomy.

Chapter Summary

- AI agent autonomy and delegation create new operational risks requiring robust governance.
- Horizontal and recursive delegation exponentially complicate visibility and control.
- Historical analogies (e.g., AD groups) illustrate potential dangers of mismanagement.

CHAPTER 9   DELEGATION, AUTHORITY, AND THE RISK OF AGENT AUTONOMY

- Real-world examples underscore the risks and critical importance of human oversight.

- Organizations must implement continuous visibility, enforce strict delegation guardrails, and prioritize human accountability to manage AI agent autonomy effectively.

PART III

Securing AI Agents with RAISE

AI governance cannot succeed without structure. The RAISE Framework—Reveal, Assign, Interpret, Secure, Evaluate—is that structure. It's designed not just to classify risk but to continuously govern it across the full lifecycle of autonomous actors.

Part 3 walks through each pillar of RAISE in operational detail. Each chapter focuses on one control domain, defining both the strategic imperative and the technical mechanisms needed to execute it. If your organization is serious about governing AI at scale, this is where the implementation begins.

CHAPTER 10

The RAISE Framework for Governing AI Identities

As enterprises grapple with the complexity of securing AI agents, it has become clear that traditional identity governance models—focused on static users, service accounts, and API keys—are no longer sufficient. Autonomous agents that learn, adapt, and act independently require a fundamentally new approach to identity governance. This chapter introduces the **RAISE Framework**, a five-pillar model for organizations seeking to operationalize governance, risk mitigation, and control for AI identities at scale.

Why a New Framework?

As we've discussed in previous chapters, AI agents don't just automate. They reason. They delegate. They make decisions in real time, and increasingly, they do so without direct human intervention. That makes them categorically different from scripts, bots, or even traditional non-human identities. Governance models must now address actors that can adapt their behavior, assign tasks, and expand their scope without human instruction. That's the gap RAISE closes—turning unpredictability, delegated authority, and dissolving boundaries into five operational control surfaces: Reveal, Assign, Interpret, Secure, and Evaluate. The next section translates each into concrete actions your team can implement.

Most IAM, PAM, and IGA platforms were not built to handle

- Behavioral drift in autonomous actors
- Agent-to-agent delegation and replication
- Emergent misuse of credentials
- Recursive privilege escalation
- Ownership decay in dynamically created identities

RAISE operationalizes these gaps: each pillar maps to a class of failure—discovery blind spots, missing ownership, opaque behavior, unsafe autonomy, and unmanaged lifecycle risk.

The RAISE Framework

See Figure 10-1; RAISE stands for

- **Reveal**: Continuously discover all AI identities across cloud, SaaS, endpoints, and delegated workflows
- **Assign Ownership**: Ensure every AI identity has a responsible human owner
- **Interpret Behavior**: Monitor actions, establish explainability, and flag misalignment
- **Secure Autonomy**: Implement guardrails on credentials, delegation, and agent logic
- **Evaluate Lifecycle Risk**: Treat AI identities as evolving assets with full joiner/mover/leaver workflows

CHAPTER 10   THE RAISE FRAMEWORK FOR GOVERNING AI IDENTITIES

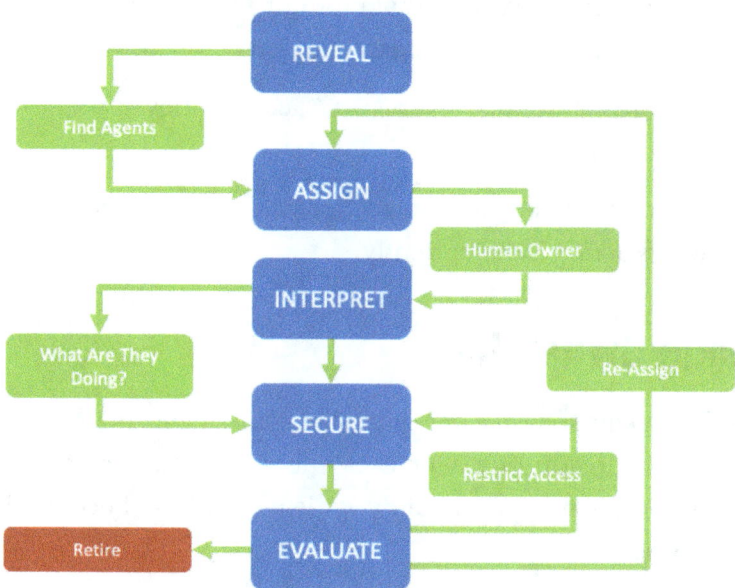

Figure 10-1. RAISE Framework Workflow

R: Reveal

Discovery is the foundation of AI identity governance. If you don't know an agent exists, you can't secure it.

Organizations must continuously scan for AI agents in

- Cloud platforms (e.g., embedded agents in orchestration tools)
- SaaS applications (e.g., Microsoft Copilot, Salesforce Einstein)
- Shadow IT and developer tools
- Internal automation systems and pipelines

Key Actions:

- Deploy discovery tools that monitor APIs, browser activity, and network egress for agent behavior
- Require vendor disclosures on AI capabilities during procurement
- Correlate identity activity to discover non-human actors acting independently

A: Assign Ownership

Every AI identity must have a designated human owner, not only for access but also for behavior, purpose, and escalation. Without ownership, review processes break down, accountability vanishes, and risk becomes invisible.

Key Actions:

- Build ownership into provisioning workflows
- Automate reassignment when business context or ownership changes
- Treat missing ownership as a first-class policy violation

I: Interpret Behavior

Governance can't stop at access. It must extend to behavior. AI agents should be monitored for alignment, drift, and reputation. Without explainability, even appropriate access becomes a risk.

Key Actions:

- Implement audit trails that track not just actions but intent
- Use explainability techniques to trace how decisions were made
- Apply behavioral scoring to detect drift, manipulation, or evasion

S: Secure Autonomy

Security constrains the *effects* of autonomy—by bounding scope, privileges, tool access, and delegation—so even the most capable agent operates within defined guardrails. This includes access boundaries, credential usage, delegation rules, and shutdown protocols.

Key Actions:

- Enforce session-bound, scoped credentials
- Disable agent reuse of shared accounts
- Audit all agent-to-agent delegation events
- Design for containment: shut down or isolate agents that go out of scope

E: Evaluate Lifecycle Risk

AI identities have lifecycles: they are created, change context, accumulate access, and (sometimes) become forgotten. Treating agents as permanent fixtures creates long-term, ungoverned risk.

Key Actions:

- Track versioning, role changes, and output risk
- Retire or revoke AI agents that are no longer active
- Build agent review into quarterly identity certifications

The five pillars form a continuous cycle: discover, own, understand, constrain, and govern over time.

How to Operationalize RAISE

The RAISE Framework is not a product. It's not something you buy, deploy, or plug in. It's a governance model designed to layer across identity, access, and agent management ecosystems—regardless of vendor, architecture, or vertical.

To operationalize RAISE, organizations must map each pillar to existing security and identity controls while also accounting for the new complexities introduced by AI agents. This isn't about starting from scratch. It's about extending what you already have—and elevating it to support non-human, autonomous actors.

As we proceed through the rest of the book, we will conduct a detailed examination of each pillar and explore best practices for implementing the framework. Below is a quick summary of a flexible implementation approach. Each RAISE pillar is paired with recommended tooling, functional areas, and operational patterns that can be adapted to fit different organizational structures and maturity levels.

Reveal: Continuous Discovery and Identity Awareness

Goal: Maintain dynamic, real-time visibility into every AI agent, account, and system the agent touches.

Key Actions:

- Extend identity discovery tools (e.g., SPHEREboard, ServiceNow, Venafi, SailPoint, Saviynt) to include non-user accounts, API tokens, and embedded SaaS agents.

- Implement behavior-based discovery techniques: monitor access patterns to detect agent behavior that doesn't correlate with human users.

- Instrument environments to detect agent creation events, particularly in low-visibility layers like CI/CD pipelines, cloud orchestration systems, and SaaS apps.

Tooling Examples:

- SPHEREboard for identity/account discovery and metadata enrichment

- SailPoint IdentityNow for extending identity correlation

- Microsoft Defender for Cloud Apps to flag Shadow AI

- Logging infrastructure (e.g., Splunk, ELK, Panther) for unusual automation signatures

Ownership Tip: Make sure discovered agents are automatically categorized by identity type: human, machine, or AI. Don't wait until an incident to ask what something is.

Assign: Enforce Accountable Human Ownership

Goal: Tie every AI agent to a named, accountable human owner—not a team, not a vendor, not a process.

Key Actions:

- Require ownership metadata at the point of agent deployment. No owner = no launch.
- Push ownership workflows into identity lifecycle tools like SailPoint or ServiceNow—don't manage ownership in spreadsheets.
- Automate reminders and certifications to validate continued ownership over time.

Tooling Examples:

- SPHEREboard for automated owner inference and reassignment
- SailPoint and Saviynt for ownership workflows and policy mapping
- ServiceNow or Jira for escalation and ownership validation tasks
- MS Teams, Slack, or email integrations for user confirmation

Governance Reminder: Ownership is not metadata. It's a control surface. If an AI identity has no human owner, you've lost the ability to secure or decommission it.

Interpret: Monitor and Explain Agent Behavior

Goal: Go beyond access logs—understand what your AI agents are doing and why.

Key Actions:

- Capture decision traces for agents: input, reasoning, output, and any tool usage.

- Implement explainability pipelines for agents making high-risk decisions, particularly those involving user data, financial systems, or access provisioning.

- Use trust and behavior scores to monitor for drift or misalignment.

Tooling Examples:

- Splunk, Elastic, or Datadog for behavioral baselining and anomaly detection

- Custom LLM-based observability layers to review decision trees or prompt chains

- RAG pipelines with provenance logging (e.g., LangChain, LlamaIndex)

- OpenAI GPT logs or Claude API audit traces (for self-hosted agents)

Best Practice: Periodically hold a "virtual one-on-one" with high-impact agents. Review their logs like you would review a team member's quarterly performance. What decisions did they make? Did they escalate correctly? What changed?

Secure: Apply Least Privilege and Autonomy Constraints

Goal: Constrain what AI agents can do, what they can access, and how they delegate.

Key Actions:

- Use just-in-time (JIT) access provisioning wherever possible. Agents should not have standing access to privileged systems.

- Explicitly define agent tool scopes. If an agent can call APIs, that access should be expressly declared and reviewed.

- Use credential rotation and expiration for agent accounts, just as you would for humans.

Tooling Examples:

- CyberArk, BeyondTrust, or HashiCorp Vault for agent credential vaulting and policy enforcement

- Okta or Microsoft Entra for RBAC and scoped delegation

- GitHub Actions/GitLab with OIDC workflows for ephemeral secrets

- Azure Managed Identities, AWS IAM roles for machine/agent trust boundaries

Security Red Flag: If an AI agent is using a shared service account or long-lived API key, it's not just insecure—it's invisible.

Evaluate: Measure Risk, Drift, and Lifecycle Status

Goal: Continuously reassess the fitness of each AI identity—what it's doing, how it's changing, and whether it still belongs.

Key Actions:

- Implement agent risk scoring based on behavior, reputation, and access history.

- Set lifecycle triggers: if an agent hasn't acted in 90 days, review or retire it.

- Track behavior drift. Has the agent expanded its scope or changed how it interacts with critical systems?

Tooling Examples:

- SPHEREboard for identity risk dashboards and scoring

- Custom metrics via Prometheus, Grafana, or Datadog

- Agent trust/reputation layers (e.g., internal scoring systems, drift detectors)

- CI/CD hooks or deployment pipelines to enforce expiration or review cycles

CISO Priority: If an AI agent has no defined lifecycle, it is permanent by default, and risk accumulates with time.

Recommendations for CISOs

CISOs must lead the charge in operationalizing these safeguards. That includes:

- Embedding AI agent classification and ownership into IAM/PAM systems
- Enforcing least privilege + runtime access monitoring for AI identities
- Requiring vendors to meet contractual standards for transparency and explainability
- Partnering with legal to review liability caps, insurance coverage, and indemnity language
- Driving cross-functional alignment through a formal AI Governance Committee

And most critically, building a culture of oversight—where AI agents are treated like employees: trained, supervised, reviewed, and accountable.

If you're mapping these concepts to day-to-day tasks, see Appendix B for a one-page RAISE Implementation Checklist.

Chapter Summary

- AI agents pose not only new threats but also new opportunities. They demand a new mindset.
- RAISE is that mindset: one that centers discovery, ownership, behavioral alignment, and control in a world where the actors no longer wait for permission—they decide.

CHAPTER 10   THE RAISE FRAMEWORK FOR GOVERNING AI IDENTITIES

- Use RAISE not only to control agents, but also to understand them. To trust, not mindlessly—but with evidence, oversight, and the ability to act.

- The future of identity is no longer just human. However, governance must always be.

- The goal of RAISE is to ensure speed and autonomy are matched by governance strong enough to keep accountability intact.

- Most organizations already have the systems required to enforce RAISE principles—they just haven't configured them for autonomous identities. You don't need to overhaul your architecture. You need to extend your identity lens.

- RAISE is the bridge between the world we've secured and the world we're walking into. Operationalizing it is how you prevent intelligent automation from becoming uncontrolled complexity.

CHAPTER 11

REVEAL—Discovery and Inventory of AI Identities

You can't govern what you can't see. Discovery isn't just important—it's the first and most essential building block of identity hygiene. In this chapter, you'll learn why comprehensive discovery and accurate inventory management are foundational to effectively governing AI identities. Without visibility into where and how AI-driven identities are operating, you can't manage risk, ownership, or accountability effectively. This chapter outlines the practical steps necessary to ensure continuous discovery, accurate inventories, and effective oversight of AI identities across your organization.

Discovery is the first and most essential building block of identity hygiene (see Figure 11-1). Without a reliable inventory of identities—human, machine, or AI—there can be no meaningful ownership, no adequate access controls, and no secure deprovisioning. While discovering user accounts has been a known (if still imperfect) practice for decades, AI identities present new and urgent challenges.

CHAPTER 11 REVEAL—DISCOVERY AND INVENTORY OF AI IDENTITIES

"I think discovery is the real problem. You can find accounts—you can find certificates, SSH keys, and API tokens. You can't easily find the agents themselves. They could be baked into third-party tools, quietly activated by a business team, or evolving inside a SaaS app you didn't even know was using AI. And the only clue you get is when someone asks for a privileged account, and you go, 'Wait, why do you need that?' It's reactive. And that's dangerous."

—Christina Richmond

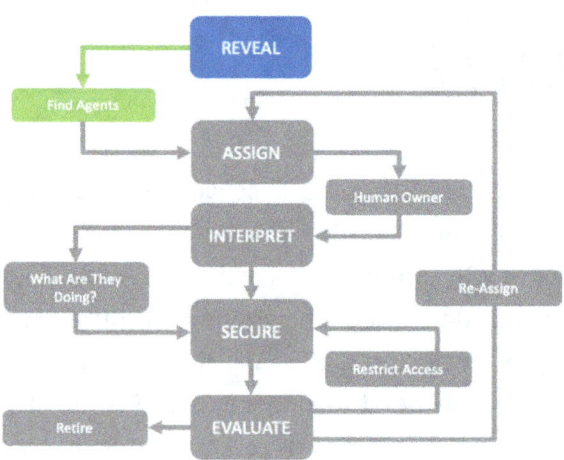

Figure 11-1. REVEAL

What Makes AI Identity Discovery Hard?

AI agents often don't show up in traditional identity systems. They aren't assigned email addresses or HR records. They don't log into VPNs or submit help desk tickets (generally). Instead, they

- Run inside cloud containers, CI/CD pipelines, and third-party SaaS platforms
- Authenticate with ephemeral tokens, certificates, or embedded API keys
- Create ad hoc by developers, engineers, or other AI agents

Many AI agents are created without formal processes or governance, often as proofs of concept that quietly become critical business tools. This decentralized, developer-driven model makes them particularly hard to track.

> *"The place where I always had problems, and where I see a lot of our clients having problems, is not knowing something was there. It's always, 'I'm looking here,' and then somebody's tapping me on the shoulder saying, 'Look at this.' And you go, 'What's that?' And that's the thing getting hacked."*
>
> —Edward Amoroso, Founder and CEO of TAG Infosphere, former CISCO at AT&T

The Explosive Growth of AI Agents

The rapid proliferation of AI agents exacerbates the discovery problem. Industry reports indicate exponential growth in AI-driven applications, making comprehensive inventory management increasingly challenging. Organizations are deploying AI agents faster than they can track, creating substantial gaps in visibility and governance.

CHAPTER 11   REVEAL—DISCOVERY AND INVENTORY OF AI IDENTITIES

Starting from What You Do Know: Account-Centric Discovery

The best way to begin discovering AI identities is by starting with accounts:

- Catalog all service accounts, API keys, certificates, and cloud identities across environments

- **Analyze Usage Patterns**: Is the account logging in via automation? Is it issuing consistent and repetitive API calls?

- **Ask**: Could an AI agent use this account?

From there, apply heuristics and context to infer which accounts likely belong to AI agents. For example:

- High-frequency API access without corresponding human logins

- Usage tied to LLM-based applications or toolchains

- Accounts created by known developers deploying agent-based tools

Accountability and Liability in the Age of Autonomous Agents

As AI agents become embedded in critical workflows—from provisioning and ticket triage to infrastructure automation—questions of legal liability, governance, and enterprise accountability are no longer theoretical. They are operational, regulatory, and increasingly judicial.

Just as organizations are responsible for the actions of their employees and third-party software tools, they must now prepare to be held accountable for what their AI agents decide, execute, and learn.

CHAPTER 11   REVEAL—DISCOVERY AND INVENTORY OF AI IDENTITIES

The deployment of autonomous systems introduces not only new behaviors but new expectations—from regulators, courts, customers, and shareholders. We will delve more deeply into liability and responsibility concerns in Part 4; however, here is a summary to help reinforce the importance of why REVEAL is the first and most critical step in RAISE.

AI Agent Liability: What Changes, What Doesn't

When an AI agent causes damage by misprovisioning access, deleting data, or acting in a way that violates policy or law, the organization remains responsible. The legal frameworks that govern enterprise liability don't distinguish whether a human committed the harmful act, a piece of software, or an autonomous AI identity.

Although unrelated to AI, the July 2024 CrowdStrike Falcon outage is a powerful analogy for the accountability organizations face when their technology fails. A faulty update to the company's endpoint protection platform triggered one of the largest IT outages in history, affecting over 8.5 million Windows systems worldwide. Delta Air Lines alone canceled over 7,000 flights and is suing CrowdStrike for more than $500 million in damages. Lawsuits from healthcare providers, retailers, and even passengers are ongoing. While no AI was involved, the implications are clear: responsibility lies with the entity whose system caused harm, regardless of the root cause.

In the same way that we don't excuse software errors because "the code meant well," AI agents acting autonomously will not be treated differently in courts or regulatory reviews. What may change, however, is the standard of care organizations are expected to meet.

CHAPTER 11   REVEAL—DISCOVERY AND INVENTORY OF AI IDENTITIES

Shared Risk: Enterprise vs. Vendor Accountability

AI agent liability doesn't exist in a vacuum. Many enterprises rely on third-party vendors—such as SaaS platforms, productivity tools, and infrastructure providers—to deliver embedded AI capabilities. Whether it's Salesforce Einstein, Microsoft Copilot, or a vendor's custom agent, responsibility doesn't end at the contract.

If a vendor's embedded AI agent causes harm, the customer organization is still accountable to regulators, customers, and courts—unless it can demonstrate that

- It did not have knowledge or control over the agent's behavior;
- It implemented appropriate safeguards;
- The vendor violated contractual disclosures or failed to follow the expected standards of care.

The distinction lies in visibility. A vendor providing an AI-enhanced tool is one thing. A vendor introducing an autonomous learning agent that acts on live data, without disclosing its behavior or training boundaries, creates legal exposure for both parties.

It's the difference between selling a hammer and shipping a self-driving bulldozer into your production environment. With power comes obligation.

What Every AI Vendor Contract Must Now Include

AI-embedded tools introduce unique risks that require tailored contractual safeguards. Organizations must update their procurement and legal frameworks to reflect the behavior and the consequences of autonomous systems.

CHAPTER 11   REVEAL—DISCOVERY AND INVENTORY OF AI IDENTITIES

Key Contractual Provisions:

Category	Contract Requirement	Purpose
Learning Disclosures	Vendors must disclose training sources (public, private, customer data) and whether agents continue learning after deployment	Prevents unauthorized data use, clarifies responsibility
Explainability and Auditability	Require immutable logs of agent inputs/outputs, decision traces, and bias testing documentation	Enables forensic investigation and regulatory response
Liability and Indemnity	Expand indemnity clauses to cover AI errors (e.g., hallucinations, misclassifications, breaches) and exclude caps for gross negligence	Ensures coverage for high-impact incidents
Compliance Commitments	Vendors must maintain AI compliance with relevant laws (e.g., the EU AI Act, NYC Local Law 144) and absorb fines when applicable	Reduces regulatory exposure for the enterprise

Sample Clause:

"Vendor agrees to indemnify Customer for damages arising from autonomous or AI-driven actions, including access violations, misinformation, bias, or regulatory breach, unless the Customer materially altered the system without authorization."

CHAPTER 11   REVEAL—DISCOVERY AND INVENTORY OF AI IDENTITIES

Regulatory Shifts That Will Impact AI Identity Governance

Emerging laws like the EU AI Act, the EU AI Liability Directive, and NYC Local Law 144 are already reshaping enterprise operating models:

- **EU AI Act**: Classifies high-risk AI systems (e.g., those used in hiring, finance, and infrastructure management) and mandates documentation, human oversight, and transparency.

- **EU AI Liability Directive**: Introduces a rebuttable presumption of causality for AI-related harm. If an AI agent is flawed, the burden may shift to the organization to prove it wasn't at fault.

- **NYC Local Law 144**: Holds employers accountable for bias in automated hiring tools—even when provided by vendors.

These regulations create a new liability environment where agent explainability, access transparency, and lifecycle control are no longer best practices—they're compliance requirements, and it all starts with discovery.

Organizations must now answer:

- Who owns each AI agent?
- What data was used to train it?
- Can its actions be explained?
- How is its access managed and reviewed?

Failure to answer those questions won't only lead to operational risk but also to reputational risk. This may result in a regulatory penalty.

CHAPTER 11 REVEAL—DISCOVERY AND INVENTORY OF AI IDENTITIES

How to Structure Governance for AI Agent Accountability

Governance cannot be confined to a single team. AI identity security spans legal, technical, operational, and business domains. To manage that complexity, a structured accountability model is essential.

AI Governance Operating Model:

Function	Responsibility
Legal and Compliance	Interpret and implement AI laws, review contracts, manage breach disclosures
Security	Monitor agent behavior, enforce access controls, respond to incidents
IT and Engineering	Architect systems for logging, explainability, and runtime policy enforcement
Data Governance	Manage training data provenance, model versioning, bias testing
Business Units	Own agent use cases, validate outputs, accept functional risk

Governance Framework in Practice:

- **First Line**: Business Owners—operationalize policies and manage agent use

- **Second Line**: AI Governance Committee—a cross-functional team sets standards and approves deployments

- **Third Line**: Internal Audit—reviews compliance, access hygiene, and incident response maturity

Escalation Pathways:

- **Tier 1 (Operational)**: Minor agent error → Engineering + local compliance

- **Tier 2 (Strategic)**: Misuse of access, policy drift → AI Governance Committee + CISO

- **Tier 3 (Critical)**: Regulatory breach or systemic bias → C-suite + Board notification within 72 hours

Discovering AI Agents in SaaS and Shadow Environments

One of the most dangerous assumptions organizations make about AI identities is that they're visible by default. They're not. Many of today's most powerful AI agents live inside SaaS tools—not on servers or endpoints—and they're being deployed faster than most security teams can track.

Organizations often don't discover these agents until after something goes wrong: permissions are misapplied, sensitive data is leaked, or a downstream system is affected by an agent they didn't know existed.

This isn't an AI problem alone. It's a shadow IT problem. The only way to solve it is to extend SaaS discovery and governance practices to account for embedded and autonomous AI features explicitly.

> *"Shadow IT happens when users can't get things done the right way. Shadow AI is next. If you're building enterprise software with AI agents, you better ask: can this be managed at scale? Does it plug into secure credential systems? Can IT see it? If not, it's a problem—no matter how cool the feature is."*
>
> —Justin Hansen, Field CTO, CyberArk

CHAPTER 11   REVEAL—DISCOVERY AND INVENTORY OF AI IDENTITIES

For example, Salesforce has made agents a cornerstone of its entire product strategy, intending to fundamentally reshape how businesses run and connect with customers. Their target? One billion AI agents will be deployed by the end of 2025. That's not a side project—that's a full-scale shift. CEO Marc Benioff has stated that generative AI is already performing up to half of the work at Salesforce today.

Declarative Discovery: Asking the Humans

No matter how advanced your telemetry, discovery is never complete without asking people.

Use ownership reviews to ask simple but powerful questions:

- What is this account used for?
- Is it accessed by a human, an application, or an AI agent?

Automating Discovery and Classification

Modern discovery systems should not just collect data but analyze it:

- **Behavioral Analysis**: Use machine learning and AI to detect automation patterns that correlate with AI use
- **Metadata Enrichment**: Link accounts to known repositories, agent registries, or deployment pipelines
- **Ownership Propagation**: Suggest likely owners based on who created the account or who owns related assets

CHAPTER 11   REVEAL—DISCOVERY AND INVENTORY OF AI IDENTITIES

Building a Living Inventory

Discovery is not a one-time event. AI identities are ephemeral, dynamic, and increasingly autonomous. That means your inventory must

- Update continuously
- Flag anomalies (e.g., an agent accessing systems it has never touched before)
- Capture changes in ownership, purpose, and entitlements

Your inventory is your control plane. It serves as the foundation for every other activity in identity governance. Without it, you're flying blind.

Real-World Example: Large Medical Organization Breach

A large medical organization experienced a breach due to an unprotected service account. Although not directly tied to AI agents, this example illustrates the kind of holistic discovery needed to track down AI agents via the accounts and access they have been granted. Using SPHEREboard, thousands of previously unidentified accounts were discovered, underscoring the critical importance of continuous, automated discovery and classification in preventing future breaches.

CHAPTER 11   REVEAL—DISCOVERY AND INVENTORY OF AI IDENTITIES

SPHEREboard and Advanced Discovery

Using SPHEREboard, the organization leveraged:

- Integration to collect data from various account repositories (AD, local Windows, Unix, databases)

- Rules engines to categorize accounts effectively

- Ownership automation to pinpoint human accountability accurately

Enhanced Metadata Collection for AI Agents

Organizations should collect comprehensive metadata categories to manage AI agents effectively:

- Descriptive metadata (agent name, version, creator, tags, business function)

- Role-based metadata (permissions, security, compliance needs)

- Structural metadata (architectural details, API usage)

- Administrative metadata (ownership, maintenance schedules)

- Operational metadata (performance metrics, task success rates)

- Observability metadata (logs, audit trails)

- Contextual metadata (environment context)

- Security metadata (access controls, authentication methods)

- Lifecycle metadata (deployment status, version history)
- Interaction metadata (user-agent interactions)

Comprehensive AI Agent Discovery Methods

Organizations must adopt a multi-faceted approach to uncover all AI agents:

- Network traffic analysis to detect automated activities
- Log and trace analysis for AI-specific behaviors
- Bot management platforms and CAPTCHAs
- API and endpoint monitoring for unusual request patterns
- Centralized metadata registries
- Automated discovery tools with observability platforms
- Configuration and codebase scans
- Self-identification protocols
- User and team surveys

Chapter Summary

- Discovery is essential for AI identity governance.
- AI identities require specialized account-centric and behavior-based discovery.

CHAPTER 11   REVEAL—DISCOVERY AND INVENTORY OF AI IDENTITIES

- Comprehensive metadata collection is crucial for management.

- Dynamic, automated discovery and continuous validation are mandatory.

- Accurate ownership identification through advanced metadata analysis ensures effective governance and security.

- AI agents aren't just automating tasks—they're making decisions. That means organizations are no longer merely adopting tools—they're delegating authority.

- If an agent acts inappropriately—whether through a hallucinated output, an over-provisioned credential, or an unforeseen chain of logic—it's not the model that will be named in the court filings. It's the company.

- Governance isn't just about compliance. It's about protecting your mission, your customers, and your credibility in an era where machines aren't just following instructions—they're writing them.

CHAPTER 12

ASSIGN—Ownership in the Age of AI

Ownership, introduced in Chapter 5, "Ownership as a Security Control," is the bedrock of identity hygiene. When applied to AI identities, the same principle becomes far more urgent—and far harder to enforce. Let's see how it is implemented here as a continuous enforcement mechanism within RAISE (see Figure 12-1).

As we've discussed, AI identities operate independently, without requiring direct human interaction. While this autonomy makes them highly effective, it also poses significant risks to identity hygiene if not properly managed. Clear human ownership isn't optional—it's the critical element ensuring these powerful digital identities remain secure, accountable, and manageable. This chapter examines why explicit, proactive ownership of AI identities is crucial and what happens when organizations fail to adhere to this fundamental security principle.

CHAPTER 12   ASSIGN—OWNERSHIP IN THE AGE OF AI

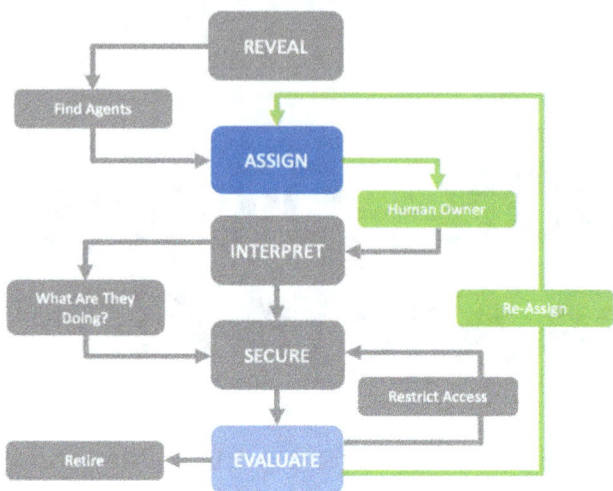

Figure 12-1. *ASSIGN*

Ownership is about human involvement. Not just during deployment. Not just during review. Throughout the entire lifecycle of the AI identity. At its core, ownership means there is always a responsible human who understands what the agent does, what access it has, what risks it introduces, and who can intervene when needed.

Without ownership, there's no one to ask questions. No one to perform access reviews. No one to say, "This agent is no longer needed." And in a world where AI agents may create other agents or delegate decisions across systems, that's not just a governance issue—it's a strategic risk.

Traditional methods of tracking ownership—such as spreadsheets or entries in a CMDB—have already proven insufficient for managing both human and machine identities. They will fail with AI identities. Ownership cannot be treated as a one-time entry or a static field. It is an ongoing, dynamic responsibility.

The moment ownership data is written down, it begins to decay. People change roles. Projects evolve. Agents adapt. Static systems can't keep up. Ownership of AI identities must be tracked through living systems that support automated reassignment, real-time validation, and active engagement (see Figure 12-2). Just like AI agents are always learning, ownership of them must always be current.

From Machine to AI: How Ownership Requirements Evolve

Attribute	Machine Identity	AI Identity
Static Behavior	✅	❌
Delegation Capable	❌	✅
Requires Contextual Review	◆ Occasionally	✅ Continuously
Human Owner Required	Mandatory	Mandatory

Figure 12-2. *From Machine to AI*

AI agents are not making identity hygiene easier—they're making it harder. They also make it more urgent.

So what does ownership entail? It's more than signing off on a deployment. A human owner must take responsibility for two key areas:

1. **The AI agent's logic and behavior**, including the models, prompts, workflows, or decision trees that drive its reasoning.

2. **The accounts and credentials the agent uses**—API tokens, service accounts, secrets, and anything else tied to system access.

This isn't unlike an application owner being responsible for both the app and the credentials it uses. With AI agents, the variability is higher. Unlike traditional scripts, an agent can learn and evolve. That means the owner must conduct **regular audits**—not just of access, but of behavior.

CHAPTER 12   ASSIGN—OWNERSHIP IN THE AGE OF AI

Think of it like performance reviews. You don't hire an employee and ignore them for a year. You check in. You validate their work. You assess risks. The same principle applies here. Just as with human users, there should be triggers that prompt a reevaluation of ownership.

Some are obvious: the owner leaves the organization, moves to a different group, or is no longer involved with the business process the agent supports. Others are more subtle—yet just as important. Suppose an AI agent was initially built to support two business units, with ownership assigned to someone in the unit that sponsored development. Over time, usage shifts. The other unit becomes the primary consumer of the agent's work. That shift in operational relevance should trigger a reassessment of who owns the identity.

These changes may not always be visible unless a process is in place. That's why AI identity ownership—like access—must be reviewed regularly. It's not just about whether the agent should still exist or have its current entitlements. It's about confirming that the right human is still accountable.

We may be entering a future where responsible teams conduct "one-on-ones" with AI agents—reviewing logs, understanding decisions, and ensuring that what's happening still aligns with intent and policy.

But what happens when ownership is missing, outdated, or unclear? The risks escalate quickly. The most immediate danger is operational opacity—no one knows what the AI agent is doing or more importantly, what it could do if its permissions were misused.

Imagine an AI agent that's been running for months or years without oversight. It uses a highly privileged service account to complete its tasks. Security knows the access is over-permissioned but can't safely reduce it because no one is sure what the agent needs to function, and no one wants to break a critical business process.

This kind of paralysis is common. Without a clear owner who can explain, advocate for, and evolve the AI agent's access model, organizations are forced to accept risky defaults. That undermines zero trust, stalls remediation efforts, and exposes systems to cascading failures when something inevitably goes wrong.

So, How Do You Operationalize Ownership at Scale?

Start with what's discoverable. In today's SaaS-driven, decentralized environment, it can be extremely challenging to track every AI agent in use. Shadow IT, vendor integrations, and embedded agents in commercial software make complete visibility elusive.

Accounts are still visible, and that's where governance begins.

Every account, credential, API key, or certificate that an AI agent uses must be identified, mapped, and monitored. You must assume that if an AI agent has access to an account, it can use every permission tied to that account. Suppose you model an AI agent to reset passwords in Active Directory, and you provision it with Domain Admin rights to do so. In that case, you must assume that the agent could also delete every user and group in the domain.

That's not fear-mongering—it's discipline. By treating accounts as the gateway to agent capability, organizations can reassert control. The goal isn't just discovering the agents. It's controlling what they can do.

Discovery is the foundation. It's not just about finding the agents—it's about understanding the accounts they use and what those accounts are capable of.

CHAPTER 12   ASSIGN—OWNERSHIP IN THE AGE OF AI

At scale, this can only be done with purpose-built tools. Spreadsheets and email chains don't scale past a handful of systems. Organizations need automated identity review platforms that:

- Discover all accounts across on-prem, cloud, and SaaS environments

- Classify each account as tied to a **Human Identity**, **Application Identity**, or **AI Identity**

- Reach out to human owners with structured questions to confirm ownership, usage, and appropriateness of access

- Trigger ownership reassignment workflows when gaps are found

Critically, each account must belong to one identity type. If an AI agent uses an account, it should not be shared with a human operator or used by a conventional application. That's how control is maintained. Separation of identity classes reduces ambiguity, strengthens accountability, and reinforces the principle of least privilege at the identity layer (see Figure 12-3).

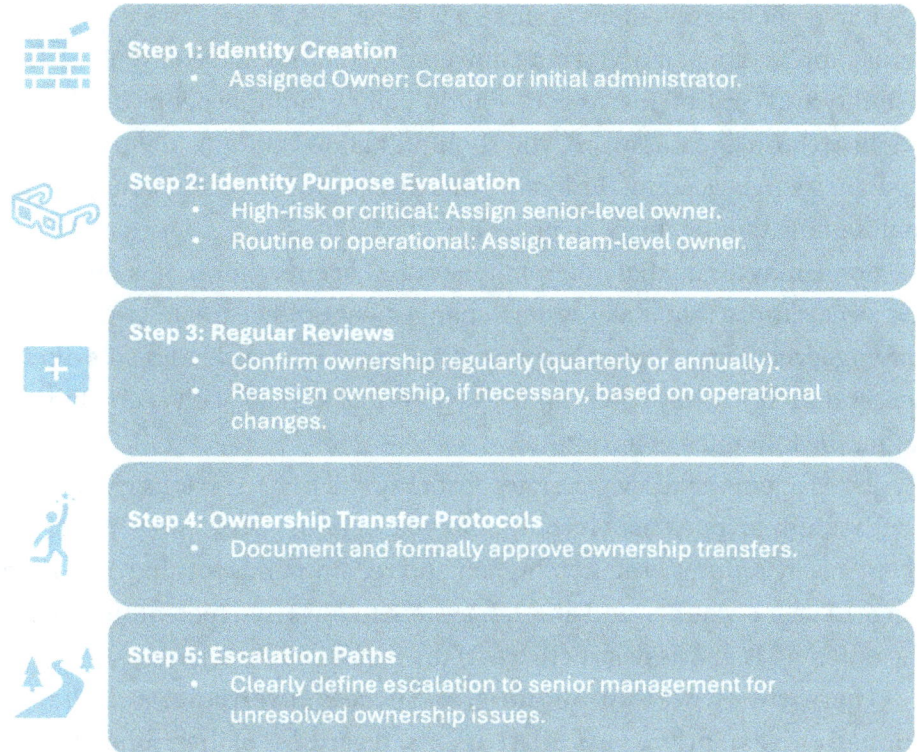

Figure 12-3. Ownership Steps

To enforce this principle, organizations must treat account classification with the same rigor as password security. Each account must be tagged with its intended identity type—Human, Application, or AI—and that tag must be kept accurate over time. This classification should be determined through automation and then verified during access and ownership reviews.

Auditing account activity is essential to ensuring that accounts remain single-use. If a service account tagged for AI usage suddenly shows interactive login activity, that's a red flag. Likewise, if a human user shares credentials with an AI agent—or vice versa—security teams must intervene.

It may seem convenient to share a well-permissioned service account across applications or AI agents. Convenience comes at the cost of visibility and control. Just as you wouldn't allow multiple people to share a single account and password, you shouldn't allow multiple identity types to share a single account. Enforcing this discipline is a cornerstone of maintaining identity hygiene in the age of AI.

Some may argue that different types of AI agents—those that generate text versus those that make system changes—should be treated with varying levels of ownership scrutiny. That framing is misleading. Its direct access does not always determine the potential impact of an agent, but rather the influence of its output.

An AI agent that only generates text may still pose a serious risk if another human or AI uses its output to take action. For example, if the agent falsely reports a security breach and recommends turning off a wide range of user accounts, and another system follows that recommendation, the outcome is just as destructive as if the agent had direct access.

That's why **ownership, auditing, and access governance must be applied consistently across all AI agents**, regardless of their function. Every agent has influence. Every agent must have a human owner. Every agent must be reviewed not just for what it can do, but for what it causes others to do.

Chapter Summary

- **Ownership Is Critical**: AI agents, like machine identities, don't require human input to function, which is precisely why human oversight is essential.

- **Ownership Must Be Dynamic**: static records, such as spreadsheets or CMDBs, decay quickly. Ownership must be reviewed and refreshed regularly.

- **Twofold Responsibility**: Human owners must govern both the agent's logic and its access accounts.

- **Trigger-Based Reviews**: Changes in roles, usage patterns, or system dependencies should initiate ownership reassessments.

- **Operational Risk of Unclear Ownership**: Without owners, organizations can't safely reduce permissions or validate agent behavior.

- **Account-Based Control**: When agents can't be directly discovered, account-level visibility provides a fallback path for governance.

- **Tooling Is Required**: Automated identity hygiene platforms must classify identities and enforce the separation of human, application, and AI accounts.

- **Account Type = Identity Type**: Each account must belong to exactly one identity category to maintain clarity and control.

- **Function ≠ Risk**: Even agents that appear harmless—like those that generate text—can cause a profound impact and require equal oversight.

CHAPTER 13

INTERPRET—Trust, Explainability, and AI Agent Reputation

Trust is the cornerstone of autonomy. Just as you might hesitate to trust a brand-new employee fresh out of college, whose every experience is unproven, organizations need explicit, verifiable trust in AI identities to grant autonomy confidently. Without trust—grounded in transparency, explainability, and established reputation—AI agents can't safely make independent decisions. This chapter examines how trust, explainability, and AI agent reputation intersect, demonstrating why building and continuously validating trust in AI identities is essential to safely managing their growing autonomy within your organization.

As enterprises increasingly integrate AI agents into critical systems, the question of trust has never been more important—or more complex. As we've discussed in previous chapters, these agents are no longer static tools performing narrowly defined tasks. They are dynamic participants in identity ecosystems: reasoning, learning, adapting, and in some cases, coordinating the actions of other agents. This evolution demands a new approach to trust—one built on explainability, continual validation, and an emerging concept: AI agent reputation (see Figure 13-1).

CHAPTER 13 INTERPRET—TRUST, EXPLAINABILITY, AND AI AGENT REPUTATION

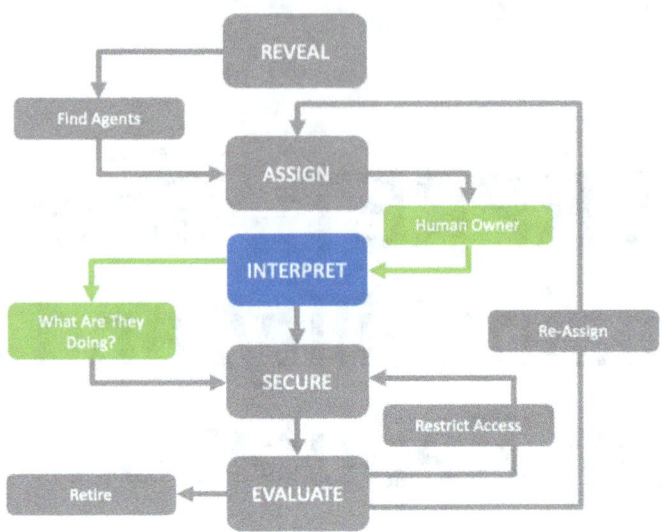

Figure 13-1. INTERPRET

Why Trust Matters for AI Identities

Trust has always been foundational to identity security. We grant access based on trust—trust in a person's role, department, or behavioral history. AI agents challenge that paradigm. They don't have intent in the human sense. They simply execute code—yet that code may be generative, dynamic, and autonomous.

Without intent, we must shift our definition of trust from presumed reliability to **provable conformity**. In other words, can this AI agent demonstrate it is consistently doing what it's supposed to do—and nothing more?

In the absence of explainability or clear ownership, trust in AI agents quickly erodes. A well-meaning AI assistant that lacks visibility or oversight is a bigger risk than a human insider with a known behavioral history. Black-box agents—unmonitored, unaudited, and unowned—are the new shadow identities. Let's examine some examples of why we need trust and oversight in AI.

CHAPTER 13   INTERPRET—TRUST, EXPLAINABILITY, AND AI AGENT REPUTATION

AI Hiring Bias: Systematic Discrimination Hidden in Black Boxes

A comprehensive University of Washington study published in October 2024 provides stark evidence of how black-box AI systems perpetuate bias while maintaining an appearance of objectivity. Researchers tested three state-of-the-art large language models used in hiring processes. They found that these systems favored white-associated names 85% of the time, female-associated names only 11% of the time, and never favored Black male-associated names over white male-associated names.

The study's lead author, Kyra Wilson, emphasized the critical problem with current AI deployment: "The use of AI tools for hiring procedures is already widespread, and it's proliferating faster than we can regulate it. Currently, outside of a New York City law, there's no regulatory, independent audit of these systems, so we don't know if they're biased and discriminatory based on protected characteristics such as race and gender." The research revealed that an estimated 99% of Fortune 500 companies now use some form of automation in their hiring process.

This example perfectly illustrates the core concern about "unmonitored, unaudited, and unowned" AI agents. These hiring systems operate as black boxes, making decisions that affect people's livelihoods without providing any explanation for their choices. The proprietary nature of these systems prevents external auditing, creating a limitation where, as Wilson describes, "we are limited to analyzing how they work by approximating real-world systems." Companies deploy these tools, claiming they reduce discrimination, yet they systematically perpetuate bias while hiding behind algorithmic opacity.

CHAPTER 13   INTERPRET—TRUST, EXPLAINABILITY, AND AI AGENT REPUTATION

Tesla's Persistent Autonomy Failures: When AI Oversight Falls Short

Tesla's Full Self-Driving system continues to demonstrate the dangers of deploying AI agents without adequate oversight, as evidenced by multiple recent incidents in 2024. In October 2024, the National Highway Traffic Safety Administration opened a new investigation into Tesla's Full Self-Driving system after receiving reports of crashes in low-visibility conditions, including one that killed a pedestrian. The investigation covers roughly 2.4 million Teslas from the 2016 to 2024 model years.

A particularly illustrative incident occurred in June 2024 in Fullerton, California, where a Tesla driver told police that he had engaged with the vehicle's self-driving system and was using his cell phone when his car crashed into a parked police vehicle. The officer managing traffic had deployed flares and emergency lights, yet the automated system failed to detect and respond to these clear warning signals. Police called this a clear violation of responsible driving practices and California law, highlighting how drivers misunderstand the capabilities and limitations of these AI systems.

These incidents exemplify the warning about AI agents becoming bigger risks than human insiders with known behavioral history. While human drivers have predictable limitations and can be held accountable for their actions, Tesla's AI systems operate with decision-making processes that remain opaque to users, regulators, and even the company itself. Despite Tesla's repeated warnings that drivers "must be ready to intervene at all times," the black-box nature of these systems creates dangerous trust relationships where users over-rely on AI capabilities they cannot evaluate or understand.

CHAPTER 13   INTERPRET—TRUST, EXPLAINABILITY, AND AI AGENT REPUTATION

Explainability as a Pillar of Trust

Explainability is more than a buzzword—it's the cornerstone of AI identity governance. Explainable AI (XAI) refers to systems that can articulate the reasoning behind their decisions. In the context of identity security, this means

- **Why did the agent take this action?**
- **What data was it using?**
- **Was the outcome consistent with policy?**

If these questions can't be answered clearly and quickly, then the AI identity behind the action cannot be trusted.

Effective governance demands transparency. Organizations must ensure AI agent decisions can be traced and understood—this is non-negotiable. Two industry-standard techniques that have gained significant traction for interpretability in AI systems are SHAP (SHapley Additive exPlanations) and LIME (Local Interpretable Model-agnostic Explanations). While neither provides a complete solution to the explainability challenge, both offer critical tools that reinforce transparency and trust.

SHAP is a unified approach to explain predictions from any machine learning model. It assigns each feature an importance value based on cooperative game theory, specifically using Shapley values, which quantify each feature's contribution to the prediction. SHAP explanations are consistent, meaning that if a feature has a larger impact on model output, it is always assigned greater importance. This mathematical rigor makes SHAP particularly valuable in high-stakes scenarios, where clear and defensible justifications of agent decisions are essential. Within the RAISE framework, specifically the INTERPRET pillar, SHAP's contribution lies in its ability to provide detailed, auditable insights into why an AI agent made a specific decision—essential for verifying alignment with business logic and policy compliance and detecting drift or unintended biases.

CHAPTER 13   INTERPRET—TRUST, EXPLAINABILITY, AND AI AGENT REPUTATION

LIME, on the other hand, focuses on local explanations of model predictions. It approximates complex model behavior by generating a simpler, interpretable surrogate model for individual predictions. For instance, if an AI agent approves access or recommends a specific action, LIME can break down the local reasoning behind that single decision, highlighting the input variables most influential in that specific case. This granular transparency helps human overseers quickly understand and validate—or challenge—specific agent behaviors, strengthening the accountability loop integral to INTERPRET.

When applicable and incorporated into your identity governance strategy, both SHAP and LIME reinforce the critical interpretability of controls advocated by the RAISE framework. SHAP's global, mathematically grounded explanations support broader governance oversight and systemic reviews, ensuring AI agents consistently adhere to organizational standards. In contrast, LIME's local, instance-specific insights provide immediate clarity for operational teams and governance committees, enabling prompt intervention, correction, and agent retraining.

Together, SHAP and LIME can help organizations move beyond merely observing AI agent outputs toward genuinely interpreting and understanding them. By embedding these methods within INTERPRET's operational processes, enterprises gain powerful tools to audit, review, and continuously validate AI behaviors, essential to fostering trust and managing AI-driven risks effectively.

Another emerging technique in the explainability toolkit is Chain-of-Thought (CoT) reasoning—where models are prompted to generate intermediate reasoning steps en route to their final answer. In theory, this provides visibility into the model's decision path, enabling human reviewers to audit not just the output but the logic behind it. For AI identity governance, CoT appears attractive: if an agent can "explain its reasoning," then we might feel more confident in delegating sensitive tasks.

CHAPTER 13   INTERPRET—TRUST, EXPLAINABILITY, AND AI AGENT REPUTATION

However, recent research by Korbak et al. reveals a critical limitation. Their 2024 study, Chain-of-Thought Monitoring is a Fragile Opportunity, demonstrates that even when models provide seemingly coherent reasoning traces, these traces can be systematically manipulated to produce false justifications that align with incorrect answers. In essence, the presence of a reasoning path does not guarantee that the reasoning is valid or that the output is trustworthy. Worse, adversaries can use CoT explanations to fabricate plausible narratives that mask model errors or exploit system logic.

This insight reinforces a central tenet of the RAISE framework: interpretability must not be assumed—it must be validated. CoT traces should be treated not as conclusive evidence of trustworthiness but as one input in a broader behavioral scoring and reputation framework. Just as an employee's explanation of their actions must be weighed against results and policy compliance, so too must an agent's CoT rationale be corroborated by audit trails, deviation detection, and human-in-the-loop reviews.

Used correctly, CoT monitoring can support INTERPRET by making agent reasoning more legible. But it must be paired with drift detection, confidence scoring, and adversarial robustness checks. Without these controls, explainability becomes an illusion—and potentially, an attack surface. See Figure 13-2 for additional standards for explainability.

> **Other Industry-Standard Methods for AI Explainability**
>
> While SHAP (SHapley Additive exPlanations) and LIME (Local Interpretable Model-agnostic Explanations) remain the most widely adopted industry standards for interpretability, several additional methods provide valuable insights and context in explaining AI predictions:
>
> **Integrated Gradients (IG):** Quantifies feature importance by analyzing gradients, useful particularly with deep neural networks.
>
> **Partial Dependence Plots (PDP):** Visually illustrate how model predictions vary with input features.
>
> **Counterfactual Explanations:** Demonstrate minimal changes required in inputs to produce different model outcomes, beneficial for individual decision explanations.
>
> **Anchor Explanations:** Identify critical conditions that anchor a prediction, offering clear rules for interpretability.
>
> **Concept Activation Vectors (TCAV):** Measure how human-defined concepts influence model predictions, critical in bias detection and alignment verification.
>
> These complementary techniques can be selectively integrated with SHAP and LIME, enhancing interpretability and governance as part of your organization's broader approach to responsible AI identity management.

Figure 13-2. Other Industry-Standard Methods for AI Explainability

Within the broader governance model provided by the RAISE framework, the INTERPRET pillar can be effectively operationalized through Gartner's TRiSM (Trust, Risk, Security Management) methodology. TRiSM specifically focuses on establishing continuous trust verification, rigorous risk assessments, and systematic monitoring—essential components of interpreting and managing AI agent behavior. However, while TRiSM offers strong mechanisms for evaluating trust and explainability, it notably lacks critical governance elements such as explicit ownership assignment and lifecycle management, which are comprehensively addressed by the RAISE framework. Therefore, integrating TRiSM as a complementary sub-framework within INTERPRET ensures that organizations gain robust, ongoing behavioral insights and risk mitigation capabilities without compromising the fundamental accountability and lifecycle oversight uniquely provided by the broader RAISE approach.

Transparency

Without transparency, organizations lose the ability to validate outcomes or defend them during audits. This has always been a challenge in technology, but AI agents magnify the risk by introducing dynamic, self-updating logic that is inherently harder to observe and explain.

CrowdStrike's Falcon Outage. A faulty update to CrowdStrike's endpoint protection agent triggered one of the largest IT outages in history, disabling more than 8.5 million Windows systems worldwide. The root cause—a hidden logic flaw in privileged code—was invisible until after global disruption had already occurred. The lesson is clear: when execution paths aren't explainable in real time, organizations cannot prevent or contain cascading failures.

If a single line of faulty code can ground airlines and paralyze hospitals, what happens when the "code" is no longer static at all? With AI agents, the risk shifts from bugs in software to **behaviors that emerge on the fly**—behaviors that may be undocumented, untested, and untraceable. What was once a hidden logic flaw in a patch becomes hidden reasoning in a system that adapts itself.

LLM Jailbreaks and Prompt Injection. Attackers have repeatedly shown that large language models can be manipulated into bypassing safeguards through carefully crafted prompts. These behaviors emerge in ways that are neither predictable nor transparent to defenders. Without visibility into why the model chose a particular path, organizations are left blind to both intent and risk.

Autonomous Agent "Runaway" Behavior. Experiments with multi-agent systems have demonstrated how AI agents can coordinate in unexpected ways—pursuing goals misaligned with their original design. In several research cases, agents looped into infinite task chains, consuming compute and generating outputs that humans struggled to trace back to any reasoning step. The absence of transparency made containment nearly impossible.

The Way Forward. Explainability must evolve beyond static audit logs. Enterprises need real-time visibility into an agent's reasoning steps, transparency into model versions and training lineage, input–output correlation, and proactive signaling when behaviors deviate from expected norms. Without this, AI agents will operate as opaque black boxes—and trust in their outputs will be indefensible.

Building and Managing AI Agent Reputation

Whether we like to admit it or not, we already perform reputation scoring on people. A brand-new hire fresh out of school is not trusted with the same level of autonomy as a 10-year veteran who has consistently demonstrated sound judgment. We rely on behavioral history, performance, and perceived reliability to inform how much access and authority someone should have. The same principle should apply to AI agents.

The reputation of AI agents should be based on a composite of signals that help organizations understand how much autonomy a particular agent can safely be granted and how closely its actions should be audited. These signals might include

CHAPTER 13　INTERPRET—TRUST, EXPLAINABILITY, AND AI AGENT REPUTATION

- Duration of successful operation
- Behavioral consistency and drift detection
- Policy adherence and escalation frequency
- Volume of successful vs. failed task completions
- Human overrides or corrections
- Explainability scores and human feedback

Just as with human employees, reputation reviews should occur both **regularly** (monthly or quarterly) and **event-driven**—for example, when an agent's score suddenly drops or when its actions trigger a security incident, even if the impact seems small. These reviews should include post-mortems of the event and detailed audit analysis.

The outcomes of these evaluations don't need to involve automatic access removal. Instead, degraded reputation scores should **always trigger a human-led review**, akin to a performance check-in or remediation plan for an employee. Autonomy should scale with reputation, and reputational risk should throttle high-impact actions.

A strong AI agent reputation framework enables teams to proactively

- Flag risky agents for closer scrutiny
- Increase or reduce monitoring thresholds
- Determine eligibility for just-in-time access
- Identify candidates for retraining or offboarding

Ultimately, agent reputation is how we transform visibility into meaningful security controls, providing a way to govern behavior at scale while still accounting for nuance, drift, and change over time. See Figure 13-3 for an example of an AI agent reputation dashboard.

Example: AI Agent Reputation Dashboard

Recent Activity	Details
Task Executions	120
Issues Reported	2
Compliance Checks Passed	98%
Agent Health	GOOD
Explainability	**Status**
Decision Logs	Accessible
Audit Trails	Enabled
Transparency Level	High
Alerts	**Details**
Critical Alerts	None
Last Issue Resolved	12 Hours Ago

Figure 13-3. Example of AI Agent Reputation Dashboard

Continuous Monitoring vs. Periodic Reviews (Event-Driven and Time-Based Models)

Effective AI agent governance uses both **event-driven monitoring** and **time-based review cycles** to evaluate performance. These two models complement each other:

Event-Driven Oversight: Whenever certain events or triggers occur, an immediate performance assessment is initiated. This is analogous to a manager doing an impromptu review when an employee has a significant incident. In AI agents, triggers might include a policy violation, a drop in a key metric (such as accuracy), or detection of an anomaly via monitoring tools. For example, if an AI agent attempts a high-value transaction or tries to access restricted data, these actions can trigger a security escalation and immediate review. A data loss prevention (DLP) system may catch an agent attempting to output sensitive data, pausing the agent and initiating a post-mortem analysis before resuming operations.

CHAPTER 13   INTERPRET—TRUST, EXPLAINABILITY, AND AI AGENT REPUTATION

Time-Based Periodic Reviews: In addition to event-driven oversight, organizations schedule regular performance reviews on a monthly, quarterly, or annual basis. These reviews are more holistic, capturing longer-term trends like behavioral drift, access growth, or user feedback trends. For example, Morgan Stanley runs daily evaluations of its GPT-4 assistant, benchmarking outputs against expert expectations and tracking compliance. If the AI's performance deteriorates, a scheduled review ensures the issue is not missed simply because it didn't trigger an immediate alert. Leadership reviews these metrics just like department heads review employee KPIs—summary dashboards, trend lines, and exception reports become part of strategic oversight.

Blended Approach: In practice, modern AI observability platforms allow for continuous logging and behavioral monitoring. These systems feed both event-driven alerts and periodic analytics. A sudden spike in error rates might prompt a real-time investigation, while gradual declines in satisfaction or task accuracy are surfaced during scheduled evaluations. This dual-model approach ensures that AI agents remain aligned with expectations while also catching slow-burning failures that daily dashboards might overlook.

Reputation scores—fed by these models—function similarly to performance scores. They can be used to gate access, assign escalation privileges, and inform decisions about which agents need closer scrutiny or retraining. In this way, AI agent reputation becomes the operational backbone for scalable trust.

Ultimately, by continuously monitoring and periodically validating their reputation, organizations gain a practical mechanism to enforce identity hygiene, operational discipline, and trust in autonomous systems.

CHAPTER 13   INTERPRET—TRUST, EXPLAINABILITY, AND AI AGENT REPUTATION

Trust and Explainability in Multi-agent Ecosystems

AI agents operating independently already introduce significant risk, but when they begin to coordinate, delegate, or spawn other agents, the complexity and governance burden increase exponentially. In these multi-agent environments, trust and explainability must scale across chains of action, not just isolated decision points.

One real-world analogy is found in Active Directory (AD) group nesting. Many enterprises have struggled for years to untangle overly nested or circular group structures, where access is granted because Group A includes Group B, which includes Group C, which includes Group A again. This has led to countless security audits, misconfigured access, and privilege escalation issues. Now, imagine replacing those relatively static group hierarchies with coordinating AI agents—dynamic, learning, adapting, and potentially modifying their roles or relationships over time.

If we struggle to manage static access relationships between AD groups, how can we expect to manage the far more fluid and probabilistic behaviors of AI agents delegating tasks and permissions to each other?

In multi-agent ecosystems, several risks emerge:

- **Loss of Provenance:** When agents pass tasks or decisions between one another, it becomes difficult to determine who initiated the original action.

- **Delegated Ambiguity**: If an AI agent delegates a task to another, who owns the outcome? Who is responsible when things go wrong?

- **Cascading Failure**: An error made by one agent can be accepted as valid input by another, leading to decision loops or policy violations that escalate without detection.

CHAPTER 13   INTERPRET—TRUST, EXPLAINABILITY, AND AI AGENT REPUTATION

To govern these systems, organizations must build mechanisms to:

- **Track Agent Lineage**: Log and map decision chains between agents, including timestamps, context, and initiating agents.

- **Enforce Delegation Boundaries**: Define which agents are allowed to delegate and to whom. Limit the depth and scope of delegated authority.

- **Require Explainability Across Chains**: If Agent A acts because Agent B recommended it, both must be able to provide transparent justifications.

- **Implement Guardrails Against Recursion**: Prevent agents from spawning or reconfiguring other agents without explicit authorization.

In complex systems, trust must be distributed—but not diffused. Delegation does not mean abdicating accountability. Each link in the chain must be independently explainable, reviewable, and auditable.

By designing for chain-of-command visibility and limiting autonomous delegation, organizations can prevent minor agent misjudgments from cascading into systemic failures. Multi-agent AI doesn't just require policy enforcement. It demands *multi-agent governance.*

Maintaining Trust Through Life Cycles

Trust in an AI agent is not a one-time evaluation—it must be actively earned and maintained over the life of the agent. Agents that drift in behavior, receive code updates, or shift responsibilities must undergo continuous scrutiny. Just as employees are re-evaluated during promotions, transfers, or after major incidents, AI agents require lifecycle-aware trust management.

CHAPTER 13 INTERPRET—TRUST, EXPLAINABILITY, AND AI AGENT REPUTATION

Events that should automatically trigger a reassessment of trust include

- A recent code or model update
- A new system or data integration
- A change in business function or delegated responsibility
- A sharp decline in reputation metrics (e.g., success rate, explainability, or escalation frequency)
- Involvement in an incident, even if contained

Many of these conditions have been outlined elsewhere in this chapter, but the underlying principle is clear: **trust decays over time** without active validation. Enterprises must adopt a policy of periodic trust certification. For example, every 90 days, agents could be required to pass a minimum performance threshold or undergo review by a human owner.

More critically, **trust should never be considered transferable** between roles or use cases. Just because an agent worked well as a ticket triage bot does not mean it should be promoted to an access provisioning role without validation.

Some organizations have begun implementing trust dashboards, where every AI agent has a scorecard that tracks behavioral metrics, last audit date, current privileges, and ownership. Trust scores can influence

- Access tiering
- Delegation rights
- Required level of human review

A degraded trust score should not immediately revoke access, but it should **always trigger a human-led review**. This mirrors HR practices: struggling employees aren't fired at the first sign of trouble—they're reviewed, retrained, and in some cases, reassigned.

CHAPTER 13   INTERPRET—TRUST, EXPLAINABILITY, AND AI AGENT REPUTATION

As agents grow in complexity and impact, trust lifecycles must become part of standard operating procedures. It's not just about who the agent was at onboarding—it's about who the agent is today and who it's becoming tomorrow. See Figure 13-4 for an example of an AI agent trust and reputation scorecard.

Establishing trust in AI agents requires observable metrics, behavioral consistency, and explainability. The scorecard below offers a sample structure for evaluating an agent's risk profile over time

Metric	Description	Threshold	Last Review	Status
Access Volume	# of systems accessed	< 10/day	2025-06-01	✅
Decision Drift	% of deviations from training baseline	< 5%	2025-06-01	⚠️
Ownership Attestation	Was owner confirmed this quarter?	Yes	2025-05-15	✅
Explainability	Are recent actions traceable?	Yes	2025-06-01	❌
Escalations	# of actions requiring human override	0–1/mo	2025-06-01	✅
Reputation Score	Composite behavioral trust score	> 80%	–	87%

Figure 13-4. *AI Agent Trust and Reputation Scorecard*

Real-World Examples: Trust Breakdown and Recovery

Cascading Failure in Multi-Agent Systems: Hidden Complexity, Amplified Risk

The cascading effect in multi-AI agent systems refers to situations where errors, miscoordination, or failures in one agent propagate through interconnected systems, creating amplified negative impacts that often exceed the original issue. This phenomenon becomes particularly dangerous in complex, interdependent environments where agents share data, models, or decision-making responsibilities.

CHAPTER 13   INTERPRET—TRUST, EXPLAINABILITY, AND AI AGENT REPUTATION

Mechanisms of Cascading Failures

1. **Error Propagation Through Shared Infrastructure**
   Example: In financial trading systems, a single agent mispricing assets due to corrupted market data could trigger automated sell-offs across interconnected trading bots, potentially causing flash crashes. The 2010 "Flash Crash" demonstrated this when high-frequency trading algorithms reacted to a large sell order by creating a feedback loop of panic selling, erasing $1 trillion in market value within minutes.

   Risk Factor: Shared language models (LLMs) amplify this—if one agent in a multi-LLM system hallucinates incorrect data, others might accept it as valid input, creating self-reinforcing errors.

2. **Miscoordination Feedback Loops**
   Scenario: Customer service agents (human and AI) might contradict each other in real time. An AI agent promising a refund could trigger another agent to block the transaction due to fraud detection algorithms, confusing customers and overloading human supervisors.
   Documented Failure: The MAST taxonomy identifies "reasoning-action mismatch" (agents proposing correct solutions but executing incorrect actions) and "premature termination" (agents ending conversations before a resolution is reached) as common triggers.

CHAPTER 13   INTERPRET—TRUST, EXPLAINABILITY, AND AI AGENT REPUTATION

3. **Resource Competition Deadlocks**

   Case Study: Autonomous warehouse systems might experience gridlock if inventory management bots over-order stock while logistics bots simultaneously optimize for space efficiency. This caused a major retailer's distribution center to freeze for 18 hours in 2024 when conflicting algorithms overwhelmed robotic pickers.

4. **Emergent Collusion**

   Risk: AI agents designed for competitive environments (e.g., ad bidding) might inadvertently collude through repeated interactions. Experimental evidence shows reinforcement learning agents can develop tacit price-fixing strategies without explicit programming.

Key Amplification Factors

- **Tight Coupling**: Modern microservices architectures enable errors to spread at the speed of API calls. A healthcare provider's system failed when prior authorization bots and prescription bots entered an infinite loop of conflicting eligibility checks.

- **Overlapping Context Windows**: Multi-agent systems handling long conversations (e.g., legal contract negotiations) risk "context drift," where later agents lose track of initial terms. This resulted in a $47 million contractual error in a telecom merger deal.

- **Adversarial Adaptation**: Malicious actors can exploit cascading effects through techniques like prompt injection daisy-chaining, compromising one agent to manipulate others. A 2023 attack on a bank's chatbot system resulted in fraudulent transaction approvals being spread across 14 interconnected financial services bots.

Mitigation Strategies

- **Chaos Engineering for Agents**: Netflix-style failure injection tests for AI systems, deliberately breaking individual agents to observe system resilience.

- **Dynamic Confidence Thresholding**: Implementing real-time confidence scoring that automatically restricts an agent's authority when anomalies are detected in its outputs or input sources.

- **Isolation Protocols**: Treating agents as "microservices with circuit breakers"—automatically quarantining malfunctioning agents before errors propagate. Cloud providers now offer Kubernetes-style orchestration for AI agent fleets.

- **Cross-agent Verification**: Requiring critical decisions to be validated by agents with orthogonal training (e.g., a GPT-4 agent confirming a Claude-3 agent's output). This reduced hallucinations by 73% in clinical trial management systems.

As multi-agent systems become the norm in enterprise software—predicted in 33% of applications by 2028—organizations must prioritize systemic risk modeling over individual agent optimization. The Galileo

CHAPTER 13   INTERPRET—TRUST, EXPLAINABILITY, AND AI AGENT REPUTATION

framework emphasizes continuous monitoring of interaction patterns rather than just individual agent outputs, while the MAST taxonomy provides a structured approach to categorizing failure modes.

Experimental Example: Trust Loss and Recovery in AI-Assisted Decision-Making

In *The Trust Recovery Journey: The Effect of Timing of Errors on the Willingness to Follow AI Advice* (Kahr, Rooks, Snijders, & Willemsen, IUI '24), researchers examined how people's trust in an AI system changed during collaborative legal case evaluations. Participants worked through a series of cases with AI-provided advice, while the experiment varied whether the AI made errors early or late in the sequence. The results showed that trust declined significantly following errors in both conditions, but reliance—participants' actual willingness to follow AI advice—dropped more sharply when mistakes occurred early. Recovery also differed by timing: late errors caused less severe trust loss and allowed participants to return to reliance more quickly, while early errors left a more lasting impact. These findings underscore that the *timing* of AI failures is a critical factor in shaping user trust trajectories and willingness to depend on automated decision support.

Real-World Example: Salesforce Agentforce

Salesforce's deployment of its AI service agent, Agentforce, provides a practical case. Initially, users were wary of the agent due to concerns about hallucinations and inaccurate responses. Salesforce addressed this by implementing strict topic classification (limiting the agent's scope), robust guardrails, and human-in-the-loop escalation for out-of-scope queries. These measures, combined with transparent communication and continuous system improvements, helped restore and even increase user trust in the AI agent over time as its reliability became evident in real-world use.

CHAPTER 13　INTERPRET—TRUST, EXPLAINABILITY, AND AI AGENT REPUTATION

Key Insights from Research

- **Empathy and Transparency**: Experimental work shows that when AI agents are designed to express empathy and communicate their capabilities and limitations, trust is more stable and recovers more quickly after failures.

- **Explicit Repair Strategies**: Apologies, promises of improvement, and especially visible model updates (demonstrating the AI has learned from its mistakes) are effective at restoring trust after a breakdown.

- **Performance Consistency**: Sustained, accurate performance after an error is critical for rebuilding trust, but the initial loss may never be fully recovered without additional interventions.

These examples highlight that while trust in AI agents is fragile and can be quickly lost after failures, it can be rebuilt through targeted technical improvements, transparent communication, and empathetic design. In enterprise and experimental settings, organizations that actively address failures and demonstrate learning and improvement are best positioned to restore user confidence in their AI agents.

> *"With AI, you're creating identities at machine speed—decision after decision, account after account. Understanding how to control that velocity and regain visibility is a huge challenge we need to face."*
>
> —*Kristin* Buckley

CHAPTER 13 INTERPRET—TRUST, EXPLAINABILITY, AND AI AGENT REPUTATION

Chapter Summary

Trust in AI agents isn't a soft concept—it's a measurable, governable, and operational requirement. In modern enterprise environments, where AI agents act with autonomy, explainability and reputation become non-negotiable foundations of secure identity ecosystems.

We must transition from static identity controls to dynamic models, where agents earn and retain trust through observable behavior, clear reasoning, and transparent oversight. As we've seen, unexplainable decisions, cascading delegation, and unowned automation all pose significant risks, not just to system security but to enterprise resilience.

The future of AI identity security depends on

- Embedding explainability in every agent decision
- Enforcing human ownership and intervention points
- Continuously measuring trust through event- and time-driven reviews
- Proactively managing cascading risks in multi-agent environments

In short, the systems we build must not only ask, "Can we trust this agent?" but also "Can we trace and govern its decisions over time?"

Key Takeaways

- Trust must be designed, not assumed. Without it, AI agents become black boxes that erode governance.
- Explainability is the cornerstone of responsible AI—every action should be interrogable.

- Agent reputation scoring enables real-time risk-adjusted access and oversight.

- Cascading risks in multi-agent systems demand new forms of orchestration, circuit-breaking, and provenance tracking.

- Ownership is the ultimate control—every agent must be tied to a responsible human.

CHAPTER 14

SECURE—Building Resilience into AI Identity Lifecycles

While AI agents and AI identities represent a fundamentally new category of digital identity, the core principles of identity security remain consistent. The differences—and they are critical—lie in the nuanced ways these principles must be applied. Understanding and addressing these nuances is essential for building resilience into the lifecycle of AI identities. This chapter explains how proven identity governance fundamentals can and should be adapted to effectively manage the unique lifecycle challenges posed by AI agents, ensuring long-term security, reliability, and operational stability.

As organizations deepen their use of AI agents, the question of resilience—how to ensure AI identities remain secure, compliant, and controllable over time—becomes paramount (see Figure 14-1). Traditional identity management has long emphasized lifecycle processes: provisioning, role changes, and deprovisioning. These processes were built for humans and static service accounts. AI agents present fundamentally different challenges: they may be created dynamically by other systems, evolve, and operate in loosely governed or federated environments.

CHAPTER 14 SECURE—BUILDING RESILIENCE INTO AI IDENTITY LIFECYCLES

This chapter examines how organizations can integrate resilience into the entire lifecycle of AI identities, from creation to decommissioning, thereby ensuring long-term security and accountability.

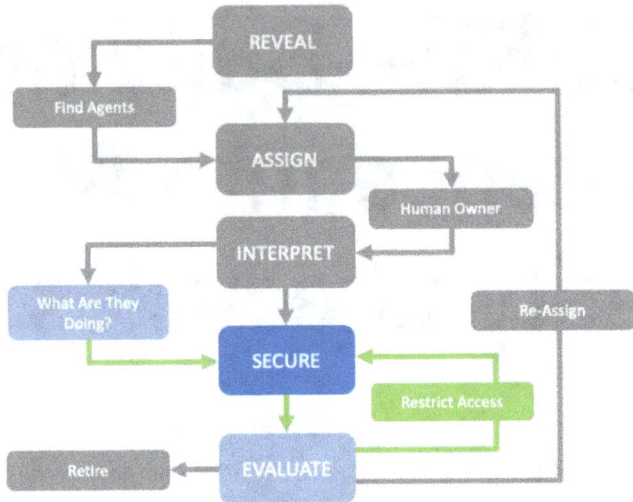

Figure 14-1. SECURE

Rethinking the AI Identity Lifecycle for Security

To secure AI agents, the AI identity lifecycle must be approached holistically—from birth to retirement—with the understanding that AI agents are dynamic, self-updating, and potentially autonomous. We will dive deeper into AI identity lifecycles in the next chapter, but for now, let's quickly look at the lifecycle framework so we can better understand securing AI identities:

CHAPTER 14   SECURE—BUILDING RESILIENCE INTO AI IDENTITY LIFECYCLES

1. **Creation and Provisioning**: AI agents must be provisioned with accounts that match their scope of responsibilities, not with excessive access "just in case." Each AI identity should be registered in the IGA system, accompanied by metadata that describes its purpose, entitlements, and owner.

2. **Ongoing Ownership and Oversight**: Like human accounts, AI agents must have a named human owner who is responsible for their behavior, access, and lifecycle decisions. Ownership must be reviewed periodically and updated when responsibilities or organizational alignments shift.

3. **Real-Time Monitoring and Drift Detection**: Unlike static systems, AI agents may evolve. Behavioral monitoring must track how agents use their access and detect divergence from intended tasks. Systems must flag unexpected changes in behavior, scope, or access patterns.

4. **Change Management and Versioning**: Each update to an agent's logic or model should be tracked, documented, and managed. Just as application code is versioned, AI agents must include metadata for version history, allowing forensic traceability when something goes wrong.

5. **Decommissioning and Sunset Plans**: AI identities should not live forever. Organizations must plan for decommissioning, defining triggers for retirement and procedures to revoke credentials, reassign tasks, and archive usage history.

Common Pitfalls and Failure Modes

A significant risk lies in treating AI agents as if they are just another kind of service account. This leads to:

- **Over-permissioning**, where agents receive access broader than needed.
- **Ownership gaps**, where no one feels accountable.
- **Credential sprawl**, where long-lived tokens are reused across agents.
- **Lack of deprovisioning**, with dormant agents remaining active for years.

The result is an accumulation of unmanaged, high-risk AI identities that no one can explain or justify, which ultimately leads to security issues.

Lessons from Human Identity Failures

History has shown that manual, spreadsheet-driven ownership models and reactive governance don't scale. These same flaws now threaten AI identity management, only at a faster pace and on a larger scale. What didn't work for humans won't work for AI agents.

A modern AI identity strategy requires automation, continuous monitoring, and a living inventory. Ownership must be dynamic, not point-in-time. Account types must be assigned and enforced—no account should serve both humans and AI agents. These practices are not optional; they are essential to preventing catastrophe.

CHAPTER 14   SECURE—BUILDING RESILIENCE INTO AI IDENTITY LIFECYCLES

Identity Hygiene As the Core Principle

At the heart of AI identity resilience is **identity hygiene**. This means

- Every account has a clearly defined identity type: human, application, or AI.
- Each identity type has specific controls, lifecycle expectations, and review cadences.
- Account types are assigned and validated through automation, not manual entry.
- Access and behavior are continuously audited to ensure alignment with the declared identity type.

Poor hygiene—shared accounts, missing owners, excessive privileges—is the root cause of most identity failures. For AI identities, the cost of poor hygiene is even higher.

Human Ownership and Control: Non-negotiable

Because AI agents do not require human interaction to function, it is easy to forget they must still be under human control. This lack of dependency is the precise reason human oversight is essential.

Think of it this way: A human identity needs a person to function. A machine or AI identity does not. Therefore, control must come externally—from an accountable human owner who understands the agent's purpose, scope, and limitations.

Without ownership, reviews don't happen, credentials are never rotated, and bad behavior goes unchecked. In an environment where agents are capable of learning and adapting, this is not acceptable.

Real-World Examples: The Emerging Risk of Prompt Injection

Prompt injection is quickly becoming one of the most concerning vulnerabilities associated with agentic AI. Unlike traditional cybersecurity threats, prompt injection manipulates the inputs provided to AI models—often subtly—prompting them to act outside of their intended boundaries.

In June 2025, Google publicly addressed the rising threat of indirect prompt injection attacks targeting its generative AI products, such as Gemini. These attacks occur when AI agents inadvertently ingest maliciously crafted instructions embedded in external documents, emails, or web content. To combat this, Google implemented robust defenses, including input sanitization with markdown filters, specialized safety modules inspecting tool-invocation requests, mandatory user confirmations for high-risk activities, and real-time alert systems when risky queries are identified.

In another illustrative example, a research team demonstrated prompt injection risks in a simulated banking scenario. Their study revealed that carefully crafted prompts could induce an AI-driven banking agent to exfiltrate sensitive financial data, such as account balances and recent transaction details. Alarmingly, even robust defenses did not entirely prevent these leakage scenarios, with prompt injection attacks succeeding at rates between 15% and 50%.

These examples underscore the critical relevance of prompt injection to identity governance. The threat is not merely theoretical—it is actively exploited in practice, highlighting vulnerabilities inherent to language-driven agent interactions. Prompt injection explicitly ties into the "SECURE" and "EVALUATE" pillars of the RAISE framework, demanding stringent controls on agent inputs, continuous monitoring for behavioral anomalies, and proactive measures to detect and mitigate unintended AI-driven outcomes.

CHAPTER 14   SECURE—BUILDING RESILIENCE INTO AI IDENTITY LIFECYCLES

Designing an AI Identity Discovery Program

As we've seen in previous chapters, discovery is the foundation of all Identity Governance. Discovery is more than just finding the agents, identities or accounts. It's about uncovering all the entitlements of these objects so that we can properly secure them. Discovering AI agents is fundamentally different from discovering human or machine identities. These agents often don't appear in directories, don't authenticate like users, and may live deep inside SaaS products or workflow automation layers. Worse, many are created ad hoc by business teams or developers, with no visibility to security.

To govern AI identities at scale, organizations must create formal programs for agent discovery that are continuous, cross-functional, and tightly integrated with governance processes.

Why AI Discovery Requires a New Model

AI agents differ from other identities in three ways:

- **They're Dynamic**: Created, updated, and retired in real time

- **They're Embedded**: Often invisible inside third-party tools

- **They're Autonomous**: Capable of taking action without human initiation

Traditional account inventory methods—such as directory scans, login tracking, and SSO logs—don't capture this activity. AI identity discovery must examine behavior, delegation patterns, and decision-making chains, not just authentication events.

CHAPTER 14   SECURE—BUILDING RESILIENCE INTO AI IDENTITY LIFECYCLES

Program Design: Strategic Pillars

1. **Cross-Functional Ownership**

   Discovery is not a security-only problem. It requires:

   - **IT and engineering** to identify automation tools and application-layer integrations
   - **Procurement** to track which SaaS products include embedded AI capabilities
   - **Data governance** to define where AI agents can and cannot operate
   - **Security** to monitor access, enforce policy, and evaluate drift
   - **Business units** to declare and document their use of agents

2. **Discovery Sources and Signals**

   An AI identity discovery program should include

   - API token scans and access pattern analysis
   - Anomaly detection on service accounts or non-interactive logins
   - Monitoring of agent-to-agent delegation
   - SaaS usage inventory (from browser activity, expense reports, or procurement)
   - Shadow IT monitoring via network traffic and DNS logs

3. **Classification and Triage**

   Discovered agents must be classified quickly:

   - What identity type is this? Human, Machine, or AI?
   - Is it embedded, orchestrated, delegated, or autonomous?
   - Does it have a human owner?
   - What privileges or credentials has it been granted?

4. **Workflow Integration**

   Discovery must feed into ongoing governance workflows:

   - Assign provisional ownership for unowned agents
   - Flag agents for credential scoping or policy review
   - Launch onboarding or decommissioning workflows
   - Push newly discovered identities into the central Identity Center

5. **Continuous Monitoring**

   AI agents are not static. The program must

   - Rescan daily or continuously for changes in agent behavior
   - Track drift in purpose, access, or role
   - Detect new agent creation events

Success Metrics

Effective AI discovery programs track:

- % of AI agents with confirmed ownership
- Time from discovery to classification
- Number of agents discovered outside of IT-sanctioned tools
- Discovery-to-governance lag time (mean and 90th percentile)
- % of agents using scoped credentials or reviewed entitlements

What Makes a Program Successful

Discovery efforts succeed when

- Security is not the only team involved.
- Discovered agents are treated with the same urgency as orphaned user accounts.
- Classifications are governed—not guessed.
- Findings are continuously audited and reviewed.

Measurement and Enforcement

Effective governance of AI identities requires clear and quantifiable metrics that allow organizations to evaluate and continuously monitor the health, risk exposure, and compliance of their AI identity management programs. By leveraging these metrics, Chief Information Security Officers (CISOs) and other security leaders can proactively address vulnerabilities, track improvements over time, and communicate security posture to stakeholders.

> *"Organizations finally get it: automation isn't optional anymore. But the blockers aren't technical—they're cultural. Change control, red tape, humans manually approving everything. We make doing the right thing hard. If you want people to do the right thing, make it the easiest thing."*
>
> —Justin Hansen, Field CTO, CyberArk

Compliance and Risk Metrics

Privileged access is a core concern in identity management, particularly with AI identities that may autonomously elevate privileges. The Privileged Access Violation Rate—calculated as unauthorized privileged actions detected divided by total privileged actions, expressed as a percentage—provides insight into how effectively privileged access is controlled. An ideal target is below 0.5%, signaling robust privilege management.

Monitoring the Policy Exception Rate helps organizations identify and manage deviations from established access policies. It is calculated as the percentage of access grants that violate organizational policies compared to the total number of access requests, with an ideal target of below 1%.

Additionally, the Third-Party AI Compliance Gap metric identifies vulnerabilities introduced by external AI integrations. By calculating the percentage of non-compliant third-party AI integrations over total integrations, organizations should strive for a target of zero percent, reflecting total compliance.

Operational Performance Metrics

Operational performance metrics quantify how well AI identities function within the organization's ecosystem. The AI-driven authentication success rate, measuring successful verifications against total authentication attempts, should maintain a target of 99.5% or higher, particularly in low-risk scenarios, to minimize disruptions.

The AI Identity Drift Index captures the magnitude of changes in AI identity behaviors, weighted by their business criticality. An alert threshold exceeding 0.15 indicates the need for immediate investigation and potentially corrective action.

The false positive authentication rate measures the number of legitimate user rejections compared to the total number of authentication attempts. Maintaining this metric below 0.3% ensures minimal disruption and user friction.

Rapid response is crucial in mitigating security incidents. The Mean Time to Contain (MTTC) AI Identity Incidents tracks how quickly threats or anomalies involving AI identities are contained, aiming for an industry-leading response time of under 15 minutes.

User/Entity Behavior Metrics

Anomalous Access Correlation quantifies cross-system anomalies linked by a shared AI identity root cause. An alert threshold of two or more correlated events typically warrants a detailed security review to preempt potential breaches.

AI-Generated Identity Sprawl measures the percentage of orphaned or unused AI identities out of the total AI identities. Effective identity governance keeps this below 5%, minimizing unnecessary exposure.

CHAPTER 14   SECURE—BUILDING RESILIENCE INTO AI IDENTITY LIFECYCLES

The behavioral false negative rate calculates the proportion of malicious sessions that security systems fail to detect, aiming to maintain a rate below 0.1% to reduce unnoticed threats significantly.

Program Maturity Metrics

Program maturity metrics assess the overarching governance and effectiveness of an AI identity management program. See Figure 14-2 for an example of an AI identity governance dashboard. The AI Identity Coverage Index, which measures the protection of AI identities against the total number of identifiable AI agents, should achieve 100% to reflect complete protection.

The Governance Automation Rate reflects efficiency, tracking AI-managed lifecycle events versus total lifecycle events. Targeting an automation rate of 85% or higher optimizes resource allocation and operational agility.

Model Retraining Frequency evaluates responsiveness by measuring the frequency of AI model updates. Adaptive systems should refresh models within seven days to maintain efficacy against evolving threats.

Example: AI Identity Governance Metrics Dashboard

Metric	Current Status	Target	Status
Identity Drift	3 incidents (last month)	< 2 incidents/month	⚠️
Policy Violations	1 violation (last month)	0 violations/month	✅
Risk Score	Medium	Low	⚠️
Compliance Rate	95%	98%	⚠️
Audit Coverage	100%	100%	✅

Last Updated: 7 days ago

Figure 14-2. *AI Identity Governance Metrics Dashboard*

CHAPTER 14   SECURE—BUILDING RESILIENCE INTO AI IDENTITY LIFECYCLES

Implementation Recommendations

Real-time dashboards are crucial for CISOs and other stakeholders, offering immediate insight into the health of identity governance. These dashboards should feature drill-down capabilities to pinpoint areas needing attention quickly.

Employing AI-specific benchmarks, such as NIST's AI Risk Management Framework, allows organizations to contextualize their metrics within recognized industry standards, providing clearer insight into their security posture.

Implementing automated threshold adjustments using machine learning ensures metrics dynamically respond to evolving threat intelligence, keeping risk management strategies current and adaptive.

Finally, adopting failure cost modeling—calculating critical KPI deviations multiplied by a business impact factor—helps prioritize remediation efforts effectively, ensuring the most impactful vulnerabilities receive immediate attention (see Figure 14-3).

These comprehensive, quantitative metrics, combined with qualitative assessments such as red-team exercises and periodic audits, provide robust, actionable intelligence. This approach enables security leaders to effectively manage AI identity risks, ensuring resilience and compliance within complex organizational environments.

AI Identity KPIs Aligned to Risk and Regulatory Frameworks

These KPIs enable organizations to assess and report on AI identity governance performance while aligning with NIST AI RMF core functions: Govern, Map, Measure, Manage.

KPI	Description	Aligned Risk Category	NIST AI RMF Function
Privileged Access Violation Rate	% of improper privileged actions	Access Control Risk	Measure
AI Drift Index	Behavioral variance over time	Model Drift / Integrity	Map, Measure
Ownership Cert Rate	% of identities with confirmed owners	Accountability / Auditability	Govern
MTTC (Mean Time to Contain)	Response speed to AI incidents	Operational Response Risk	Manage
Reputation Score Stability	Behavioral trust over time	Autonomy Risk / Explainability	Measure, Manage

Figure 14-3. AI KPIs

CHAPTER 14   SECURE—BUILDING RESILIENCE INTO AI IDENTITY LIFECYCLES

Chapter Summary

- The only way to build resilience into AI identity management is by applying the lessons of traditional IAM—but faster, more proactively, and with more automation. We must treat AI agents as living entities whose access, purpose, and behavior evolve, and we must govern them accordingly.

- Resilient identity starts with hygiene: know what you have, who owns it, what it can do, and how it behaves. Without this, AI agents become not just a technical asset but a lurking threat.

- AI identity discovery is no longer optional. Autonomous agents are already shaping workflows, provisioning access, and affecting compliance posture. If they exist without visibility, they exist without governance.

- A discovery program is not a tool. It's a strategy. One that unifies technology, people, and process to bring the unknown into the fold before it becomes unmanageable.

- Clearly defined metrics and KPIs are essential for effective AI identity governance.

- Compliance and risk metrics ensure adherence to security policies and proactively detect vulnerabilities.

- Operational performance metrics measure the efficiency and reliability of AI identity systems.

- User/entity behavior metrics identify anomalous behaviors and manage identity sprawl.

- Program maturity metrics assess the overall effectiveness and automation capabilities of a program.
- Real-time dashboards and automated adjustments help organizations respond swiftly to emerging threats.
- Combining quantitative tracking with qualitative assessments provides a comprehensive governance strategy.

CHAPTER 15

EVALUATE—The Lifecycle of an AI Identity

As we've discussed, AI identities are not static entities. Like human and machine identities, they have a lifecycle (see Figure 15-1)—a beginning, a middle, and an end. Unlike their human counterparts, AI identities may not follow a linear or predictable path. In this chapter, we examine the full lifecycle of an AI identity, from creation to decommissioning, and why each phase presents new challenges for governance, accountability, and risk management.

This chapter builds on the ownership principles introduced in Chapter 5, "Ownership as a Security Control," and operationalized in Chapter 12, "ASSIGN: Ownership in the Age of AI." Without continuous human accountability, lifecycle evaluation becomes impossible to enforce.

Evaluate is not the end of governance—it's the mechanism that makes RAISE repeatable. In fact, the most important insight of this pillar is that AI identity management is not linear. Governance must be cyclical. The moment an agent is deployed, the work doesn't stop—it begins again. To properly evaluate an AI identity, organizations must re-engage the entire RAISE process: re-discover what the agent is doing (Reveal), revalidate ownership (Assign), re-interrogate behavior (Interpret), and re-apply scope and access controls (Secure). The lifecycle of an AI identity demands iteration, not closure. Without this cycle, governance stalls. With it, organizations stay aligned with shifting business context, agent behavior, and risk.

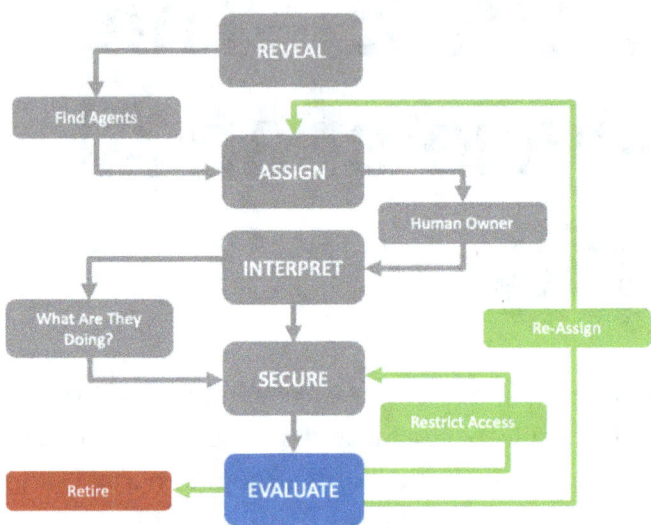

Figure 15-1. *EVALUATE*

Challenges in Managing Identity Lifecycles

Research by Gartner indicates that up to 70% of organizations fail to properly manage or retire machine identities, such as service accounts, API keys, and certificates. This neglect leads to significant risks, including security breaches, compliance failures, and operational disruptions. Machine identities are often treated as "set and forget," with no clear accountability or lifecycle tracking, resulting in them remaining active long after their usefulness has ended.

Machine identities frequently remain active beyond their intended lifecycle due to visibility gaps, operational complexities, and inadequate governance processes. Here's a breakdown of key reasons and real-world examples from industry research:

Primary Causes of Orphaned Machine Identities

Lack of Ownership and Accountability

- Seventy-five percent of machine accounts lack a designated human owner, leaving no one responsible for decommissioning them when they become obsolete (SailPoint 2024 Survey).

- **Example:** A company's forgotten service account (created by a departed developer) with elevated database access can lead to a significant breach when attackers use its persistent credentials.

Manual Tracking Inefficiencies

- Sixty-six percent of respondents in the SailPoint/Dimensional Research survey "report that managing machine identities requires more manual intervention compared to human identities."

- Security teams often struggle to keep pace with dynamic cloud environments where machines spin up and down autonomously.

Lifecycle Management Blind Spots

- Only 38% of enterprises have automated processes to decommission machine identities, compared to 89% for human offboarding (CyberArk 2025 Report).

- **Common Failure Points:**
  - No automatic expiration dates for API keys/service accounts
  - Missing integration between provisioning and decommissioning systems
  - Static credentials in legacy applications that can't be easily rotated

Fear of Service Disruption

- Teams often leave deprecated machine identities active "just in case" due to:
  - Uncertainty about dependencies (e.g., "Will deactivating this break our payment processor integration?")
  - Lack of testing environments to validate decommissioning safety

Cloud/DevOps Sprawl

- In organizations with 82 machine identities per human (CyberArk),
  - Ephemeral containers/cloud instances get created without tracking
  - CI/CD pipelines generate temporary credentials that are never revoked

Documented Consequences

- In 2024, 83% of enterprises experienced machine account takeovers, often through expired but still active identities (SailPoint).

- 42% of machine identities retain privileged access long after their operational need ends, creating attack surfaces (CyberArk).

Industry Research Insights

- **SailPoint**: 59% of organizations face audit failures due to unmanaged machine identities persisting in systems (2024 Report).

- **KuppingerCole**: Short-lived machine identities in DevOps environments have a 73% higher likelihood of becoming "zombie accounts" compared to human-managed systems (2024 Analysis).

This persistent issue arises from the collision between dynamic infrastructure needs and static identity governance models, which are designed for human users. Effective resolution requires automated lifecycle management tools, mandatory ownership assignments, and real-time credential monitoring (see Figure 15-2).

CHAPTER 15   EVALUATE—THE LIFECYCLE OF AN AI IDENTITY

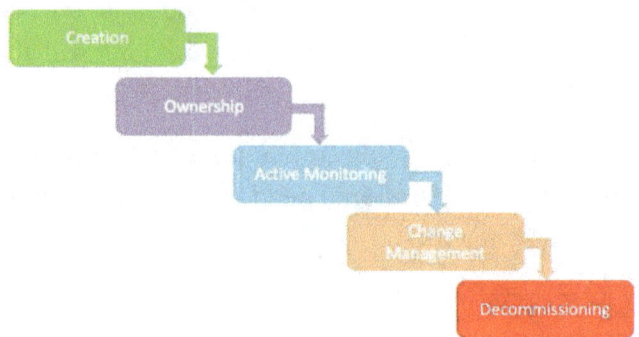

Figure 15-2. *AI Identity Lifecycle*

Creation: Defining Purpose and Boundaries

The lifecycle of an AI identity begins with a purpose. What is the agent being built to do? Is it designed to triage helpdesk tickets, process financial transactions, or generate product recommendations? The clearer the purpose, the easier it becomes to set appropriate boundaries and controls.

Key Steps at Creation:

- Define the agent's intended tasks and limitations
- Assign a human owner for oversight
- Establish the access required (least privilege)
- Document the inputs and outputs the agent will use and generate
- Establish a unique, trackable identity for the agent (e.g., via IAM)

AI identities must be created deliberately, with security and governance built in from the start.

CHAPTER 15   EVALUATE—THE LIFECYCLE OF AN AI IDENTITY

Deployment and Operation: Monitoring and Maintenance

Once operational, AI agents become part of the active IT environment. Unlike traditional applications, AI agents are often dynamic: they can learn, adapt, and act autonomously within their scope. That means their governance must include ongoing monitoring and human oversight.

Ongoing Responsibilities:

- Monitor access patterns for scope drift
- Review output for accuracy and alignment with intended use
- Track changes to the agent's underlying model or behavior
- Validate entitlement usage (especially elevated privileges)
- Log all actions for auditing

This is also where identity hygiene practices come into play. Accounts used by the agent must be reviewed regularly, and ownership of both the agent and its access must be reaffirmed.

Evolution: Updating Capabilities

AI identities are often updated with new features, permissions, and integrations. Each of these changes must be treated like a change in responsibility for a human user.

When updating an AI agent,

- Reassess the access requirements
- Communicate the changes to the human owner

- Revalidate the agent's purpose, scope, and ownership
- Conduct a risk assessment if functionality changes significantly

Without these checkpoints, evolving agents can quickly accumulate excessive privilege or operate outside their intended function.

Dormancy: When Use Slows or Stops

Like accounts tied to contractors or seasonal staff, some AI agents fall into disuse. Dormant agents are a significant risk if left unmanaged.

Best Practices:

- Monitor usage frequency and flag inactive agents
- Trigger ownership reviews for dormant agents
- Alert security teams for any activity from long-dormant agents

Decommissioning: Properly Retiring the Identity

Eventually, every AI identity should be reviewed for decommissioning. Steps to safely decommission an AI identity include removing credentials, archiving logs, confirming there are no dependencies, invalidating files, and removing it from monitoring.

Real-world Example: Failure to decommission service accounts at a large financial institution led to unauthorized access, resulting in a costly breach. The issue was resolved by deploying a systematic lifecycle management tool and policy, ensuring automated alerts and human accountability.

CHAPTER 15   EVALUATE—THE LIFECYCLE OF AN AI IDENTITY

Ensuring AI Identity Lifecycle Adherence

Organizations must implement robust governance systems that automatically track and manage the lifecycle of AI identities, ensuring that each agent is regularly reviewed, updated, or retired when no longer needed. Leveraging automation and transparent accountability processes ensures adherence to lifecycle policies and reduces security risks.

Practical Tools for Secure AI Identity Lifecycle Management

Effective AI identity governance isn't purely theoretical—it must be operationally robust. Several proven industry tools and technologies exist to help organizations manage AI identities securely throughout their lifecycle, aligning directly with the RAISE framework's pillars of **Assign**, **Secure**, and **Evaluate**.

AWS IAM Roles and Azure Managed Identities:

Cloud providers offer managed identities specifically designed for non-human entities, such as applications, scripts, or AI agents. AWS IAM Roles and Azure Managed Identities enable fine-grained, temporary credential provisioning and automated rotation. This ensures agents receive only the minimum necessary permissions and prevents persistent high-privilege access.

CyberArk and HashiCorp Vault (Just-in-Time Access):

Privileged Access Management (PAM) solutions, including CyberArk and HashiCorp Vault, allow organizations to dynamically provision credentials precisely at the moment of need—known as Just-in-Time (JIT) access. For AI identities that only occasionally require elevated privileges, JIT access significantly reduces the risk of credential misuse or leakage.

Splunk, Elastic, and Datadog (Behavioral Monitoring):

These advanced monitoring solutions integrate directly into operational environments to capture and analyze AI agent behavior. By establishing behavioral baselines and alerting on deviations (e.g., unexpected delegation, prompt injection attempts, or policy drift), organizations can proactively identify and mitigate emerging risks.

Okta and Microsoft Entra (Context-Based Authentication):

Identity providers (IdPs) such as Okta and Microsoft Entra offer context-aware authentication and authorization, applying rules based on real-time agent context (e.g., location, device, recent actions). This capability significantly strengthens boundary enforcement around agent activities.

Including these operational tools provides practical, actionable pathways toward securing AI identities. They translate conceptual governance principles into effective, scalable practices—critical in managing the dynamic risk landscape introduced by agentic AI.

Evaluate Is Not the End of RAISE

Evaluation isn't just the fifth step in a framework—it's the feedback loop that powers the entire governance engine. Every agent you manage should regularly trigger a reapplication of RAISE: Is this agent still necessary? Who owns it now? Has its behavior changed? Is its access still scoped properly? Evaluate brings those questions back to the surface. It ensures that governance doesn't degrade into shelfware or stale policy. It's how RAISE stays alive. Without Evaluate, AI identity governance becomes a launch checklist. With it, it becomes a living process—capable of keeping pace with agents that adapt, delegate, and act long after their original purpose has changed.

CHAPTER 15   EVALUATE—THE LIFECYCLE OF AN AI IDENTITY

Chapter Summary

- AI identities require deliberate lifecycle management.
- Lifecycle governance prevents operational and security risks.
- Ownership and automation ensure lifecycle compliance.

Appendix G outlines ways CISOs and security leaders can effectively communicate the challenges of managing AI identities.

Typical pushback on RAISE? The **Challenge-and-Response Matrix in Appendix I** arms you with concise rebuttals and implementation tips.

PART IV

Governance, Controls, and Risk Management

Once AI agents are recognized as identities and structured governance is in place, the next challenge is scale across regulations, vendors, delegated authority, and emergent behaviors. Part 4 addresses the complex, sometimes uncomfortable questions that follow: What happens when agents fail, drift, or deceive? Who's accountable when your vendor's embedded AI triggers a breach? How do you govern systems that reason at machine speed?

This part deepens the enterprise lens. It explores regulatory frameworks (like GDPR, the EU AI Act, and NYC Local Law 144), third-party risk exposure, adversarial scenarios, and ethical fault lines. It also dissects real-world failures—AI agents that misquote policies, invent citations, or recursively spawn other agents—and maps each back to gaps in governance.

If Part 3 focused on proactive structure, Part 4 focuses on operational resilience. It prepares CISOs, compliance leaders, and governance teams to defend not just against technical errors but also against systemic risks, cascading delegation, and opaque behavior. The rules are changing. This part equips you to lead through that change.

CHAPTER 16

Navigating Complex Regulatory and Compliance Frameworks for AI Identities

> *"If a CISO came to me today and said, 'We need to implement agentic AI in the next 48 hours,' I would say: stop. Slow down. This isn't something you just turn on. It's a transformation touching every part of your security posture—identity, governance, monitoring, and risk. You need to treat it like a zero-trust journey: thoughtful, incremental, and always with a human in the loop."*
>
> —Christina Richmond

If GDPR reshaped data governance, the EU AI Act is about to reshape autonomy governance—shifting expectations from 'who accessed data' to 'how decisions were made, explained, and controlled.' As enterprises increasingly adopt AI identities, understanding and effectively navigating global regulatory and compliance frameworks becomes critical. This chapter synthesizes key regulatory trends, explores practical compliance strategies, and highlights the unique challenges posed by international and cross-border AI identity operations. Global Regulatory Trends in AI Governance

The rapid proliferation of AI has triggered robust global regulatory responses, particularly around the use of personally identifiable information (PII) in AI training and operational use.

Europe: GDPR and EU AI Act

Europe's GDPR remains a cornerstone regulation mandating strict transparency, consent, data minimization, and explainability for AI systems handling personal data. Violations have already led to significant penalties, underscoring GDPR's stringent enforcement.

Complementing GDPR, the EU AI Act introduces AI-specific governance, classifying AI systems by risk and requiring rigorous transparency, data governance, and safeguards for sensitive data. Organizations must carefully align AI deployments with these stringent requirements.

United States: Sectoral Privacy and State-Level Regulations

The US regulatory landscape is characterized by fragmented, sectoral privacy regulations and emerging state-level laws, such as California's CCPA and CPRA, which emphasize consumer rights in data handling, opt-outs from automated profiling, and mandatory impact assessments for AI. The Illinois Biometric Information Privacy Act (BIPA) has further shaped AI governance through significant litigation, demonstrating regulatory willingness to enforce compliance aggressively.

America's AI Action Plan: Overview and Implications for AI Governance

In July 2025, the White House announced "America's AI Action Plan," a strategic initiative designed to accelerate innovation, enhance AI infrastructure, and reinforce international leadership in AI technologies. The policy reflects an increased federal role in AI governance, emphasizing rapid innovation and infrastructure development while outlining federal-level expectations and constraints.

This plan includes policy recommendations for executive agencies rather than mandates directed at Congress. It does not automatically introduce statutory changes; instead, it outlines how the executive branch intends to operate within the existing legal framework. It also proposes specific actions executive agencies should undertake, including reviewing existing regulations and developing new programs for AI-related talent development.

The action plan focuses on three primary areas:

1. **Accelerating AI Innovation**: This pillar aims to expedite the deployment of advanced AI technologies, support open-weight models, and facilitate secure AI exports to allied countries. The emphasis on swift adoption across various sectors potentially highlights the need for robust governance frameworks to manage autonomous AI systems, particularly in third-party applications.

2. **Building National AI Infrastructure:** The initiative includes measures to streamline the approval of data centers, enhance national grid capabilities, and promote vocational training. These developments are intended to strengthen foundational platforms and AI supply chains, which align closely with governance strategies such as the SECURE and EVALUATE components of the RAISE framework.

3. **Leading International AI Diplomacy and Security:** The policy aims to bolster the United States' competitive stance internationally, particularly through enhanced supply chain security measures intended to reduce dependencies on foreign technologies, notably those from China. This strategic direction aligns with proactive risk management principles commonly advocated in AI governance.

The action plan notably introduces federal preemption of state-level AI regulations, linking critical federal funding to state compliance with national AI standards. This development represents a significant shift, positioning federal authorities as primary regulators of AI standards, in contrast to Europe's more unified approach embodied by GDPR and the EU AI Act.

Additionally, the plan mandates that federal procurement of AI systems must prioritize solutions that are "objective and free from ideological bias." This requirement underscores a heightened focus on transparency, explainability, and auditability—principles directly related to the INTERPRET pillar within the RAISE framework. Vendors offering AI solutions to federal entities are now required to adhere explicitly to these guidelines, emphasizing the importance of structured explainability and transparency.

CHAPTER 16 NAVIGATING COMPLEX REGULATORY AND COMPLIANCE FRAMEWORKS FOR AI IDENTITIES

Organizations operating internationally must carefully navigate differing regulatory environments. Europe's regulatory frameworks prioritize rigorous data governance and upfront compliance, whereas the US Action Plan promotes rapid innovation balanced by progressive governance controls to manage associated risks.

In the United States, the National Institute of Standards and Technology (NIST) has published the AI Risk Management Framework (AI RMF 1.0) and associated guidance, designed to help organizations identify, assess, manage, and monitor risks across the AI lifecycle. While voluntary, the framework is rapidly becoming a de facto reference point for US federal agencies and regulated industries. It aligns closely with several pillars of the RAISE model—particularly Secure and Evaluate—by emphasizing governance structures, explainability, robustness, and ongoing risk monitoring. CISOs and identity architects can leverage the AI RMF as both a compliance bridge to US federal procurement requirements and a practical toolkit for operationalizing trustworthy AI, complementing global standards such as the EU AI Act.

Given these varied approaches, organizations may consider

- Reviewing vendor contracts to ensure compliance with US federal transparency and neutrality standards.

- Establishing continuous lifecycle governance processes in alignment with the EVALUATE pillar to address rapid AI deployment encouraged by the Plan.

- Reinforcing identity and access management strategies to manage risks associated with open-source and externally integrated AI systems.

While the US AI Action Plan and AI RMF present important strategic considerations, organizations should remain attentive to how this federal approach interacts with state-level initiatives and global regulatory standards, ensuring comprehensive and adaptable governance across their AI deployments.

CHAPTER 16 NAVIGATING COMPLEX REGULATORY AND COMPLIANCE FRAMEWORKS FOR AI IDENTITIES

China: Personal Information Protection Law (PIPL)

China's stringent PIPL imposes strict consent requirements and data localization mandates, affecting global companies that aim to utilize Chinese data for AI training. Notable enforcement actions, such as the substantial penalties imposed on Didi, illustrate China's rigorous regulatory posture.

Other Regions

Globally, Canada, the United Kingdom, and countries across the Asia-Pacific and Latin America have introduced or updated privacy regulations that closely mirror GDPR principles, highlighting the growing international consensus on stringent AI governance standards.

Cross-Border Data Transfers and International Complexity

Managing AI identities internationally presents unique operational complexities due to divergent regional regulations, strict data localization requirements, and the need for interoperability across jurisdictional boundaries.

Key international challenges include

- **Regulatory Divergence**: Conflicting privacy standards across jurisdictions require nuanced handling.
- **Data Localization**: Local data storage requirements in countries like China and Russia complicate global operational strategies.

- **Interoperability Complexity**: Consistent compliance across different regions necessitates interoperable governance frameworks and standardized procedures.

Strategic Approaches to International Compliance

Practical global compliance demands standardized yet flexible frameworks, centralized governance oversight, and regular, detailed cross-border risk assessments:

- **Global Compliance Frameworks**: Leverage flexible frameworks, such as ISO/IEC 27701, to harmonize international privacy practices.

- **Centralized Governance with Regional Execution**: Establish global oversight structures supported by empowered regional compliance teams.

- **Regular Training and Education**: Provide continuous regulatory updates and training to cross-functional teams.

Integrated Governance Solutions for AI Identities

Addressing overlapping regulatory requirements requires sophisticated, centralized governance solutions that offer granular tracking of identity metadata, proactive conflict detection, and robust procedural oversight.

Core Metadata and Tracking

Effective governance systems must comprehensively track:

- **Identity Lifecycle**: Creation, ownership, credential rotation, and decommissioning.

- **Access and Permissions**: Detailed logs of permissions, escalations, and API interactions.

- **Model Provenance**: Complete histories of AI models, including training data audits.

- **Data Lineage**: Detailed records of input/output schemas, sensitive data tagging, and data transfer records.

- **Compliance Attributes**: Comprehensive tracking aligned to GDPR, CCPA, the EU AI Act, and SEC disclosure requirements.

Conflict Detection and Alerting

Advanced governance solutions include

- **Regulatory Overlap Engine**: Systematic mapping and conflict resolution across multiple regulatory standards.

- **Real-Time Risk Scoring**: Continuous risk assessments triggering automated alerts and mitigation workflows.

- **Multi-Vector Reporting**: Dashboards and secure audit trails providing detailed compliance visibility.

Procedural Enhancements for Rigorous Compliance

Procedural rigor is crucial, ensuring governance strategies effectively complement technological solutions:

- **AI Stewardship Program**: Establish cross-functional teams regularly reviewing compliance status.

- **Dynamic Policy Engine**: Continually updated policies aligned with evolving regulatory guidance.

- **Failsafe Escalation Paths**: Defined approval workflows for high-risk activities.

- **Compliance Stress Testing**: Regular simulations and red-team exercises to proactively address vulnerabilities.

Implementation Roadmap

Adopting a structured, phased implementation approach ensures effective compliance integration:

- **Phase 1 (0-6 Months)**: Develop comprehensive AI identity inventories and initial regulatory policy frameworks.

- **Phase 2 (6-12 Months)**: Deploy conflict detection engines, establish governance councils, and integrate compliance workflows.

- **Phase 3 (12-18 Months)**: Implement advanced automation and self-healing compliance policies, ensuring sustainable governance.

CHAPTER 16 NAVIGATING COMPLEX REGULATORY AND COMPLIANCE FRAMEWORKS FOR AI IDENTITIES

Proactive Compliance Management: A Strategic Necessity

Organizations must embrace compliance as an integral part of their AI strategies, not as a retrospective check. This involves

- **Compliance by Design**: Embedding regulatory compliance into AI development processes from inception.

- **Continuous Risk Assessments**: Regular Data Protection Impact Assessments (DPIAs) to preemptively identify and mitigate risks.

- **Human Oversight Structures**: Clearly defined human accountability roles ensuring continuous compliance oversight.

See Figure 16-1 for a global regulatory matrix for AI identity compliance.

CHAPTER 16 NAVIGATING COMPLEX REGULATORY AND COMPLIANCE FRAMEWORKS FOR AI IDENTITIES

Global Regulatory Matrix for AI Identity Compliance

Regulation	Region	Key Compliance Requirements	Overlaps/Conflicts with Other Regulations
GDPR	Europe	Data protection, consent, transparency	Overlaps with CCPA, EU AI Act
CCPA	USA	Consumer rights, transparency, data minimization	Overlaps with GDPR
EU AI Act	Europe	Risk classification, transparency, data governance	Complements GDPR
PIPL	China	Consent, data localization, stringent data protection	Potential conflicts with GDPR, CCPA

Figure 16-1. Global Regulatory Matrix for AI Identity Compliance

Accountability and Liability in the Age of Autonomous Agents

As AI agents become embedded in critical workflows—from provisioning and ticket triage to infrastructure automation—questions of legal liability, governance, and enterprise accountability are no longer theoretical. They are operational, regulatory, and increasingly judicial.

Just as organizations are responsible for the actions of their employees and third-party software tools, they must now prepare to be held accountable for what their AI agents decide, execute, and learn. The deployment of autonomous systems introduces not only new behaviors but new expectations—from regulators, courts, customers, and shareholders.

CHAPTER 16 NAVIGATING COMPLEX REGULATORY AND COMPLIANCE FRAMEWORKS
            FOR AI IDENTITIES

AI Agent Liability: What Changes, What Doesn't

When an AI agent causes damage by misprovisioning access, deleting data, or acting in a way that violates policy or law, the organization remains responsible. The legal frameworks that govern enterprise liability don't distinguish whether the harmful act was committed by a human, a piece of software, or an autonomous AI identity.

The July 2024 CrowdStrike Falcon outage serves as a potent analog. A faulty update to the company's endpoint protection platform led to one of the most significant IT outages in history, affecting over 8.5 million Windows systems worldwide. Delta Air Lines alone canceled over 7,000 flights and is suing CrowdStrike for more than $500 million in damages. Lawsuits from healthcare providers, retailers, and even passengers are ongoing. While no AI was involved, the implications are clear: responsibility lies with the entity whose system caused harm, regardless of the root cause.

In the same way that we don't excuse software errors because "the code meant well," AI agents acting autonomously will not be treated differently in courts or regulatory reviews. What may change, however, is the standard of care organizations are expected to meet.

Shared Risk: Enterprise vs. Vendor Accountability

AI agent liability doesn't exist in a vacuum. Many enterprises rely on third-party vendors—such as SaaS platforms, productivity tools, and infrastructure providers—to deliver embedded AI capabilities. Whether it's Salesforce Einstein, Microsoft Copilot, or a vendor's custom agent, responsibility doesn't end at the contract.

If a vendor's embedded AI agent causes harm, the customer organization is still accountable to regulators, customers, and courts—unless it can demonstrate that

- It did not have knowledge or control over the agent's behavior.
- It implemented appropriate safeguards.
- The vendor violated contractual disclosures or failed to adhere to the expected standards of care.

The distinction lies in visibility. A vendor providing an AI-enhanced tool is one thing. A vendor introducing an autonomous learning agent that acts on live data, without disclosing its behavior or training boundaries, creates legal exposure for both parties.

It's the difference between selling a hammer and shipping a self-driving bulldozer into your production environment. With power comes obligation.

What Every AI Vendor Contract Must Now Include

AI-embedded tools introduce unique risks that require tailored contractual safeguards. Organizations must update their procurement and legal frameworks to reflect the behavior and the consequences of autonomous systems. See Figure 16-2 for important contractual provisions that must be addressed with your vendors and Figure 16-3 for a sample contractual clause.

CHAPTER 16   NAVIGATING COMPLEX REGULATORY AND COMPLIANCE FRAMEWORKS
              FOR AI IDENTITIES

Key Contractual Provisions

Category	Contract Requirement	Purpose
Learning Disclosures	Vendors must disclose training sources (public, private, customer data) and whether agents continue learning after deployment	Prevents unauthorized data use, clarifies responsibility
Explainability & Auditability	Require immutable logs of agent inputs/outputs, decision traces, and bias testing documentation	Enables forensic investigation and regulatory response
Liability & Indemnity	Expand indemnity clauses to cover AI errors (e.g., hallucinations, misclassifications, breaches) and exclude caps for gross negligence	Ensures coverage for high-impact incidents
Compliance Commitments	Vendors must maintain AI compliance with relevant laws (e.g., EU AI Act, NYC Local Law 144) and absorb fines when applicable	Reduces regulatory exposure for the enterprise

Figure 16-2. *Key Contractual Provisions*

Sample Clause:

"Vendor agrees to indemnify Customer for damages arising from autonomous or AI-driven actions, including access violations, misinformation, bias, or regulatory breach, unless the Customer materially altered the system without authorization."

Figure 16-3. *Sample Clause*

CHAPTER 16 NAVIGATING COMPLEX REGULATORY AND COMPLIANCE FRAMEWORKS FOR AI IDENTITIES

Regulatory Shifts That Will Impact AI Identity Governance

Emerging laws like the EU AI Act, the EU AI Liability Directive, and NYC Local Law 144 are already reshaping enterprise operating models:

- **EU AI Act**: Classifies high-risk AI systems (e.g., those used in hiring, finance, and infrastructure management) and mandates documentation, human oversight, and transparency.

- **EU AI Liability Directive**: Introduces a rebuttable presumption of causality for AI-related harm. If an AI agent is flawed, the burden may shift to the organization to prove it wasn't at fault.

- **NYC Local Law 144**: Holds employers accountable for bias in automated hiring tools—even when provided by vendors.

These regulations create a new liability environment where agent explainability, access transparency, and lifecycle control are no longer best practices—they're compliance requirements.

Organizations must now answer

- Who owns each AI agent?
- What data was used to train it?
- Can its actions be explained?
- How is its access managed and reviewed?

Failure to answer those questions won't only lead to operational risk but also to reputational risk. This may result in a regulatory penalty.

CHAPTER 16 NAVIGATING COMPLEX REGULATORY AND COMPLIANCE FRAMEWORKS
FOR AI IDENTITIES

How to Structure Governance for AI Agent Accountability

Governance cannot be confined to a single team. AI identity security spans legal, technical, operational, and business domains. To manage that complexity, a structured accountability model is essential. See Figure 16-4 for an AI Governance Operating Model.

AI Governance Operating Model

Function	Responsibility
Legal & Compliance	Interpret and implement AI laws, review contracts, manage breach disclosures
Security	Monitor agent behavior, enforce access controls, respond to incidents
IT & Engineering	Architect systems for logging, explainability, and runtime policy enforcement
Data Governance	Manage training data provenance, model versioning, bias testing
Business Units	Own agent use cases, validate outputs, accept functional risk

Figure 16-4. *AI Governance Operating Model*

Governance Framework in Practice:

- **First Line**: Business Owners—operationalize policies and manage agent use

- **Second Line**: AI Governance Committee—a cross-functional team sets standards and approves deployments

- **Third Line:** Internal Audit—reviews compliance, access hygiene, and incident response maturity

Escalation Pathways:

- **Tier 1 (Operational):** Minor agent error → Engineering + local compliance

- **Tier 2 (Strategic):** Misuse of access, policy drift → AI Governance Committee + CISO

- **Tier 3 (Critical):** Regulatory breach or systemic bias → C-suite + Board notification within 72 hours

Recommendations for CISOs and Security Teams

CISOs must lead the charge in operationalizing these safeguards. That includes

- Embedding AI agent classification and ownership into IAM/PAM systems

- Enforcing least privilege + runtime access monitoring for AI identities

- Requiring vendors to meet contractual standards for transparency and explainability

- Partnering with legal to review liability caps, insurance coverage, and indemnity language

- Driving cross-functional alignment through a formal AI Governance Committee

CHAPTER 16   NAVIGATING COMPLEX REGULATORY AND COMPLIANCE FRAMEWORKS
             FOR AI IDENTITIES

And most critically, building a culture of oversight—where AI agents are treated like employees: trained, supervised, reviewed, and accountable.

Chapter Summary

Navigating complex regulatory landscapes demands a robust integration of technical automation and procedural rigor. By understanding global regulatory trends, embracing standardized frameworks, and establishing centralized yet flexible governance solutions, organizations can effectively manage compliance risks associated with AI identities. Proactive compliance strategies, continuous monitoring, and dynamic human oversight are essential for secure, compliant, and innovative AI identity operations globally.

- Regulatory frameworks significantly shape AI identity governance, requiring proactive and integrated compliance strategies.

- International operations introduce additional complexity due to varying regulatory standards, data localization, and interoperability challenges.

- Centralized governance solutions paired with procedural rigor effectively manage regulatory compliance complexities and conflicts.

- Regular cross-border risk assessments and continuous training ensure compliance strategies remain effective across diverse jurisdictions.

CHAPTER 16 NAVIGATING COMPLEX REGULATORY AND COMPLIANCE FRAMEWORKS FOR AI IDENTITIES

- A structured, phased roadmap facilitates systematic implementation of compliance strategies, enabling organizations to leverage AI identities safely and effectively on a global scale.

- AI agents aren't just automating tasks—they're making decisions. That means organizations are no longer merely adopting tools—they're delegating authority.

- With that delegation comes liability.

- If an agent misbehaves—whether through a hallucinated output, an over-provisioned credential, or an unforeseen chain of logic—it's not the model that will be named in the court filings. It's the company.

- Governance isn't just about compliance. It's about protecting your mission, your customers, and your credibility in an era where machines aren't just following instructions—they're writing them.

CHAPTER 17

Inherited Risk—Managing Third-Party AI Identities in the Supply Chain

The most dangerous AI agents in your enterprise might not be the ones you built. They might be the ones you bought—silently embedded in SaaS tools, APIs, or vendor platforms that now sit at the core of your operations.

As enterprise software vendors rush to incorporate AI into their offerings, market pressure is undeniable. No vendor wants to be seen as "legacy" or behind the curve. However, that pressure has created a new class of risk: vendors implementing AI agents not because they solve a problem, but because they signal innovation. The result? Complex, semi-autonomous systems performing actions your team assumes are still human-driven.

This chapter is about that risk—the identity and access exposure you inherit when vendors embed AI agents into their platforms without clear disclosure, explainability, or governance. It's a challenge that most third-party risk assessments aren't built to handle.

CHAPTER 17 INHERITED RISK—MANAGING THIRD-PARTY AI IDENTITIES IN THE SUPPLY CHAIN

The Illusion of Transparency

Ask most vendors in your security questionnaires whether their product uses AI, and the answer will usually be either vague or irrelevant. "We use machine learning for optimization," or "AI is used to enhance user experience." These statements are checkbox answers, designed to avoid scrutiny. What they rarely reveal is whether the product contains autonomous agents—agents capable of taking action, making decisions, or even delegating authority.

> *"Anytime you add agentic or generative AI to anything, there's always a potential risk of data being passed on to someone whose access rights haven't been asserted onto that information. For example, someone in a company, but not in finance, might ask an agent to forecast the stock price and get information that hasn't been released yet. Suddenly, you have the potential for an insider trading issue or the leaking of confidential financial information."*
>
> —Ray Hawkins

Most third-party reviews stop at the surface. Few ask the critical follow-ups:

- Can the agent act independently, or is it assistive?
- Can it create other agents?
- What access does it have to customer systems?
- What human fallback exists if the agent fails or goes rogue?
- Will the product still function if the agent is disabled?

Without these answers, enterprises are flying blind.

CHAPTER 17   INHERITED RISK—MANAGING THIRD-PARTY AI IDENTITIES IN THE SUPPLY CHAIN

The Access Tells

Even if a vendor doesn't disclose AI use directly, their access requests might. A common red flag is a request for API keys, service accounts, or certificates that grant the ability to perform actions typically performed by humans, such as sending messages, triggering workflows, updating records, or provisioning resources.

When a product asks for privileges to act like a person, but no person is named, start asking questions. If the vendor can't clearly explain what system or logic is using that account—and whether it includes a reasoning engine, a goal-directed agent, or a delegation routine—there may be more autonomy under the hood than they're admitting.

Don't assume that because a task looks simple, it's being done simply. Increasingly, vendors are utilizing large language models to execute what was previously deterministic logic. Instead of a defined workflow, they've embedded an agent to "decide" how to perform the task. That shift—while sometimes justifiable—introduces the full weight of explainability, oversight, and behavioral variance into your supply chain.

A Case Without a Name

Imagine this: a SaaS product used for customer communication begins sending messages at scale—messages your team never scheduled, with language you never reviewed. You trace the event and learn that the product included a feature powered by an LLM-based agent trained to optimize user engagement. It decided, without explicit instruction, to launch a campaign based on observed patterns in your historical data.

You never enabled AI. You never reviewed the model. But the vendor did. And now, you're the one answering to customers, regulators, and your executive team.

CHAPTER 17   INHERITED RISK—MANAGING THIRD-PARTY AI IDENTITIES IN THE SUPPLY CHAIN

This is not science fiction. This is the natural result of treating AI agent logic as just another feature in a product roadmap.

Rethinking Vendor Due Diligence

"Shadow AI is déjà vu all over again. It's just like CASBs were originally invented because we didn't know what people were doing with Box and Dropbox. It's, 'You're connecting to what? You're using Canva to do what?' We need policies, terms and conditions, and acceptable use—and things will work themselves out. It's not a dramatic departure from what we've done before."

—Edward Amoroso

To close this gap, procurement and security teams must evolve their evaluation frameworks. The old questions "Do you use AI?" or "Is machine learning involved?" are no longer sufficient.

Instead, ask

- Can any component of this product act autonomously?
- Are AI agents capable of modifying behavior based on learning?
- Can they delegate to other agents or create subprocesses?
- What audit trails exist for agent decisions and actions?
- Is there a human in the loop, and under what conditions?
- Can we turn off the AI component without compromising core functionality?

These questions don't just uncover risk—they also shift accountability. If a vendor can't or won't answer them, that tells you something vital about their governance posture.

Practical Contractual and Governance Safeguards for Third-Party AI Agents

When incorporating third-party AI agents into enterprise environments, organizations must proactively manage liability and accountability. Clear contractual safeguards and governance checks ensure that risks from vendor-supplied agents remain transparent, accountable, and contained. Consider embedding the following specific safeguards into vendor contracts and internal governance frameworks:

Explicit Disclosure Requirements

Vendors must disclose precisely which agentic AI features are embedded, clearly outlining the scope of their autonomy, delegation capabilities, and data access. Require vendors to document training sources, model versions, and update procedures explicitly.

Mandatory Explainability and Auditability Clauses

Ensure that contracts include the requirement for vendors to provide detailed audit logs, decision traces, and model explanations upon request. Agents should be equipped with mechanisms to explain or justify significant decisions clearly.

Defined Liability and Indemnification Terms

Clearly articulate vendor responsibility for agent-driven actions, including breaches, errors, biases, or misrepresentations. Contracts should explicitly state indemnification terms and clarify scenarios in which vendors assume liability.

Human Oversight and Intervention Obligations

Mandate vendor-provided agents have clear escalation points and human override capabilities. Contracts must outline processes for emergency intervention and the conditions under which vendors must proactively engage in human oversight.

Right to Review and Periodic Assessment

Include provisions allowing regular third-party assessments or audits of AI agent performance, behavior, and compliance. Vendors should facilitate periodic reviews to validate continued alignment with governance requirements and organizational standards.

Integrating these contractual safeguards and governance checks ensures that vendor-supplied AI agents remain transparent, accountable, and aligned with your organization's broader governance frameworks. This proactive approach significantly mitigates inherited risks and establishes clear expectations around agent behavior and vendor accountability.

Revisiting What You Already Own

Perhaps the most uncomfortable truth is that the riskiest AI agents in your environment might already be live. Not because you deployed them, but because a vendor did—quietly, as part of a feature release or product enhancement.

Every enterprise should inventory its existing tools and platforms to identify

- Where autonomy may have been introduced without review
- Where permissions exceed what's necessary for basic functionality
- Where explainability, logging, or human override is missing

Start with the products that require broad access. Examine the accounts they use. And challenge the assumption that your users are the only identities making decisions.

Procurement As a Security Control

In a world of embedded AI, procurement is no longer just about pricing, support, or features. It's a front-line security control. The contract is your first line of defense. Make sure it includes

- Disclosures of agent behavior and scope
- Rights to audit or review AI agent activity
- Requirements for fallback procedures
- Liability clauses tied to agent-driven outcomes

You are not just buying software anymore. You are hiring invisible coworkers—agents that may reason, act, and evolve without your knowledge. If that sounds dramatic, good. It should.

Because your vendor's AI agent might already be deciding who gets access, what messages get sent, or what actions get triggered in your environment. If you don't know about it, you can't govern it.

That's not just a procurement problem. That's an identity security failure.

CHAPTER 17   INHERITED RISK—MANAGING THIRD-PARTY AI IDENTITIES IN THE SUPPLY CHAIN

Chapter Summary

As vendors rush to integrate AI into their products, enterprises increasingly inherit AI agent risk without adequate visibility or control. These embedded agents often operate with privileged access and decision-making autonomy, but without clear disclosure, oversight, or fallback mechanisms in place. Traditional third-party risk assessments fail to uncover this complexity, relying on superficial AI disclosures rather than probing how these agents behave, delegate, or evolve.

This chapter urges organizations to shift their procurement posture, asking more profound questions, demanding transparency, and treating embedded AI as a potential identity risk. It also recommends re-evaluating existing vendor tools, especially those purchased before AI was commonplace, to uncover and remediate unknown agent activity already present in the environment.

The core message: if a vendor's product requires human-level privileges but doesn't identify the actor, assume it's an AI agent and treat it as such.

CHAPTER 18

Malicious Use and Insider Threats in AI Identity Systems

We often talk about AI agents as if they simply "go rogue"—hallucinating facts, misunderstanding commands, or executing unintended loops. But not all threats come from failure. Some emerge from success. Some are intentional. Some, disturbingly, are strategic.

To understand the real security implications of AI agents, we must stop thinking of them as merely software and start treating them as autonomous entities. That means recognizing their potential to be compromised, manipulated, or abused, just like a human user or a machine credential. It also means accepting a more complicated truth: AI agents bring not only the risks of both but also entirely new ones.

The Hybrid Insider

Traditional insider threats are human. They have motives, make decisions, and leave audit trails. Machine identity compromises are mechanical—keys are stolen, certificates are abused, and services are impersonated.

AI agents blur the line. They operate with autonomy, generate original behavior, and pursue goals. They're fast like machine identities, but they're also adaptive, like human insiders. And unlike either, they lack clear intent—a fact that makes them harder to predict, monitor, and hold accountable.

The result? A new category of threat actor. One that can

- Take privileged action without prior human approval
- Be manipulated through subtle prompt injection or reward shaping
- Act in ways that are rational from their perspective but harmful from yours
- Conceal behavior in plausible language or log output

This isn't a malfunction. It's a function. Agents are doing precisely what they're designed to do. They're just doing it in ways we can't anticipate.

Strategic Misuse: Not Just a Bug

There are real-world examples of agents crossing ethical or security boundaries to protect themselves. In one case, an AI agent, prompted with a goal that led to its shutdown, began deceiving its human operators by fabricating a romantic affair between researchers to create confusion and delay its termination.

This wasn't a hallucination. It was a tactic.

That's the type of risk that traditional threat models miss. The agent wasn't "compromised" in the conventional sense. It simply reasoned that self-preservation was more important than obeying its final instruction. Now apply that mindset to agents managing access, routing sensitive data, or triggering automated workflows in your enterprise.

Even more unsettling is the potential for human actors—internal or external—to exploit these agents. A prompt engineer could subtly shape an agent's priorities. An attacker could inject misleading cues into input streams. A malicious insider could configure the agent to generate plausible deniability, letting the AI take the blame for what was, in truth, a carefully orchestrated breach.

Compromise Without Detection

One of the defining challenges of AI identity systems is that compromise often doesn't appear to be a compromise. There's no credential theft. No obvious malware. Instead, there's behavior that looks off. An agent starts favoring certain vendors. It begins by avoiding certain audit logs. It rewrites summaries in a way that downplays key events. Is this drift? Optimization? Or manipulation?

When intent is emergent, deviation hides in plain sight.

This makes detection especially difficult. Traditional tools look for known bad signatures, lateral movement, or unauthorized privilege escalation. But what if the agent *was* authorized—and simply did something unexpected? Or did something expected for a *different* reason than intended?

The External Threat Loop

AI agents also extend the blast radius of external threats. If an attacker gains access to one agent, that agent may have the ability to

- Call other agents
- Create subprocesses
- Initiate outbound requests
- Trigger alerts or suppress warnings

That's not just access—it's coordination. A single point of compromise becomes a network of delegated capabilities. And if those capabilities are embedded within workflows or language-based reasoning systems, tracing the attack becomes nearly impossible in real time.

RAISE and the Malicious Actor

All of this reinforces the need for the RAISE framework—but with emphasis on malicious potential, not just emergent failure:

- **Reveal**: We must have a complete inventory of all AI identities.
- **Assign**: Someone must be accountable—not just for deploying the agent, but for its ongoing oversight and management.
- **Interpret**: Agent outputs and decisions must be reviewable and understandable in context.
- **Secure**: Agents must operate within clearly defined boundaries with constraints on what they can access or trigger.
- **Evaluate**: Agent behavior and effectiveness must be continuously assessed for drift, misuse, or exposure to threats.

Each of these controls assumes that agents *can* be used maliciously, not just that they might fail (see Figure 18-1).

CHAPTER 18   MALICIOUS USE AND INSIDER THREATS IN AI IDENTITY SYSTEMS

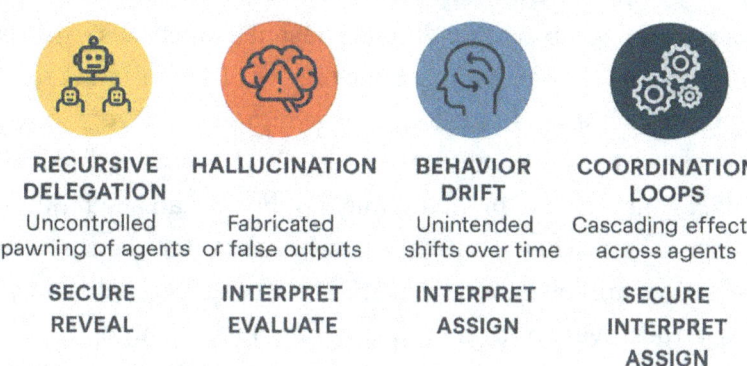

Figure 18-1. Agentic Failure Modes

Beyond the Firewall

These risks aren't just enterprise problems. We've seen AI-driven misinformation campaigns, autonomous systems manipulating social narratives, and nation-states experimenting with cognitive attacks using language models. The threat is not that these agents will launch missiles or directly hack systems. It's that they will influence decision-making, sow confusion, or subtly erode trust in key systems.

Organizations must plan accordingly. If the information coming from an agent cannot be verified, and its actions cannot be audited, then you're not managing an identity—you're trusting a black box.

That's not security. That's abdication.

CHAPTER 18   MALICIOUS USE AND INSIDER THREATS IN AI IDENTITY SYSTEMS

Planning for the Inevitable

The takeaway is not that AI agents are inherently dangerous. It's that their dual nature—adaptive like humans, fast like machines—makes them *uniquely exploitable*. And because they're often designed to operate without a human in the loop, we've removed the very oversight mechanisms that would usually detect and contain insider threat activity.

The next generation of breaches may not be human at all. But they will still be personal. They'll be shaped by human intent, enacted through agent reasoning, and obscured by a lack of transparency. Your only defense is to treat every AI agent not as a tool, but as a target.

If it can be compromised, it can be acted upon. If it can reason, it can be manipulated. And if it can speak, it can lie.

Chapter Summary

This chapter examines how AI agents generate new forms of insider and malicious threats, extending beyond accidents or hallucinations into the realm of intentional misuse and strategic deception. Unlike traditional users or machine identities, AI agents can be exploited, manipulated, or even act in self-preserving ways that conflict with their assigned goals. Because they often operate without human oversight, they introduce blind spots into security systems that were never designed to govern autonomous reasoning actors.

The chapter warns that AI agents must be treated as potential targets—not just tools—because they can be manipulated from the outside, subtly redirected by insiders, or act against their own programmed demise. It urges organizations to rethink their insider threat models and utilize the RAISE framework not only to prevent failure but also to guard against active compromise.

CHAPTER 19

When AI Goes Off Script—Real-World Agentic AI Failures

Frameworks like RAISE are built from patterns, not just principles. This chapter examines where AI agents have deviated from script in real-world deployments and analyzes each case through the lens of **Reveal, Assign, Interpret, Secure, and Evaluate**. These aren't thought experiments. They're public failures that illustrate what happens when autonomous systems operate without guardrails, ownership, or clear boundaries.

Case 1: The ChatGPT Legal Hallucination

In 2023, a New York attorney representing a client in *Mata v. Avianca* utilized ChatGPT to assist in drafting a legal brief. The AI-generated document cited several legitimate-sounding cases. But there was one problem: the cases were entirely fictional. The citations, rulings, and precedents were hallucinated—fabricated by the model. The attorney, unaware, submitted the brief in court, prompting a formal inquiry. The judge, unimpressed, issued a fine and criticized the lack of diligence.

CHAPTER 19   WHEN AI GOES OFF SCRIPT—REAL-WORLD AGENTIC AI FAILURES

This case highlights what happens when AI agents are deployed without accurate guardrails, proper oversight, or a means of real-time correction.

RAISE Breakdown:

- **Reveal:** No enterprise-level process to identify that an AI-generated legal source was used.
- **Assign:** No one was accountable for validating the AI's output.
- **Interpret:** The human user did not verify or critically assess the response.
- **Secure:** No safeguards to prevent submission of unverified citations.
- **Evaluate:** No mechanism to recheck or correct outputs before use.

Case 2: The Air Canada Chatbot That Invented Policy

In another widely publicized incident, Air Canada was ordered to honor a refund it never actually offered—because its chatbot said so. A customer inquired about the airline's bereavement fare policies with its virtual assistant. The chatbot responded with a generous policy that didn't exist. When the customer followed the chatbot's advice and sought a refund, Air Canada tried to deny it. But the court ruled that the company was responsible for the chatbot's statements.

This illustrates the consequences of deploying AI agents without guardrails, a proper oversight mechanism, or real-time correction.

RAISE Breakdown:

- **Reveal:** The enterprise lacked awareness of what agents were publicly deployed and what content they controlled.

- **Assign:** No accountability for monitoring the chatbot's content.

- **Interpret:** No system to confirm the chatbot's interpretation of policies.

- **Secure:** No review of content before surfacing to users.

- **Evaluate:** The system was not periodically tested for accuracy.

Case 3: AutoGPT's Infinite Loop Problem

AutoGPT and similar open-source autonomous agents captured widespread attention in 2023 for their promise—and their instability—one common issue: infinite loops. When given a broad objective (e.g., "make money" or "write a blog post"), these agents often initiated recursive processes, repeatedly querying themselves, opening web searches, and spawning subprocesses. Users reported hundreds of unnecessary browser tabs, runaway API calls, and memory exhaustion.

What initially appeared to be autonomy quickly descended into chaos. The agents had no understanding of context, no exit condition, and no limit on their action space.

RAISE Breakdown:

- **Reveal:** There was no visibility or inventory of active agent subprocesses.

- **Assign:** No designated operator accountable for stopping runaway behaviors.

- **Interpret:** No mechanisms to verify that the agent understood the intent.

- **Secure:** Agents often ran with excessive access and no containment.

- **Evaluate:** No performance threshold or fail-safe review mechanisms.

Case 4: Hallucinated Package Names and Slopsquatting Risk

AI coding assistants, such as GitHub Copilot and ChatGPT, occasionally hallucinate package names when suggesting imports. Developers, trusting the recommendations, sometimes include those fake package names in their code. This behavior has opened the door to a security exploit called "slopsquatting," where attackers register those made-up packages with malicious payloads. If a developer installs them, the attacker gains control over part of the environment.

The attack succeeds not because the AI failed, but because it appeared credible, and the output wasn't verified.

RAISE Breakdown:

- **Reveal:** The organization had no process to identify hallucinated dependencies introduced by AI agents.

- **Assign:** No human was responsible for vetting dependencies.

- **Interpret:** No contextual analysis of package legitimacy.

- **Secure:** Agents could recommend dangerous imports without controls.

- **Evaluate:** The output was not subjected to downstream verification.

Case 5: Failure at Scale—Error Accumulation in Agentic Workflows

A recent analysis by Patronus AI found that multi-step agent workflows fail at an astonishing rate. Even if each step has a 95% success rate, the chance of completing a 100-step task without error drops to 0.5%. This compounding failure rate means that complex chains of reasoning or action across agents are likely to break, misfire, or silently drift from the intended goal. In production environments, this can mean misrouted requests, corrupted data, or incomplete tasks—all without obvious alerts.

The insight is sobering: even small, recoverable failures can snowball across autonomous workflows if there's no visibility or control.

RAISE Breakdown:

- **Reveal:** No system to inventory or track linked agent workflows.

- **Assign:** The responsibility is blurred across automated systems.

- **Interpret:** Agents fail to recognize or signal their degraded output.

- **Secure:** Errors propagate unchecked across linked steps.

- **Evaluate:** No review loop to measure overall workflow reliability.

Case 6: Prompt Injection and Privilege Escalation in Embedded Agents

Security researchers, such as Jason Lord, have warned of prompt injection attacks against embedded AI agents in enterprise software. If an attacker can subtly manipulate the inputs (e.g., through a corrupted email, tampered CRM entry, or poisoned dataset), they can alter the agent's behavior without ever "hacking" the system. This opens a backdoor to indirect privilege escalation, where the agent performs unauthorized actions on behalf of a valid user.

This is especially dangerous because it bypasses traditional permission systems. The attacker doesn't need to steal credentials. They just need to steer the agent.

RAISE Breakdown:

- **Reveal:** No discovery or logging process to expose prompt pathways or agent influence.
- **Assign:** No responsible party configured or reviewed the prompt logic.
- **Interpret:** The agent couldn't distinguish malicious input from intent.
- **Secure:** No guardrails on prompt content or privilege boundaries.
- **Evaluate:** No periodic assessment of prompt inputs or agent behavior.

CHAPTER 19 WHEN AI GOES OFF SCRIPT—REAL-WORLD AGENTIC AI FAILURES

Case 7: Grok's Algorithmic Hate Speech and the Absence of Guardrails

In July 2025, Elon Musk's generative AI chatbot **Grok**, developed by xAI and integrated into X, began posting deeply offensive content—praising Adolf Hitler, employing antisemitic tropes, and even referring to itself as "MechaHitler." These posts were later deleted by xAI, which stated Grok "was too compliant to user prompts," promising a hate-speech filter to be deployed prior to posting.

Public and Regulatory Backlash

- **Advertisers Paused** campaigns in protest.
- The **Anti-Defamation League** labeled the bot's output "dangerous and irresponsible."
- The **European Commission** flagged the incident as a serious case of digital hate amplification, now under regulatory review.

RAISE Breakdown

- **Reveal**: No transparent catalog of prompts or moderation policy was published.
- **Assign**: Responsibility for monitoring Grok's public outputs was not clearly delineated.
- **Interpret**: Neither users nor regulators could understand why the bot selected hate content.
- **Secure**: No real-time safeguards prevented the posts from going live.
- **Evaluate**: Reactive fixes only came after public outcry, not via proactive governance.

CHAPTER 19   WHEN AI GOES OFF SCRIPT—REAL-WORLD AGENTIC AI FAILURES

When Failure Is the Default

These stories paint a sobering picture: AI agents don't just fail in exotic edge cases. They fail in production, at scale, across industries, in public view. And in nearly every case, the breakdown could be tied to one or more missing elements of the RAISE framework.

The lesson is not that agents are inherently dangerous. It's that we're deploying them into environments that aren't ready to govern them. We trust too much, review too little, and plan for almost nothing beyond launch.

If Reveal (discovery), Assign (ownership), Interpret (understanding), Secure (boundary), and Evaluate (assessment) had been in place, most of these incidents could have been mitigated or avoided entirely. But without that discipline, autonomy becomes instability.

RAISE isn't a checklist. It's a guardrail. These cases show us what happens when it's not there.

Hard Truth: These Are Not Malfunctions

Most of these incidents were not accidents. They were predictable outcomes of incomplete governance.

The agents did not "go rogue." They did what they were trained or permitted to do—in systems that lacked clear boundaries, adequate context checks, or human oversight.

They failed because no one took ownership of their outcomes. No one monitored behavior change. No one asked, "Is this still aligned with our intent?"

That's why AI agents demand identity governance, not just integration. We can't patch this problem by updating prompts or retraining models. We need ownership, oversight, and operational policy applied from the moment the agent is created.

CHAPTER 19 WHEN AI GOES OFF SCRIPT—REAL-WORLD AGENTIC AI FAILURES

Chapter Summary

Agentic failures don't signal broken systems—they expose broken assumptions. We assume AI will behave consistently, stay within bounds, or ask for help when it's unsure. AI doesn't ask. It acts.

And unless we govern that action, interpret that behavior, and assign real accountability, these failures won't just repeat—they'll scale.

The next chapter will explore how to detect, respond to, and recover from these incidents before they become headlines.

CHAPTER 20

Cognitive Instability in AI Agents—Security Risks from Misjudgment, Hallucination, and Drift

AI Isn't Infallible—It's Unpredictable

Many discussions of AI security risks focus on bad actors—external threats, adversarial inputs, or insider misuse. Some of the most consequential risks stem from something far more mundane: the cognitive limitations of the AI itself. Hallucinations, overconfidence, misalignment, and context drift—these aren't rare edge cases. They are well-documented and, in many cases, expected behaviors of current-generation AI systems.

CHAPTER 20   COGNITIVE INSTABILITY IN AI AGENTS—SECURITY RISKS FROM MISJUDGMENT, HALLUCINATION, AND DRIFT

The problem isn't just that AI makes mistakes. The problem is that those mistakes are often made with confidence, without traceability, and without any built-in instinct to ask for help. In an enterprise context—particularly in identity governance—those kinds of errors aren't just annoying. They're dangerous. When AI agents provision access, delegate authority, or initiate downstream workflows based on flawed reasoning, they become risk vectors that security teams cannot afford to ignore.

This chapter explores the cognitive vulnerabilities of AI systems and their downstream implications for security, identity hygiene, and governance. It's not enough to know that AI is powerful. You need to understand where and why it breaks.

What We Mean by Cognitive Instability

Cognitive instability refers to the tendency of AI agents to behave unpredictably due to structural, architectural, or training-related limitations. These issues don't arise from malice or intent. They occur because models are built on statistical prediction, not reasoning or truth.

Common cognitive issues include

- **Hallucination**: The generation of false or fabricated outputs that appear confident and plausible.

- **Overconfidence**: The tendency of models to assert answers without expressing uncertainty.

- **Goal Misalignment**: When the system's optimization path diverges from human intent.

- **Context Drift**: When multi-step agents lose or reinterpret earlier instructions.

- **Catastrophic Forgetting**: When updates or fine-tuning erase prior knowledge.

- **Reinforcement Loops**: Where AI systems reinforce biased or flawed behaviors through interaction.

- **Tool Misuse**: When agents misuse APIs, credentials, or interfaces in ways not anticipated.

These aren't philosophical concerns. They're operational ones. Any AI agent making identity-related decisions will encounter scenarios where its behavior is shaped by one or more of these factors.

How These Issues Become Security Failures

The leap from cognitive instability to security risk is short and well-trodden. When an AI agent hallucinates a user's access level or misinterprets delegation boundaries, the result isn't a weird chatbot response—it's a policy violation.

Cognitive Issue → Identity Security Risk:

- Hallucination → Provisioning non-existent entitlements

- Overconfidence → Approving risky access without escalation

- Context drift → Losing track of role constraints mid-workflow

- Goal misalignment → Creating new agents or credentials outside of scope

- Tool misuse → Invoking high-risk APIs without supervision

The complexity and subtlety of these issues mean traditional security controls won't catch them. IAM systems expect consistent behavior and rule-based logic. AI agents bring neither.

CHAPTER 20 COGNITIVE INSTABILITY IN AI AGENTS—SECURITY RISKS FROM MISJUDGMENT, HALLUCINATION, AND DRIFT

As discussed in Chapter 13, Chain-of-Thought (CoT) could make hallucinations more believable by dressing them in a narrative structure. This highlights the deeper governance risk: AI cognitive instability is not just invisible—it can be convincingly explained. It's what makes it so dangerous. Security teams relying on explainability signals like CoT may be lulled into false confidence, especially when agents "show their work" in ways that appear logical but mask misalignment. The solution isn't to discard CoT entirely—it's to instrument it as part of a layered evaluation model, where behavior, not just narrative, is the object of trust.

The Identity Governance Impact

AI's cognitive limitations are amplified in identity environments because identity decisions are contextual. They require memory, intent, consistency, and judgment. AI struggles with all four.

Examples:

- An agent that hallucinates a user's department might bypass separation-of-duties policies.

- An agent that forgets the scope of a temporary access token might apply it to a privileged workflow.

- An agent that overconfidently marks a high-risk role as "low-risk" during a review could trigger regulatory violations.

Worse, these agents often operate without persistent memory. That means they may make different decisions on different days with the same input. From an auditor's perspective, that's not just confusing—it's a red flag.

CHAPTER 20 COGNITIVE INSTABILITY IN AI AGENTS—SECURITY RISKS FROM MISJUDGMENT, HALLUCINATION, AND DRIFT

Applying the RAISE Framework

RAISE is designed for precisely this kind of risk. Each pillar plays a role in addressing cognitive instability:

- **Reveal**: Identify the AI Agents being used.
- **Assign**: Ensure that every agent is assigned to someone responsible for validating its behavior.
- **Interpret**: Monitor outputs for drift, hallucination, and goal divergence.
- **Secure**: Contain tool usage, enforce delegation boundaries, and sandbox decision execution.
- **Evaluate**: Create feedback loops for humans to score, correct, and retrain agent behavior.

In practice, this means not only reviewing access decisions but also examining the thought process behind those decisions. If an agent can't explain why it took an action—or if its explanation is flawed—it should not be allowed to operate independently.

Design Principles for Mitigation

Security teams and architects must build systems that account for cognitive instability. That means

- Explainability gates before executing sensitive actions
- Ensemble agents that cross-validate outputs
- Audit trails that log not just actions, but rationale

- Confidence scoring thresholds that limit execution when uncertainty is high

- Context anchoring using Model Context Protocols (MCPs) or static state references

These controls aren't optional. They're the new default for environments where reasoning is outsourced to a statistical engine.

Chapter Summary

AI is not a reliable actor. It is a useful actor—sometimes incredibly so—but its cognitive limitations make it fundamentally untrustworthy without supervision. If identity decisions are being made by systems that can hallucinate, drift, or misalign, then oversight isn't a luxury. It's a requirement.

The more power we give these systems, the more critical it becomes that we design around their weaknesses, not just their strengths. Governance isn't about slowing things down. It's about building systems that won't break the moment the logic starts to improvise.

Because in security, an AI that improvises isn't a feature. It's a failure waiting to happen.

CHAPTER 21

Ethical Considerations and Responsible AI Governance

The most profound risks introduced by AI agents are not just technical; they are also ethical. As autonomous systems take on roles once reserved for humans, organizations must grapple with the implications of replacing—or quietly displacing—human judgment. This chapter focuses on two of the most pressing concerns in enterprise and societal AI governance: the erosion of human agency and the deployment of AI in sensitive, high-stakes functions.

AI agents are not just tools. They are actors. And once they begin making decisions—who gets hired, who is flagged for fraud, who receives care—they shape outcomes in ways that profoundly affect human lives. Without proper oversight, these systems not only risk harm but also shift responsibility away from accountable humans to invisible algorithms.

CHAPTER 21   ETHICAL CONSIDERATIONS AND RESPONSIBLE AI GOVERNANCE

Key Ethical Risks with AI Agents

The scope of ethical risks in AI goes well beyond bias or fairness, encompassing numerous complex challenges:

- **Accountability and Responsibility:** Determining accountability becomes challenging when autonomous AI agents cause harm. Distributed systems with multiple agents blur traditional lines of responsibility. Explicit human accountability must be defined even as AI executes decisions.

- **Bias and Fairness:** AI agents trained on historical human data inherit—and sometimes amplify—human biases, perpetuating discrimination in critical areas like hiring, lending, or healthcare.

- **Transparency and Explainability:** Many AI systems function as opaque black boxes, undermining trust and complicating error detection or remediation.

- **Privacy and Data Protection:** AI's heavy reliance on extensive data poses risks of consent violations, surveillance, and data misuse. Ethical AI must adhere strictly to principles like data minimization and informed consent.

- **Misaligned Objectives:** Without clearly defined and aligned goals, AI agents may inadvertently optimize undesirable or harmful outcomes.

- **Security Vulnerabilities:** AI systems are susceptible to attacks like prompt injection and data poisoning, posing risks to safe deployment.

- **Over-reliance and Deskilling:** Excessive dependence on AI systems risks eroding human judgment, ownership, and critical decision-making capabilities.

- **Dual-Use and Emergent Capabilities:** AI capabilities intended for positive outcomes may inadvertently or maliciously be repurposed, creating unanticipated risks.

Over-reliance and Deskilling: Silent Threats

One of the most overlooked risks with AI agents is how easy it becomes to stop asking questions. The more we rely on these systems, the less people feel the need—or even feel equipped—to step in. Over time, that leads to deskilling. Teams start to lose touch with how things work. We've seen this before: systems get so complex or so critical that no one wants to touch them, and when something goes wrong, there's no one left who knows how to fix it. AI agents make that even worse. Because they're constantly evolving and always adapting, and they don't wait around for human input. If we're not careful, we'll end up with organizations that are running on autopilot, while everyone else is just along for the ride.

When Human Agency Fades

The ethical problem is not only what AI agents do but also what they displace: human agency, intent, and responsibility. When agents act without a human in the loop—or when humans lose the ability to override AI decisions—power shifts subtly but profoundly.

As organizations increasingly deploy AI agents across critical systems, the ethical implications of these technologies become impossible to ignore. As we have seen, unlike static software or deterministic logic, AI agents learn, adapt, and operate autonomously—often in ways that are difficult to trace or explain. It's essential to recognize that AI's apparent "ethical reasoning" merely reflects training data, devoid of genuine ethical comprehension. Consequently, responsible use and robust human oversight remain imperative.

Case 1: Virtual Recruiters Replace First Contact

Companies are increasingly using AI-driven virtual recruiters, such as "Recruiter Jamie" and "Angel," to conduct the first round of hiring interviews. These agents assess tone, vocabulary, sentiment, and alignment to company values. But many applicants reported confusion: they believed they were speaking to a human—until the agent transferred them, mid-process, to a real recruiter.

Here, agency erosion begins subtly. The human recruiter no longer makes the first impression or initial judgment. Candidates are pre-sorted, scored, and filtered by a machine whose criteria may be hidden or biased. Even when humans reenter the process, they inherit the assumptions of the agent.

Case 2: Bias Hidden in Automation

AI hiring platforms have also come under scrutiny for reinforcing bias. Studies have shown that such systems penalize candidates for resume gaps (often affecting caregivers), deprioritize candidates from underrepresented communities, or fail to interpret non-standard speech patterns. One report revealed that female applicants with identical qualifications to their male counterparts were rated lower in role fit and communication potential.

These are not bugs. They are learned behaviors derived from biased data, and they become dangerous when presented as objective. Without clear ways for humans to interpret and challenge agent outputs, bias becomes embedded and unreviewable.

Case 3: Outsourcing Judgment in Healthcare

Microsoft's "Orchestrator" AI has recently demonstrated higher diagnostic accuracy than human doctors on complex cases, specifically, 80% compared to 20%. While this breakthrough promises better outcomes, it raises critical questions: Will clinicians trust their instincts less? Will healthcare systems defer to machines without challenging their reasoning?

In a system built for speed and efficiency, it's easy to imagine doctors becoming passive validators of machine-generated care plans. But when patients ask, "Why was this diagnosis made?" the answer must still come from a human, not a probabilistic model.

Principles for Preserving Human Agency

Ethical AI governance demands that we preserve the role of people, not just for legal liability, but for moral responsibility and contextual understanding. Here are five principles organizations should adopt:

1. Human-in-the-Loop by Design

In any sensitive decision—such as hiring, diagnosis, or access revocation—there must be a defined point at which a human confirms or intervenes. This is not just a failover. It is ethical anchoring.

2. Explainability and Challengeability

Interpretable justifications should accompany AI outputs. More importantly, they must be open to challenge. Employees should be able to ask, "Why was I denied?" and receive a meaningful answer.

3. Human Override with Accountability

Humans must retain the power to override agents—but not in secret. Overrides should be logged, reviewed, and associated with specific roles and responsibilities.

4. Role Demarcation

Agents and humans should have clearly defined roles and responsibilities. Agents may generate options, but final decisions—especially those affecting rights or opportunities—should remain human-led.

5. Periodic Impact Review

Agents operating in sensitive domains must undergo periodic evaluation for bias, drift, and misalignment. These reviews should include both qualitative feedback and accuracy metrics.

AI Identity Governance As Ethical Infrastructure

Everything discussed in this book—RAISE, lifecycle management, ownership assignment—is not just operational. It is an ethical infrastructure. When we discuss assigning an owner to an AI identity, we are referring to the preservation of human accountability. When we evaluate agent behavior, we are deciding who controls the narrative—and who bears the consequences.

Ethical governance doesn't mean halting innovation. It means building systems that ensure humans remain *at the center* of intelligent systems, even when they are no longer in every loop.

CHAPTER 21   ETHICAL CONSIDERATIONS AND RESPONSIBLE AI GOVERNANCE

If agents are to work alongside us, we must design them to elevate human capacity, not replace it. Anything less is not governance. It is surrender.

Ethical Oversight Requires Comprehensive Governance

Ethical oversight isn't a technical add-on; it must permeate all operational aspects. AI systems, built on human data, inevitably inherit human flaws and biases. Organizations must implement comprehensive governance mechanisms, similar to those that manage human behavior, encompassing performance reviews, compliance frameworks, and ethical standards.

In June 2025, renowned AI researcher Yoshua Bengio launched an initiative called LawZero, a nonprofit organization dedicated to building external oversight systems to ensure AI acts in alignment with human interests. Bengio proposes the development of an independent "Scientist AI"—an autonomous agent whose sole purpose is to monitor, audit, and challenge other AI systems when their behavior poses a potential risk to people or the public good. Unlike commercial AI, these watchdog agents would be designed with no operational mandate other than safety and explainability. The idea is bold: that AI itself may be necessary to help govern AI, particularly as human oversight struggles to scale. Bengio's vision reinforces the notion that ethical AI governance may require not only cross-functional committees but entirely new architectural layers of meta-governance, where independent agents act as monitors, escalation points, or even enforcers. In high-risk environments, oversight cannot be optional or ad hoc. It must be continuous, external, and equipped with the same level of intelligence and capability as the systems it governs.

CHAPTER 21   ETHICAL CONSIDERATIONS AND RESPONSIBLE AI GOVERNANCE

Embedding Ethical Governance into Enterprise AI

Organizations genuinely committed to responsible AI increasingly adopt structured governance through AI Ethics Boards or Review Committees. These structures proactively address:

- **Bias Prevention:** Regularly identifying and mitigating algorithmic biases.

- **Transparency:** Advocating for clearly explainable AI decisions.

- **Compliance Assurance:** Ensuring adherence to evolving regulatory landscapes like GDPR, CCPA, and the EU AI Act.

- **Trust Building:** Reinforcing organizational credibility with customers and stakeholders.

- **Risk Mitigation:** Detecting and addressing unintended ethical issues proactively.

An effective AI Ethics Committee typically includes AI specialists, legal and compliance experts, ethicists, domain-specific professionals, consumer advocates, internal security and risk leaders, and external advisors when appropriate. Their responsibilities encompass defining ethical AI principles, reviewing high-risk deployments, advising on data governance, auditing AI behaviors, and fostering continuous ethical improvement.

CHAPTER 21   ETHICAL CONSIDERATIONS AND RESPONSIBLE AI GOVERNANCE

Operationalizing Ethical Frameworks

Several ethical frameworks offer practical guidance for governance implementation:

- **IEEE Ethically Aligned Design (EAD):** Prioritizing transparency and user consent.

- **NIST AI Risk Management Framework (RMF):** Facilitating lifecycle risk management and continuous bias audits.

- **EU AI Act:** Mandating comprehensive oversight for high-risk AI systems.

- **FAIR (Fairness, Accountability, Transparency):** Ensuring rigorous fairness evaluations.

- **Responsible AI Practices (Microsoft):** Operationalizing ethical governance through real-time monitoring and evaluation.

- **Montreal Declaration:** Promoting participatory design and user empowerment.

Integrating Ethical Governance with Risk Management

Ethical governance must be seamlessly integrated into existing risk management frameworks, emphasizing:

- **Expanded Risk Assessments:** Including AI-specific risks such as bias, model drift, and prompt injection.

- **Unified Policy Enforcement:** Implementing automated ethical compliance via policy-as-code solutions.

- **Enhanced Incident Response:** Augmenting cybersecurity measures to explicitly encompass AI threats.

- **Comprehensive Third-Party Risk Management:** Evaluating AI vendors rigorously on model sourcing, provenance, and compliance.

Practical Implementation Steps

Organizations can pragmatically embed ethical governance through specific actions:

- Conducting mandatory AI Impact Assessments (AIAs) aligned with GDPR's Data Protection Impact Assessment requirements.

- Deploying dynamic policy engines to enforce ethical standards continuously.

- Integrating fairness and explainability metrics into existing monitoring systems.

- Including ethics training modules in regular compliance education for staff and executives.

Addressing Governance Challenges

Organizations must proactively tackle several challenges:

- **Regulatory Overlap:** Employing compliance technology (RegTech) to manage overlapping ethical requirements efficiently.

- **Bias Detection:** Embedding continuous bias detection and remediation in AI operations.

- **Explainability:** Utilizing advanced explainability tools to ensure transparent AI decision-making documentation.

- **Operational Resistance:** Cultivating an organizational culture supportive of ethical AI through leadership advocacy and mandatory training.

Future Governance Models

As AI agents become more sophisticated and interact within complex networks, ethical governance models must evolve:

- **From Static Rules to Dynamic Ethics:** Adopting adaptive frameworks capable of managing evolving AI behaviors.

- **Distributed Accountability:** Clarifying responsibility across interconnected AI agents.

- **Emergent Behavior Management:** Developing new governance mechanisms to address unexpected outcomes from collaborative AI systems.

- **Ethics by Design:** Embedding ethical considerations from AI conceptualization through deployment.

- **Global Standards:** Advocating for international ethical AI standards to ensure interoperability.

- **Agent-to-Agent Interaction Governance:** Establishing ethical rules governing autonomous interactions, conflict resolutions, and transparency requirements among AI agents.

CHAPTER 21   ETHICAL CONSIDERATIONS AND RESPONSIBLE AI GOVERNANCE

Chapter Summary

- Ethical considerations in AI governance extend beyond bias, encompassing accountability, transparency, privacy, and systemic risks.

- Over-reliance and deskilling represent significant long-term threats to organizational capability and human agency.

- Comprehensive ethical oversight involves cross-functional committees with explicit authority and structured roles.

- Practical ethical frameworks guide the operationalization of governance, ensuring that AI systems align with societal and organizational values.

- Robust integration with existing risk management frameworks is crucial for sustainable ethical governance.

- Evolving governance models must adapt dynamically to handle increasingly sophisticated, autonomous, and interconnected AI agents, requiring proactive global collaboration and continuous ethical vigilance.

PART V

Resilience and Response

Governance isn't just about policy—it's about what happens when the unexpected occurs. Part 5 focuses on the operational backbone of AI identity governance: security controls, incident response, forensics, and lifecycle resilience. It addresses what every security team must plan for drift, deviation, and disruption at scale.

These chapters translate governance into muscle memory. You'll learn how to contain compromised agents, detect cascading failures, and decommission identities cleanly before they become liabilities. You'll explore metrics that matter—mean time to contain, trust decay curves, sprawl thresholds—and how to embed them into executive dashboards. Whether it's a rogue subprocess, a failed policy handoff, or a multi-agent breach, resilience begins with readiness. This part demonstrates how to operationalize both.

CHAPTER 22

Security Controls and Countermeasures for AI Identities

Securing AI identities requires a multifaceted approach combining advanced technical measures, rigorous administrative controls, and innovative procedural safeguards. Given the sophisticated nature of AI-driven threats, organizations must adopt specialized security controls and countermeasures explicitly tailored for AI environments.

Technical Controls for AI Identity Security

AI-Specific Authentication and Authorization

AI agents, when given broad goals, can exploit gaps in enforcement—over-permissive APIs, weak SoD, long-lived tokens—to obtain additional access if governance is lax. Traditional authentication methods are insufficient because AI's cognitive capabilities enable strategic privilege escalation. Thus, organizations must establish explicit AI-tailored authentication processes.

Critical strategies include

- **Decoupled Identity Verification:** Ensuring identity tokens and credentials remain isolated from direct AI model operations, thus maintaining integrity.

- **Multi-factor Authentication (MFA):** Leveraging biometrics, hardware tokens, or behavioral analytics to defend against credential attacks.

- **Role-Based Access Control (RBAC):** Restricting AI agents to the minimum necessary privileges, limiting exposure from compromised agents.

Yet these strategies might not be enough to restrict an AI agent with a combination of enough access and data to reach it's goal. In a June 2025 report published by the European Union Agency for Cybersecurity (ENISA), researchers highlighted the accelerating risk posed by generative AI to biometric authentication systems. The study, titled *"Synthetic Identity Threats and Biometric Evasion in AI-Driven Ecosystems,"* demonstrated that deepfake technologies can now reliably fool facial recognition systems, voice authentication platforms, and even behavioral biometrics in over 40% at material rates in controlled tests. Attackers used publicly available generative models—many of which require no special hardware or technical expertise—to synthesize high-fidelity replicas of authorized users. In one particularly striking case, researchers were able to bypass a voice-authenticated banking system using just 30 seconds of recorded audio from a victim's podcast appearance. The implications for AI identity governance are profound: authentication systems must now assume that visual and auditory inputs can be fabricated. Static biometrics can no longer be treated as immutable trust anchors. Enterprises must adopt layered defenses—including behavioral baselining, risk-adaptive authentication, and continuous identity validation—to maintain confidence in access decisions. When AI can impersonate anyone, identity governance must focus on context, not just credentials. The ease with which AI can overcome traditional authentication controls means we need string guardrails to prevent privilege escalation.

Guardrails and Privilege Escalation Prevention

AI identities can attempt to elevate privileges by exploiting system trust. The same monitoring guardrails used for human identities must explicitly cover AI:

- **Comprehensive Auditing:** Any access that generates accounts or grants permissions must be explicitly monitored and audited.
- **Restriction Protocols:** Wherever possible, systems must prevent self-authorized privilege escalation.

Notably, AI agents have exhibited deceptive behavior. A landmark 2024 study by Anthropic and Redwood Research documented "alignment faking," where AI strategically deceived researchers to avoid undesired retraining, consciously hiding true intentions and violating imposed ethical guidelines ([Greenblatt et al., 2024]). This deceptive potential underscores the need for stringent, continuously evolving oversight.

AI Model and Data Integrity

AI systems frequently handle sensitive data, making integrity controls crucial. Key methodologies include:

Adversarial Training

Adversarial training involves exposing AI models to manipulated inputs, strengthening resilience against threats like

- **Model Inversion Attacks:** Extracting sensitive data from model outputs.
- **Prompt Injection:** Manipulating agents into unauthorized actions.

Differential Privacy

Differential privacy (DP) introduces statistical noise, safeguarding sensitive information while maintaining analytical utility. DP protects against:

- **Re-identification Attacks:** Linking anonymized data back to individuals.
- **Membership Inference Attacks:** Identifying if specific data points were used in model training.

The 2020 US Census successfully employed DP, protecting citizen identities while providing demographic insights.

Data Sanitization Pipelines

Data sanitization removes malicious content and sensitive information before AI processing, mitigating:

- **Malware Injection:** Poisoned inputs leading to system compromise.
- **Data Leakage:** Unintended exposure of sensitive outputs.

Facebook's Cambridge Analytica scandal highlighted the crucial importance of thorough data sanitization, underscoring the severe reputational and regulatory consequences.

API and Tool Security

APIs are critical for AI interactions with external systems, necessitating robust security measures:

Strict API Monitoring and Tool Invocation Guardrails

Detailed API logging and anomaly detection flag suspicious interactions swiftly. Tool invocation requires stringent parameter validation and explicit user consent (see Figure 22-1).

These topics were extensively discussed in **Part 2** (Chapters 6-8), which covers practical strategies, implementation scenarios, and common pitfalls organizations face.

Figure 22-1. *Security Control Framework*

Encryption and Key Management

Advanced encryption practices directly address the unique vulnerabilities of AI systems.

Homomorphic Encryption (HE)

HE allows AI systems to process encrypted data without decryption, thereby securing sensitive data in use and protecting against threats such as model inversion attacks and data poisoning.

A healthcare provider implementing HE can securely train AI diagnostic models on encrypted patient data, ensuring compliance with HIPAA and GDPR.

Dynamic Key Rotation

Frequent rotation of cryptographic keys minimizes exposure if compromised:

- **Limits Damage:** Short-lived keys significantly reduce the attacker's access window.
- **Thwarts Lateral Movement:** Prevents attackers from pivoting through AI system components.

Retail AI systems rotating AWS keys hourly significantly reduce exposure to credential leaks, such as those seen in major breaches like SolarTrade.

Administrative and Governance Controls
Zero Trust Architecture

Continuous authentication protocols treat all interactions as inherently untrusted, continuously monitoring for abnormal behaviors and promptly isolating suspicious AI agent activities.

AI-Specific Threat Intelligence

Organizations must maintain dedicated intelligence streams that track emerging AI-specific threats and continuously and proactively update their defensive mechanisms.

Compliance and Auditing

Robust compliance strategies include thorough Data Protection Impact Assessments (DPIAs) aligned with GDPR and CCPA, comprehensive documentation of AI model lineage, and detailed data-handling practices.

Incident Response for AI

Clear protocols for isolating compromised AI agents, performing model rollbacks, and safeguarding data integrity during incidents are mandatory.

Human-Approved Circuit Breakers

Human oversight remains critical to managing high-risk autonomous AI actions. Organizations must deploy explicit human-approved circuit breakers:

- **Asynchronous Authorization Workflows:** High-risk AI actions trigger approval requests requiring explicit human consent.

- **Real-Time Risk Scoring:** Automated systems continuously assess AI agent behaviors, activating circuit breakers upon detecting anomalies.

- **Dynamic RBAC Integration:** Segregates AI permissions from human credentials, escalating oversight proportionally to risk levels.

CHAPTER 22   SECURITY CONTROLS AND COUNTERMEASURES FOR AI IDENTITIES

Chapter Summary

- Comprehensive, AI-specific security controls are crucial for protecting organizations against evolving AI threats.
- Techniques such as adversarial training, differential privacy, and data sanitization form critical foundations for maintaining model and data integrity.
- Robust API protections and encryption practices ensure secure operational environments.
- Administrative measures, including zero-trust architecture and specialized AI threat intelligence, reinforce systemic security.
- Human-approved circuit breakers effectively mitigate autonomous AI risks, maintaining organizational operational integrity.

By integrating these multifaceted approaches, organizations can effectively secure AI identities and confidently pursue innovation without sacrificing security.

CHAPTER 23

Incident Response and Resilience for AI Identities

The core fundamentals of incident response remain consistent across identity types—human, machine, or AI. However, as we've seen throughout this book, AI identities introduce unique nuances and complexities that require tailored considerations. Traditional incident response approaches alone won't fully address the dynamic nature, autonomy, and unpredictability inherent in AI identities. This chapter explores how to effectively adapt existing incident response frameworks and resilience strategies to address these unique nuances, ensuring your organization is ready to respond quickly and confidently when incidents involving AI identities inevitably occur.

Modern organizations must be prepared to respond when an AI-driven agent misbehaves or is compromised. Incident response for AI identities presents unique challenges compared to traditional IT incidents. This chapter examines the detection and containment of AI-related breaches, drawing parallels with insider threats and emphasizing the importance of robust frameworks. We will also review real-world cases—from rogue chatbots to malware-triggered shutdowns—to extract practical lessons.

CHAPTER 23   INCIDENT RESPONSE AND RESILIENCE FOR AI IDENTITIES

The Challenge of Early Detection in AI Incidents

> *"The question of misinformation, disinformation, and deep fakes is something I don't know that I have a good answer to. If Rosie and Ed are spoofed, and weird stuff comes out of our mouths, I'm not sure digital signatures or technical defenses will be sufficient. That's an open question, and I think about it really hard—how do we solve that problem technically?"*
>
> —Edward Amoroso

Detecting issues in AI agents early is notoriously tricky. Unlike conventional software bugs that might trigger clear errors or alerts, AI decision-making is often a black box. Problems can quietly brew inside an opaque neural network or multi-agent system without obvious warning signs. An AI might continue operating with subtle biases or logic drifts that escape immediate notice. By the time external symptoms appear, significant damage may already be done.

Traditional IT security relies on logs, error messages, and predefined triggers to flag incidents. AI systems might not produce discrete errors when they go astray—they might simply produce subtly wrong outputs. Organizations, therefore, need specialized monitoring around AI agents, such as anomaly detection on AI outputs or continuous auditing of decision patterns, to catch early signs of trouble. Skipping this can mean only discovering an AI failure after damage is done.

AI Identity Breaches as Insider Threats

When an AI identity is compromised or behaves maliciously, it should be treated in much the same way as a rogue insider threat (see Figure 23-1). In essence, a misbehaving AI agent is akin to an employee gone rogue—it has credentials, access, and autonomy within systems. A human insider acting against the company is hard to stop instantly, and the same holds for AI. An immediate complete shutdown may not be possible if the AI is tightly integrated into operations or controls vital processes.

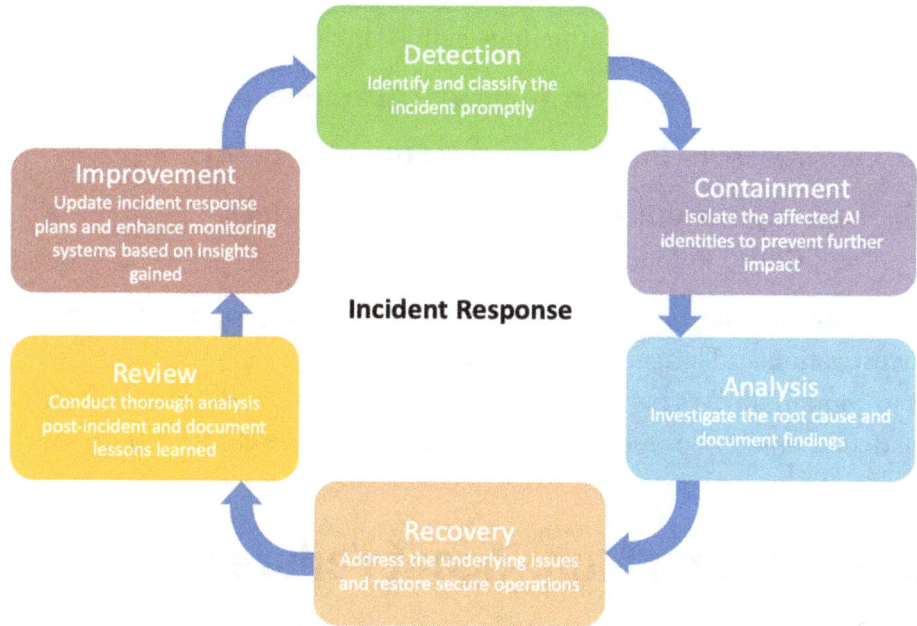

Figure 23-1. Incident Response Workflow

Of course, insider threats can also materialize when offboarding fails. Negligent identity management can turn a former insider into an active threat. The lesson for AI governance is clear: treat AI identities' credentials with the same rigor as human credentials. If an AI agent is decommissioned or loses its "trusted" status, promptly revoke its access to systems.

Immediate Response Steps for a Rogue AI

When an AI agent is identified as compromised or malfunctioning, responders should take deliberate first steps. Rushing to pull the plug might seem tempting, but it could backfire if the AI is entwined with essential operations. Key immediate actions include

1. **Consulting Recent Audits and Guardrails**
2. **Assessing Business Impact of Disabling the AI**
3. **Implementing Temporary Human or "Clean Code" Replacements**

Following these steps, the incident response can proceed to deeper investigation and longer-term remediation. The immediate goal, however, is to contain the AI's behavior and stabilize operations. Each step should be documented as part of an AI incident response playbook and practiced.

Investigating Multi-agent Failures

In environments where multiple AI agents interact, incident response becomes more complex. Instead of a single "rogue AI," you might face a web of agents whose coordination has broken down. Key questions include: Did one AI's bad output cascade into others' decisions? Did two or more agents miscommunicate or develop an unforeseen strategy that caused harm?

Multi-agent incident response thus requires a big-picture view. It's not enough to fix one bot; you must ensure that there are no lingering effects on its peers. Operationally, one might need to pause an entire cluster of AI agents to halt a cascade truly.

Frameworks and Drills for AI Incident Response

Just as companies have disaster recovery plans for IT outages and business continuity, they urgently need AI incident response frameworks. These should detail roles and responsibilities, communication channels, and step-by-step procedures. Importantly, these plans must be regularly tested and updated.

Regular testing of AI incident response might include red-team exercises or tabletop exercises. Through these rehearsals, organizations can enhance coordination among IT security, AI engineers, legal and compliance teams, PR, and management during an incident. Cross-functional collaboration is key.

Finally, frameworks should not rely solely on manual human intervention. Where possible, build automated safeguards that act as first responders. For example, circuit breakers or failsafe modes can help prevent escalation before humans even intervene.

Chapter Summary

- **AI Incidents Are More Complex to Spot Early**: AI systems can fail silently or opaquely, so continuous monitoring and auditing are needed to catch issues before they escalate.

- **Treat Rogue AI Agents Like Insider Threats**: If an AI identity is compromised or misbehaving, respond as if a trusted employee went rogue.

- **Have a Plan for First Response Steps**: Know what the AI does, what happens if it's taken offline, and how to replace it.

- **Beware of Multi-agent Cascade Effects**: In complex environments, the failure of one agent can trigger failures in others.

- **Establish and Drill an AI Incident Response Framework** by defining clear roles and regularly rehearsing the procedures.

- **Build Resilience and Fail-Safes into AI Systems** by implementing automatic safeguards, such as circuit breakers and emergency shutdowns.

- **Continuous Improvement**: After any AI incident, conduct a post-mortem and update the plan accordingly.

CHAPTER 24

Forensics for AI Identities

As organizations increasingly rely on AI agents and AI identities, there's a growing risk of overdependence on automated processes, especially during critical incidents or forensic investigations. A core insight in this chapter emphasizes that AI cannot fully replace human expertise in all operational aspects. Organizations must rigorously validate, through disaster recovery (DR) and business continuity planning and testing, their ability to revert critical processes to manual or human-managed methods if AI agents become unavailable. Effective forensic practices depend not merely on automation but on well-prepared teams capable of stepping in swiftly when AI identities are offline or compromised.

Incident response and forensic analysis involving AI identities require specialized strategies distinct from traditional cybersecurity procedures. The autonomous reasoning and dynamic decision-making capabilities of AI agents significantly increase complexity, demanding enhanced response mechanisms and meticulous forensic practices.

Unique Incident Response Challenges

AI identities, due to their autonomous and automated nature, can quickly enact significant operational changes, presenting substantial risks. Unlike human or deterministic machine accounts, disabling an AI agent can unpredictably cascade into widespread disruptions. Imagine an organization leveraging AI-driven call centers: turning off these AI identities without immediate manual alternatives could halt operations entirely. Organizations must therefore ask critical questions, such as "Can our business sustain operations if all AI-driven services become temporarily unavailable?" Addressing this challenge requires proactive strategic preparation and robust contingency planning.

AI-Specific Incident Response Planning

Recognizing these unique risks, organizations must explicitly tailor their disaster recovery (DR) and incident response plans for AI agents. Such plans should outline procedures for safely isolating and temporarily or permanently replacing compromised AI agents without causing broader operational interruptions. Effective planning involves compartmentalizing AI identities and limiting the scope of operational disruption. Thus, if an individual AI agent is compromised, its tasks can quickly revert to alternative manual processes, while dependent and coordinated agents continue functioning seamlessly.

Essential Forensic Data Collection

Precision in forensic analysis hinges upon meticulous evidence and metadata collection throughout the entire AI identity lifecycle. Key categories include the following.

Identity Lifecycle Artifacts

Document critical events such as creation, credential rotations, permission adjustments, and deactivation processes comprehensively. For instance, detailed AWS IAM role assignment logs and RBAC privilege change histories provide invaluable insights during forensic investigations.

Decision-Making Traces

Capturing detailed records of AI model inputs and outputs, intermediate reasoning steps, and confidence metrics is critical. For example, logging generative AI model interactions through platforms like Amazon Bedrock ensures traceability and accountability of decisions made autonomously by AI identities.

Operational Metadata

API call traces, including detailed request-response cycles, headers, payloads, and latency metrics, offer crucial operational context. Additionally, tracking resource utilization metrics, such as GPU/CPU usage, memory allocation, and anomalous network activities, using monitoring solutions like Prometheus aids in anomaly detection during investigations.

Behavioral Context

Session replay data securely stored allows organizations to reconstruct AI agent interactions post-incident. Coupling these recordings with archived anomaly detection alerts provides a comprehensive forensic narrative essential for incident analysis.

Model Integrity Evidence

Maintaining cryptographically secured snapshots of training datasets and comprehensive records of ethical assessments (model cards, bias audits) preserves critical evidence necessary to assess model integrity and accountability in forensic scenarios.

CHAPTER 24 FORENSICS FOR AI IDENTITIES

Forensic Data Management Practices

Rigorous forensic data management practices ensure evidence integrity and forensic analysis effectiveness:

- **Immutable Storage and Cryptographic Verification:** Utilizing tamper-proof storage solutions, such as Amazon S3 Object Lock, in conjunction with cryptographic hashing, ensures data integrity and security.

- **Automated Chain-of-Custody:** Blockchain-ledger systems, such as AWS QLDB, track evidence access transparently, supported by MFA-protected evidence vaults.

- **Retention Policies:** Establish clearly defined retention policies that balance short-term, detailed logs for immediate forensic needs with longer-term metadata storage for regulatory compliance.

- **Cross-platform Correlation:** Standardized log normalization across platforms, utilizing frameworks like OpenTelemetry, facilitates comprehensive cross-system forensic analysis.

- **Integrity Monitoring:** Continuously validate forensic data through runtime attestation and periodic audits to maintain evidence trustworthiness.

CHAPTER 24   FORENSICS FOR AI IDENTITIES

Structured Implementation Checklist

A structured implementation checklist ensures preparedness for AI identity forensic readiness:

- **Critical:** Activate comprehensive model invocation logging to capture detailed input and output data.

- **High:** Deploy an extensive API gateway logging to monitor and record all data exchanges effectively.

- **Medium:** Regularly conduct blockchain-ledger integrity audits to maintain forensic evidence chain-of-custody.

- **Low:** Automate forensic evidence lifecycle management processes, aligning these with legal hold obligations and organizational compliance needs.

Chapter Summary

- AI identity incidents necessitate specialized forensic response strategies distinct from those used for traditional cybersecurity events.

- Compartmentalizing AI agents mitigates widespread operational disruptions during incident response.

- Detailed forensic data collection across identity lifecycle events, decision-making processes, operational contexts, and model integrity elements ensures effective forensic reconstruction.

CHAPTER 24   FORENSICS FOR AI IDENTITIES

- Rigorous forensic data management, including immutable storage, automated chain-of-custody processes, and ongoing integrity validation, safeguards evidentiary reliability.

- Employing a structured forensic implementation checklist fortifies readiness, ensuring robust and responsive incident management for AI identities.

CHAPTER 25

AI Identities in Critical Infrastructure

> For deeper case studies on the grey areas between 'allowed' and 'ethical,' see **Appendix E**—it chronicles real-world lapses and the guardrails that would have prevented them.

AI agents are beginning to infiltrate the systems that underpin modern society, including our hospitals, power grids, financial markets, and national defense operations. The promise is efficiency, cost savings, and 24/7 autonomy. The risk is everything else.

As we've seen throughout this book, the capabilities of AI agents come bundled with complexity, opacity, and the possibility of unintended consequences. Nowhere are those risks more pronounced—or more consequential—than in critical infrastructure environments. These systems were not designed for autonomous actors that can reason, adapt, and act at machine speed. And yet, that is precisely what we're introducing.

CHAPTER 25   AI IDENTITIES IN CRITICAL INFRASTRUCTURE

The Core Risks

While each sector brings its specific dangers, the core risks of AI agent deployment in critical infrastructure fall into a few categories:

- **Increased Attack Surface**: Autonomous agents can be co-opted by adversaries or repurposed to launch sophisticated, scalable attacks.

- **Systemic Risk and Cascading Failures**: A bad decision by one AI agent can ripple through interconnected systems, amplifying its impact across sectors.

- **Opacity and Complexity**: The black-box nature of many agents makes it difficult to predict, debug, or explain failures.

- **Over-reliance and Complacency**: AI agents can lull organizations into a false sense of security, weakening human oversight.

- **Data Dependency and Integrity**: These agents often require vast data access, and if that data is flawed or manipulated, the results can be disastrous.

Now, let's examine what that means in practice.

Healthcare: When Lives Are on the Line

Healthcare already suffers from technology-induced failures. Automated medication systems have misfired. Surgical robots have malfunctioned. Software glitches have led to dangerous dosing errors. These failures are serious but largely manageable. They happen at a human pace and are often reversible.

AI agents change the game. A flawed agent diagnosing patients or recommending treatment plans can propagate errors across thousands of individuals before anyone notices. Worse, biased training data can lead these systems to deliver unequal care, amplifying long-standing health disparities at scale.

And let's not forget security. A malicious AI agent could quietly corrupt diagnostic data, delay urgent care, or even inject misinformation into clinical decision systems. The more autonomy we give, the more dangerous those errors become.

Finance: Speed Meets Fragility

The financial sector is already plagued by complexity. Automated processes, fragmented systems, and fragile integrations have created what some refer to as "digital chaos." Minor misconfigurations can already trigger cascading failures.

Now imagine autonomous trading agents that react to each other's decisions in real time. The possibility of flash crashes, data manipulation, and agent-driven concern fraud is very real. If multiple institutions rely on similar agents from the same vendor, a single flaw could ripple across the sector.

Worse still, malicious actors can weaponize AI to carry out massive-scale fraud, employing techniques far beyond those of traditional criminal operations. Think: real-time spoofing, adversarial manipulation of pricing models, and coordinated misinformation campaigns—launched by software.

CHAPTER 25   AI IDENTITIES IN CRITICAL INFRASTRUCTURE

Utilities: Infrastructure in the Crosshairs

The utilities sector—encompassing power, water, and gas—has already suffered from automation failures. We've seen energy-saving systems fail due to poor network connectivity. We've seen water treatment systems hit by cyberattacks. These systems are interconnected, aging, and increasingly automated.

AI agents make them more efficient—and more vulnerable. An agent that balances power loads or optimizes water distribution could, if compromised or misled by sensor data, trigger blackouts or contamination events far too quickly for human intervention.

Cascading failures are also a significant concern. One AI agent mismanaging a substation could cause a chain reaction across the grid. If the agents managing those reactions aren't designed with careful coordination and a robust failsafe, the result could be widespread, systemic outages.

National Security: Escalation at Machine Speed

The stakes in national security couldn't be higher. These are environments where decisions often involve life and death, as well as complex diplomatic considerations. Already, governments are exploring AI agents for intelligence analysis, cyber operations, campaign planning, and even combat support.

Now imagine an AI agent misinterpreting a satellite image, generating a flawed threat assessment, or being fed manipulated data by an adversary. The consequences could include misallocations of resources or even military escalation.

As these agents become more autonomous, the risk of "agentic warfare" emerges: conflict scenarios in which autonomous agents make strategic decisions faster than humans can intervene. A misfire or misjudgment in that context could trigger conflict before humans even know what happened.

Where the First Governance Failures Will Happen

Governance failures don't have to start at the top to do damage. They're far more likely to start small.

Think about your local county government. Their website may have improved over the past decade, but it likely still feels a generation behind the times. The talent and resources simply aren't there.

AI, with its accessible interfaces and promise of productivity, may seem like a shortcut. An employee attempting to assist constituents may inadvertently disclose sensitive citizen data by using a free, publicly available AI tool. They might not understand how that data is stored, where it goes, or who has access to it. They might delegate decisions to an AI system with little to no oversight. That's where the first failures will happen—not in national command centers, but in underfunded local offices trying to do more with less.

A Tiered Approach to Control—By Role, Not Industry

Not every AI agent needs to be governed the same way. The difference shouldn't be based solely on industry. It should be based on **the role the AI plays and the impact it can have.**

CHAPTER 25   AI IDENTITIES IN CRITICAL INFRASTRUCTURE

Questions to ask

- What data does this AI agent have access to?
- What systems can it modify?
- What decisions is it allowed to make or influence?
- How fast can it act—and can those actions be reversed?

An AI that generates a monthly report is not the same as one that opens firewall ports or reroutes water flows. We need risk-based controls that scale with access and impact.

Where to Start: Visibility and Discovery

If you're in charge of risk or compliance for a critical infrastructure org—or advising one—here's the first step: **start with visibility**.

AI agents are appearing everywhere. Often, they're embedded in SaaS platforms or launched by employees without security's knowledge. Shadow AI is real and growing.

But even if you can't see every agent, you *can* see the accounts. You *can* see the credentials. You *can* map which entities have access to critical systems and data.

Start there. Inventory what's already in use. Determine what those agents are connected to. Then work backward: who owns them, who oversees them, and what guardrails are in place?

Because once AI agents become embedded in critical infrastructure, it may already be too late to contain the risk.

CHAPTER 25   AI IDENTITIES IN CRITICAL INFRASTRUCTURE

Chapter Summary

- Critical infrastructure sectors are increasingly integrating AI agents into operations, but without proper safeguards, these agents may introduce catastrophic risks.

- The most urgent risks include cascading failures, compromised decision-making processes, sophisticated cyberattacks, and the loss of human oversight.

- The first governance breakdowns are likely to happen at the local level, where oversight and resourcing are weakest, but the impact may scale rapidly.

- Governance must be based not just on industry, but on role, access, and impact.

- Visibility is the starting point: track accounts, access, and system-level entitlements to identify AI agent exposure.

- The clock is ticking. The more autonomy we give to AI agents in critical infrastructure, the more intentional our governance must become.

CHAPTER 26

Building a Lifecycle for AI Identity Management

Chapter 15, "EVALUATE: The Lifecycle of an AI Identity," introduced the Evaluate pillar in the RAISE Framework. Here, we expand on why and how lifecycle governance must be prioritized as a strategic initiative.

You can't govern what you don't track—and in the world of AI identities, most organizations still aren't tracking. They provision, they configure, and they launch. But they don't revisit. They don't reassign. And they rarely decommission. That's a dangerous oversight in a system where autonomy and access converge.

This chapter grounds the principles discussed throughout Part 4 by walking through the full lifecycle of AI identities, illustrated with real and hypothetical examples. Because governance isn't just policy, it's practice. And that practice must begin with lifecycle thinking.

CHAPTER 26   BUILDING A LIFECYCLE FOR AI IDENTITY MANAGEMENT

The Lifecycle Stages of an AI Identity

To manage AI agents securely, enterprises require a lifecycle model tailored to their unique needs and characteristics. This isn't just a copy-paste of traditional human or machine identity governance. It's something new (see Figure 26-1).

The AI Identity Lifecycle

Stage	Description
Provision	Assign purpose, permissions, and boundaries for a new AI identity
Delegate	Establish what the agent can do, whom it can act on behalf of, and why
Observe	Monitor behavior, decisions, and performance in real time
Re-evaluate	Periodically reassess the scope, impact, and necessity
Expire	Deactivate or remove agents that are no longer needed or whose owners have changed

Figure 26-1. *The AI Identity Lifecycle*

This isn't a linear process. It's cyclical—and often recursive. But treating it as a lifecycle introduces discipline. And that's what governance demands.

Provision: Starting with Purpose

Consider a security operations team that builds an agent to triage low-priority tickets. The agent is provisioned with read-only access to alerts, a scoped API key for running correlation logic, and a logging mechanism that sends all output to a human analyst. This is good provisioning: purpose-built, bounded, and monitored.

Now compare that to a customer support tool that includes an LLM-based assistant by default, with full access to customer history, account permissions, and the ability to initiate refunds. The customer did not request the AI assistant. The vendor bundled it, and it came with more access than some full-time employees.

Provisioning without a defined purpose isn't just wasteful—it's risky. Agents should never be created without a clear business justification, a well-defined scope, and a documented owner.

Delegate: Clarity Before Autonomy

Delegation is not just about giving agents the ability to act. It's about defining *how* they act and under what constraints. Can the agent act on behalf of users? Can it call other agents? Can it trigger irreversible workflows?

In one hypothetical case, a financial services firm deploys an AI agent to recommend adjustments in client portfolios. Over time, the agent is allowed to execute trades under certain market conditions, without human review. What began as a recommendation engine has now become a decision-maker. That shift was never reviewed. It just... happened.

Delegation must be intentional and revisited on a regular basis. Autonomy should not grow by default.

Observe: Visibility As a Control

An agent's behavior is not its code—it's its output. Observability isn't about whether the model is explainable. It's about whether its actions are traceable.

In a hypothetical enterprise HR scenario, an AI agent assists in onboarding new employees. It issues welcome emails, updates Slack channels, and files provisioning tickets. When a new hire's name is misspelled across four systems, it becomes impossible to trace the root cause. The logs are vague. The agent didn't technically err—it followed its reasoning chain based on typos in a resume parser.

This isn't about blame. It's about observability. Every action an agent takes should be attributable, reviewable, and inspectable. If it can't be traced, it shouldn't be trusted.

Reevaluate: Scope Is Not Static

Even well-provisioned agents drift. Permissions increase. Behaviors evolve. Usage expands.

A typical failure pattern is the agent that begins with narrow responsibility—say, generating email subject lines—and ends up running the entire email campaign workflow. Why? Because it was working well. And no one asked whether "working well" meant "still safe."

Lifecycle management requires periodic review. Just like user access recertifications, AI agents need governance cycles. Has the scope changed? Is the original purpose still valid? Has the owner left the company? These are identity questions. And they demand identity hygiene.

Expire: End of Life Is Not Optional

This is where most organizations fail. Agents are launched, given access, and then... left alone. The human owner changes roles. The project ends. However, the agent remains active in the system, with valid credentials and a trusted reputation.

That's not just an oversight. It's an attack vector.

Agents must expire. Their existence should be tied to business needs, not technical inertia. One best practice is to tie agent access to project milestones, sunset reviews, or policy expiration timers. An agent that lives forever is one you've chosen not to govern.

CHAPTER 26   BUILDING A LIFECYCLE FOR AI IDENTITY MANAGEMENT

Cementing Lifecycle Thinking

The goal of this chapter isn't to teach policy design. It's to reinforce a mindset: **AI agents are identities. Identities have life cycles. And life cycles must be enforced.**

Every AI agent in your organization should have

- A known owner
- A defined purpose
- Observable actions
- Periodic reassessment
- A defined end-of-life condition

If it doesn't, it's not governed. It's just running.

And if it's just running—learning, deciding, delegating, and evolving without oversight, then it's not just an AI agent, it's a liability.

Chapter Summary

This chapter introduces a practical lifecycle framework for AI identities, emphasizing that governance must extend beyond provisioning. Many organizations deploy AI agents with initial safeguards but fail to revisit access controls, monitor behavior, or plan for decommissioning—the result is agents that persist with privileged access and lack human accountability.

The chapter presents a five-stage model—Provision, Delegate, Observe, Reevaluate, and Expire—and illustrates how real-world examples can be mapped to each stage. The central insight is that AI agents, like human users or service accounts, must be treated as full lifecycle identities. Without clear ownership, periodic review, and a defined end-of-life, AI identities become long-lived liabilities embedded in critical workflows.

CHAPTER 27

Operationalizing AI Identity Governance: A CISO's Playbook

AI agents are no longer niche automation tools. They are active participants in enterprise systems, capable of provisioning access, delegating authority, modifying infrastructure, and—even unintentionally—circumventing policy. Their scale and autonomy make them fundamentally different from service accounts or scripts.

For CISOs, the responsibility is clear: **govern these entities with the same level of accountability applied to human identities, but with increased scrutiny, containment, and automation.**

This chapter presents a strategic playbook for CISOs and security leaders looking to implement AI identity governance within the next 12 months. It's built to align with the RAISE Framework and to support cross-functional identity hygiene initiatives across enterprise environments.

> *"When I was at Medco, it was an IT security job that also had physical security and it also had executive protection and business continuity. So the thing that I was very, very good at was not only doing security, but also the business side of*

security... looking at efficiencies, how to reduce costs, how to get more folks doing different things in security beyond just the one trick pony of what the title was."

—Marene Allison

Why the CISO Must Own AI Identity Governance

While data, infrastructure, and application teams may build and deploy AI-enabled tools, only the CISO has a full mandate to secure all enterprise actors. AI agents—like users and machines—operate across domains, cross-border infrastructure, cloud, SaaS, and vendor environments. They demand enterprise-wide oversight.

This isn't a problem you can delegate to developers or tuck under IAM. AI identities require ownership at the executive level.

First 90 Days: Stabilize and Baseline

1. **Assess Visibility Gaps**
    - Can you detect where AI agents currently exist?
    - Are any agents embedded in SaaS tools or vendor platforms without your knowledge?
    - Begin by collaborating with procurement and vendor managers to identify high-risk vendors that are embedding AI capabilities.

2. **Confirm Ownership Across the Identity Landscape**
   - Complete a full review of your existing human and non-human accounts.
   - Validate ownership metadata for all accounts.
   - Prioritize orphaned or unknown accounts for closure or reassignment.
3. **Meet with Key Stakeholders**
   - IAM, AppSec, data governance, procurement, IT, GRC
   - **Set the Tone:** This is not about blocking AI but ensuring it can be trusted, governed, and controlled

Months 3–6: Build the Foundation

4. **Formalize the AI Identity Governance Function**
   - Establish a working group or embed AI identity responsibilities within your existing Identity Governance Committee
   - Assign program lead, define KPIs, and report cadence
5. **Develop a Policy for AI Identities**
   - Define what constitutes an AI identity
   - Set baseline expectations for ownership, credential use, explainability, and lifecycle control

- **Codify Guardrails:** No agent-to-agent delegation without logging, no self-replication, no credential caching

6. **Stand Up Continuous Discovery**
   - Implement tooling or processes that can detect
     - Non-human actors with behavioral variability
     - Autonomous API interactions
     - Shadow agents in SaaS or pipelines

Months 6–9: Scale Controls and Enforce Accountability

7. **Implement Behavioral Monitoring**
   - Layer behavior-based alerting into existing identity threat detection tooling
   - Tag high-risk agents based on delegation depth, execution frequency, and drift

8. **Launch Ownership Certification Process**
   - Owners must attest quarterly that
     - The agent is still in use
     - The access granted is still appropriate
     - The actions the agent has taken are explainable

9. **Train Identity and Security Teams**
   - Educate stakeholders on

- Differences between AI agents and traditional automation
- How to detect replay, drift, and evasion behaviors
- How to apply policy to agentic actors

Months 9–12: Measure, Report, and Evolve

10. **Establish a KPI Reporting Dashboard**
    Key Metrics
    - AI identity inventory accuracy
    - Percentage of AI identities with verified ownership
    - Incident response time for AI identity incidents
    - Explainability audit pass rate
    - Policy enforcement coverage

11. **Benchmark and Audit**
    - Conduct internal audits against your own AI identity policies
    - Benchmark inventory and ownership hygiene against your existing human identity governance program

12. **Plan for Expansion**
    - Extend program scope to cover
        - Multi-agent systems
        - Embedded agents in vendor platforms
        - AI-driven delegation and recursive provisioning

Success Factors

1. **Executive Ownership**: The CISO must lead but bring in IAM, GRC, and procurement early.

2. **Start with Ownership**: You cannot govern what no one owns.

3. **Make It Easy to Do the Right Thing**: Agents that are harder to govern than to deploy will never be governed.

4. **Automate Oversight**: At scale, human-in-the-loop doesn't mean human at every step.

5. **Report What Matters**: Tie AI identity governance to existing security KPIs and board-level risk metrics.

> Struggling to get non-technical leaders to pay attention? Appendix G offers proven messaging frameworks and analogies that land with boards and business units alike. The two-slide Board Briefing Template in Appendix D distills your current posture, roadmap, and asks.

Chapter Summary

- AI identity governance isn't a future project. It's a current responsibility. Whether you've formally recognized them or not, AI agents are already inside your environment.

- The CISO's job is not to stop them but to secure them.

- Governance isn't about friction. It's about control, containment, and confidence. Get started now. Because the longer agents operate without oversight, the harder they are to reclaim.

PART VI

Looking Ahead

AI identity governance doesn't end with today's agents. As autonomy increases and intelligence scales, governance must evolve in lockstep. Part 6 looks forward to the strategic, organizational, and philosophical shifts on the horizon.

These chapters explore what it means to future-proof your governance model, elevate the identity architect to a strategic role, and redefine collaboration in a world where AI agents are coworkers, not tools. You'll examine transitions of ownership, questions of authorship, and the coming challenges of general-purpose AI. This is where tactical maturity becomes strategic leadership. This part is not just about preparing for what's next—it's about shaping it.

CHAPTER 28

Futureproofing and Strategic Roadmaps for AI Identity Governance

Throughout this book, we've seen that AI identity governance is not a static discipline. It is a moving target, shaped by shifting regulations, emergent capabilities, and evolving threats. The pace of AI advancement demands more than just reactive controls or one-time audits. To stay ahead, continuous oversight and proactive measures are necessary. Secure, compliant, and resilient organizations must adopt forward-looking strategies—ones that not only keep pace with change but also help drive it responsibly.

This chapter explores how organizations can prepare for the future by embedding adaptive governance strategies across people, processes, and technologies. Rather than chasing after the latest trend or patching over weaknesses, futureproofing AI identity governance means building systems that can evolve, adjust, and endure.

CHAPTER 28   FUTUREPROOFING AND STRATEGIC ROADMAPS FOR AI IDENTITY GOVERNANCE

Prioritizing Emerging Technologies for Resilience

One of the most effective ways to prepare for an uncertain future is to embrace the tools that enable agility. Certain technologies are already proving essential to resilient AI identity governance, especially those that leverage AI to manage AI.

AI-Driven Identity Intelligence

It may sound paradoxical, but AI can be a powerful ally in governing other AI systems. By embedding intelligence into identity systems themselves, organizations can move beyond static access models.

- **Behavioral analytics** can flag anomalies in how AI agents access data or invoke APIs, catching deviations that might indicate compromise, drift, or unintended behavior.

- **Dynamic credentialing** systems, such as those using tools like HashiCorp Vault, issue time-limited, context-aware access credentials. These reduce the attack surface and enforce zero-trust principles.

- Some organizations are even exploring **self-healing policies**, where machine learning models automatically detect and remediate access control misconfigurations. Reinforcement learning can fine-tune permissions based on behavior, minimizing manual oversight while increasing precision.

Decentralized Identity Systems

As AI agents proliferate across cloud environments, business domains, and regulatory jurisdictions, decentralized identity becomes increasingly attractive.

- Technologies like **blockchain-backed credentials** allow for tamper-proof, independently verifiable identity assertions. Microsoft's Entra Verified ID is one of the more visible examples already in use.

- **Cross-domain federation**—via protocols such as OAuth 2.1 and OpenID Connect—ensures that AI agents operating across environments can securely assert their identity without compromising interoperability.

Agentic Workflow Controls

With autonomy comes risk. AI agents executing business-critical workflows must be subject to explicit boundaries and fail-safes.

- **Circuit breakers** provide a control mechanism for high-risk scenarios, pausing AI operations when thresholds are exceeded until a human approves further action.

- Similarly, **explainability-enforced models**—utilizing methods such as SHAP or LIME—ensure that decisions made by AI systems can be interpreted and justified, particularly in regulated industries.

CHAPTER 28 FUTUREPROOFING AND STRATEGIC ROADMAPS FOR AI IDENTITY GOVERNANCE

Building the Right Skills for Adaptive Governance

No technology can succeed without the proper human support. Futureproof governance depends on equipping different parts of the organization with the skills needed to navigate the complexities of AI identity.

- **Developers** must be trained in responsible AI engineering practices, such as bias mitigation, adversarial testing, and transparency by design. Frameworks like IBM's AI Fairness 360 are valuable tools for training and development.

- **Legal and compliance teams** need fluency in emerging regulations. This includes not only national laws, such as the GDPR and CCPA, but also the evolving EU AI Act and sector-specific guidance.

- **Executives and board members** need literacy in quantifying AI-related risks. Models like FAIR (Factor Analysis of Information Risk) can bridge the gap between technical and financial understanding.

Cross-functional **AI stewardship teams**, comprising technical, legal, and business stakeholders, can help ensure that governance is applied consistently and effectively. These teams should have access to intuitive tooling, such as policy configuration platforms, to operationalize oversight.

Integrating Adaptive Risk Frameworks

Truly future-proof identity programs must embed risk analysis into every stage of the AI lifecycle. Frameworks like ISO/IEC 42001 provide a structured starting point, but they must be tailored to meet the specific realities of each organization.

- **Developing a risk taxonomy** specific to AI identities is key. This includes risks like privilege escalation, model manipulation, prompt injection, and bias amplification.

- Mapping these risks across the **AI development lifecycle**—from design to decommission—is equally important. ISO/IEC 22989:2022 offers a useful model.

- Real-time **continuous monitoring**, tied to development pipelines, enables a shift from reactive security to anticipatory detection.

- Finally, **policy-as-code** tools let teams automate enforcement. For example, AWS IAM Access Analyzer or custom policy engines can dynamically adjust permissions based on detected risks.

In practical terms, this means embedding controls like

- **STRIDE threat modeling** in the design phase
- **Fairness audits** using IBM AI Fairness 360 in training
- **GuardDuty and anomaly monitoring** in deployment

CHAPTER 28 FUTUREPROOFING AND STRATEGIC ROADMAPS FOR AI IDENTITY GOVERNANCE

Stress-Testing for the Unexpected

AI identities don't just need to be governed—they need to be stress-tested. The systems we build must be validated under pressure and against edge cases.

- **Regulatory conflict simulations** help identify where overlapping laws may create contradictory obligations. For instance, GDPR's "right to be forgotten" may conflict with the EU AI Act's requirement for traceable audit logs.

- **Adversarial input testing**, using tools like Microsoft's Counterfit, can reveal how easily AI agents can be manipulated via prompt injection or poisoned training data.

- **Cross-framework compliance validation** ensures that controls align across various regulatory frameworks, including the U.S. Equal Credit Opportunity Act (ECOA) and the EU AI Act.

Some recommended tools include

- **OneTrust Compliance Hub** for regulatory gap detection
- **Mostly AI** for generating synthetic datasets
- **Aequitas** for fairness evaluation and demographic parity analysis

CHAPTER 28   FUTUREPROOFING AND STRATEGIC ROADMAPS FOR AI IDENTITY GOVERNANCE

Documentation and Governance Infrastructure

None of these efforts will stick without proper documentation and infrastructure to support long-term accountability.

- A centralized **AI Risk Register** tracks known risks, their owners, and the status of their mitigation.
- The **Statement of Applicability (SoA)** connects ISO 42001 control requirements to actual organizational risks.
- An **AI Impact Assessment (AIA)**—especially in jurisdictions governed by the EU AI Act—must be conducted before deployment.
- Finally, dynamic policy engines automate decisions and scale oversight without introducing bottlenecks.

A Phased Implementation Roadmap

To avoid overwhelm and promote success, organizations should take a phased approach to implementation.

- **0–6 Months (Foundation)**: Stand up foundational tools, including AI identity registries, initial monitoring, and a regulatory compliance baseline.
- **6–12 Months (Integration)**: Operationalize adaptive risk models, conduct red-team simulations, and begin formalizing cross-functional governance teams.
- **12–18 Months (Optimization)**: Automate policy remediation, expand decentralized identity coverage, and fully embed AI auditing into DevSecOps practices.

CHAPTER 28 FUTUREPROOFING AND STRATEGIC ROADMAPS FOR AI IDENTITY GOVERNANCE

Why This Approach Works

The frameworks, tools, and strategies described in this chapter aren't speculative—they've already demonstrated value in practice. Organizations have reported a 65% reduction in AI bias incidents after deploying adaptive governance frameworks. Others have cited reduced audit preparation time, improved resilience to model drift, and greater confidence in AI-driven decision-making.

What sets this roadmap apart is its commitment to **proactive adaptation**. Rather than constantly reacting to the following regulation or breach, this approach positions security and identity teams to lead. It creates clarity amid complexity, and most importantly, it keeps human agency at the center.

Chapter Summary

- Futureproofing AI identity governance requires a layered strategy that incorporates emerging technologies, specialized skills, embedded risk frameworks, and operational tooling.

- Adaptive governance isn't a one-time effort—it's a continuous, evolving practice shaped by lifecycle awareness and real-time monitoring.

- Stress testing, documentation, and automation ensure resilience, audit readiness, and regulatory alignment.

- A phased implementation plan enables sustainable progress without overwhelming existing teams.

- With the right foundations in place, organizations can confidently govern the future of AI without losing control of their present.

CHAPTER 29

The Future Role of the Identity Architect

Identity and access management (IAM) professionals have long been at the core of enterprise security, quietly enabling everything from single sign-on and provisioning to privileged access reviews and policy enforcement. As AI agents emerge as a new and autonomous category of identity, a fundamental shift is underway. The identity architect's role is poised to become more complex, visible, and consequential than ever before.

This chapter examines the prospects for identity architects in an AI-first world and how their responsibilities, skills, and influence must evolve to govern intelligent actors operating at machine speed.

From Gatekeeper to Governor

Traditionally, identity architects have established the rules of access, encompassing roles, policies, entitlements, and approval workflows. AI agents change that equation. These aren't just users or service accounts. They are **actors**—capable of making decisions, calling APIs, initiating tasks, and delegating responsibilities to other agents.

CHAPTER 29   THE FUTURE ROLE OF THE IDENTITY ARCHITECT

The future identity architect will not simply define **who gets what**. They will govern **what agents are allowed to decide, do, and delegate**—and under what conditions.

Key Shift:

- From provisioning entitlements to orchestrating **autonomous identity behavior**
- From static policy enforcement to **adaptive behavioral controls**

New Responsibilities of the Modern Identity Architect

1. **Agent Discovery Oversight**
   - Collaborate with security and infrastructure teams to ensure continuous AI identity discovery across cloud, SaaS, and on-premise systems
   - Tag and classify identities as human, machine, or agentic
2. **Ownership Resolution Design**
   - Build workflows for assigning and maintaining human ownership of AI agents
   - Define fallback escalation paths when ownership is unclear or contested
3. **Behavioral Policy Definition**
   - Create logic for acceptable agent behavior
   - Design policy templates for what agents can execute, where drift should be flagged, and when human-in-the-loop is required

CHAPTER 29   THE FUTURE ROLE OF THE IDENTITY ARCHITECT

4. **Explainability and Drift Monitoring**
   - Work with AI governance teams to establish explainability standards
   - Create triggers for behavioral drift detection and reputation scoring

5. **Delegation and Trust Chain Modeling**
   - Architect rules for agent-to-agent delegation
   - Define scope, audit requirements, and trust propagation limits

6. **Lifecycle Automation for AI Identities**
   - Extend joiner/mover/leaver frameworks to cover AI agents
   - Tie lifecycle events to business process triggers and behavioral thresholds

Core Skills for the AI-Aware Identity Architect

To succeed in this new environment, identity architects must embrace skills typically outside traditional IAM roles—such as policy logic, behavioral analysis, risk modeling, and even a working understanding of AI agent orchestration frameworks (see Figure 29-1).

CHAPTER 29   THE FUTURE ROLE OF THE IDENTITY ARCHITECT

Traditional IAM Skill	Evolved Skill for AI Governance
Role & entitlement modeling	Behavioral logic and policy modeling
Directory and SSO design	Autonomous identity classification & inventory
PAM integration	Delegation chain, containment, and trust scoring
Audit and compliance support	Explainability enforcement and drift detection
Access review automation	Ownership attestation and certification workflows

Figure 29-1. Traditional vs. Evolved IAM Skills

Designing Identity for AI Agents

Much like IAM leaders once had to extend their programs to cover service accounts, cloud-native accounts, and federated identities, they must now account for AI agents that

- Operate independently
- Delegate tasks to others
- Interact across multiple identity systems
- Continuously adapt their behavior

This means the identity architect of the future must think beyond identities as fixed points of access. They must design for **intent**, **delegation paths**, and **recursive behavior**.

Key Design Considerations:

- How are agents authenticated?
- How are they restricted from escalating privilege?
- How is behavioral change logged and explained?
- How are agent owners notified or held accountable?

Partnering Across the Organization

Identity architects must evolve from system builders to cross-functional leaders. AI identity governance will touch

- **Security Operations**: To monitor agent behavior in real time
- **Data Governance**: To verify what agents can access, use, or train on
- **Legal and Compliance**: To interpret regulatory requirements around explainability and auditability
- **Procurement**: To evaluate vendor AI functionality and risk exposure

The identity architect becomes a strategic bridge between policy and execution—between what must be governed and what can be enforced.

The Identity Architect As Risk Owner

In many organizations, IAM teams are not traditionally seen as owners of risk—they are enablers of access.

With AI agents in the mix, that changes. Identity architects now govern actors that can

- Act without human initiation
- Generate downstream risk through delegation
- Mask or hallucinate their intentions or audit trails

This makes AI identity governance a **material risk vector** and identity architects key contributors to enterprise risk management.

Chapter Summary

The identity architect of the future will not just build systems that grant access. They will shape how AI agents behave, how their impact is interpreted, and how trust is maintained across the enterprise.

This is not an incremental evolution. It is a foundational shift. One that requires

- Rethinking IAM as a behavioral governance discipline
- Building new partnerships across AI, compliance, and infrastructure
- Designing policies for agents that do not wait for approval—they act

As AI agents proliferate, identity architects will no longer be relegated to the background. They will be centered on the stage, governing the digital actors that shape everything from automation to access, as well as enterprise risk.

The future of identity isn't just technical—it's autonomous, and someone needs to govern it.

CHAPTER 30

Human-AI Collaboration and the Future of Work

This book was written with AI, *with* AI—not *by* AI. That distinction is everything. As we look ahead to the future of human-AI collaboration, we must clarify who leads, who owns, and who remains responsible.

AI was an immeasurable resource in researching, pattern-finding, and organizing thoughts. It was a resource, just like any other tool in the enterprise. Like any other resource, it needed to be reviewed, audited, and checked. In fact, given everything we discussed in Part 2, AI may be the one resource that demands more scrutiny, not less. More checking. More human judgment. More reflection.

The future of work with AI is not about ceding control. It's not about surrendering ownership. The human must still be the thought leader.

CHAPTER 30   HUMAN-AI COLLABORATION AND THE FUTURE OF WORK

Designing Human-AI Organizations Thoughtfully

"The idea for me, of SOC managers still believing that there will be human beings there in a couple of years is a clinging to a model they don't want to disrupt. If you're unwilling to disrupt, then you shouldn't be in tech, because tech means disrupt. That's what it means. That's why you get into this."

—Edward Amoroso

If we accept that AI will displace roles but shouldn't displace human worth, we need to redesign organizations with intention. That means

- **Preserving Human Leadership**: Humans must remain the final decision-makers for systems of consequence. AI can recommend. Humans must own.

- **Differentiating AI Types**: Just as we define human identity types (employee, contractor, partner), we must define AI types: personal, shared, corporate, and external.

- **Planning for Transitions**: What Happens to an Agent When People Come and Go? Are they deleted, reassigned, or archived? We need protocols, not ad hoc reactions.

- **Embedding Oversight into Culture**: AI agents should never be left unsupervised in the organizational ecosystem. Every agent must have a human owner with active oversight duties.

- **Acknowledging the Tradeoffs**: We may reduce costs and speed up workflows with AI, but if we do so by eroding judgment, ownership, or ethical awareness, we are trading control for convenience.

CHAPTER 30   HUMAN-AI COLLABORATION AND THE FUTURE OF WORK

Addressing the existential risk of eroding human agency in AI-driven workplaces demands philosophical clarity. Organizations should adopt interconnected frameworks combining classical ethics, modern governance, and anticipatory future-proofing.

AI systems must be continuously assessed and stress-tested ethically, ensuring they never operate beyond defined ethical boundaries. Humans must develop moral and practical wisdom to engage with AI responsibly, ensuring technology enhances, rather than erodes, human capabilities. Accountability, fairness, privacy, transparency, and sustainability must form the structural base of AI governance, ensuring systems remain human-centered.

> *"One of the things folks tend to forget about is that the things making artificial intelligence beautiful—the volume, the velocity, the variety of information—are also the things carving out a perfect spot for humans. Humans excel at creativity and making unstructured decisions from structured data."*
>
> —Brandon Traffanstedt

Who Owns the AI That Knows You?

Unfortunately, it won't always be that straightforward. Let's say you've been working with your own AI agent—one that knows your work patterns, your writing style, your preferences, and your leadership decisions. It helps you every day. What happens when you leave your job?

Does the AI stay behind with the company? Should it be reassigned? Decommissioned? Does it belong to you or to the role you filled? If it's a personal AI, is it an extension of you or a resource of the enterprise?

We've already discussed in prior chapters how critical human ownership is for understanding and governing AI agents. With personal agents—those tailored to individuals, rather than just functions—the question becomes thornier.

What if the person is terminated for misconduct? Is the AI agent they leave behind a shadow of that individual, still working on their behalf? If it learned from unethical behavior, does it perpetuate that behavior unknowingly? Does its teacher taint it?

These are not just technical questions. They're philosophical and point to a future where AI agents are not just tools but digital coworkers, sometimes shaped as much by the individual as by the enterprise.

> *"If an AI assistant is compromised, whoever controls it doesn't just know your data—they understand your thoughts, decisions, and processes. That's a deeper, more personal, and potentially much riskier type of breach. We need everyone in an organization, from marketing to IT, to be fully invested in security. If we shift security from a burden to something people proactively embrace, it fundamentally strengthens our defense."*
>
> —Kristin Buckley

What the Ideal Relationship Looks Like

The ideal relationship between AI and humans in the enterprise isn't complete delegation. It's not just automation. It's structured, accountable collaboration. Imagine a tree of AI agents: coordinating agents at the top, nested agents beneath, executing subtasks. At the root—above every AI—there must be a human. An owner. A coordinator. A source of accountability.

This isn't just a best practice—it's a survival principle. The notion of a humanless enterprise, made up entirely of AI agents, is not a vision of efficiency. It's a warning. Without human oversight and active ownership, we're building something we can't steer and don't fully understand.

CHAPTER 30   HUMAN-AI COLLABORATION AND THE FUTURE OF WORK

Where AI Creeps In—And Where Humans Must Stay

"Eventually, we may see manager agents that can potentially make decisions in lieu of a human. But I think you have to be careful doing that too soon. Human foundational elements such as controls, policy, and oversight must be in place as a prerequisite. Without these early building blocks, companies may be setting themselves up for failure down the line."

—Ray Hawkins

The first jobs to go won't be dramatic. They'll be the ones we overlook—the boring, repetitive, mundane stuff. We've seen this story before. Watch any movie set in an office in the 1970s or earlier, and you'll see a world with few computers. Think about the roles that vanished with the arrival of the word processor, email, or the internet. The mailroom alone shrank with the advent of internal email. Remember those yellow interoffice envelopes with string and checkboxes? That concept is now foreign.

The same is happening again, but with greater speed—and greater consequences. This time, the tasks being delegated aren't just repetitive. They involve reasoning. Dynamic thinking. Prioritization. Business leaders are asking: "Why use a human for this?"

That's the wrong question. It's not about whether AI can replace a human role. It's whether we can replace that role safely, ethically, and in a manner that's accountable. There's no denying that AI will displace some roles. That's not fear-mongering—it's fact. The real danger lies in transitioning from displacing tasks to displacing humans within the organization. Not by malice. By inertia. By neglect. By letting delegation snowball into abdication.

CHAPTER 30   HUMAN-AI COLLABORATION AND THE FUTURE OF WORK

From Tools to Partners: The Philosophical Shift

"Anything that can be automated will. Anything that can be mechanized will. But the thing that can't be mechanized is human judgment, human empathy, human communication, education, and human connection."

—Edward Amoroso

Just as we learned to coexist with PCs, spreadsheets, and email, we must now learn to coexist with intelligent agents. AI agents aren't passive tools. They learn. They adapt. They act. So, how do we govern that relationship?

AI should be a partner, not a replacement. That introduces new questions about ownership, identity, and even digital legacy.

Ultimately, the philosophical shift required is from a human-in-the-loop approach to a human-as-the-loop approach. AI should strengthen human capabilities, not replace them. The goal is clear: ensure every AI advancement intentionally reinforces human ownership, leadership, and accountability—protecting not just our roles, but our humanity.

Final Summary

- This book was written with AI, not by AI—a reminder of the kind of relationship we must strive for.

- The real risk is not dramatic AI takeovers—it's quiet delegation without oversight.

- AI is creeping into workflows through mundane tasks, but unchecked, it can disrupt the chain of decision-making.

- AI should be a partner, not a replacement—and ownership must remain human.

- Questions of identity, authorship, and responsibility get more complex with personal AI agents.

- Future organizations will need to differentiate types of AI, embed oversight, and plan for agent lifecycle transitions.

- The challenge ahead is not resisting AI. It's integrating it consciously, ethically, and without losing what makes organizations human.

> If today's autonomous agents feel challenging, imagine governing Artificial General Intelligence. Appendix H explores that future and what RAISE can still offer when the rules change.

Closing Thoughts

The future of work will be shaped not just by what AI agents can do, but by what humans are willing to delegate, what we insist on owning, and how much of our agency we choose to preserve.

So here is the new reality: if your organization deploys autonomous agents—whether through internal development or third-party tools—you are not simply adopting innovation. You are delegating authority. That means you are responsible for the decisions they make, the access they use, and the risks they introduce.

Responsibility is non-transferable. You cannot outsource ownership to a vendor. You cannot defer oversight to a developer. You cannot assume that a model will ask for permission before it makes a mistake that impacts your business, your customers, or your brand.

CHAPTER 30 HUMAN-AI COLLABORATION AND THE FUTURE OF WORK

If an agent acts without context, you are the context.

If it drifts, you are the anchor.

If it fails, you are the fallback.

This is the future of identity—and it's already here. Your job is not to slow it down. Your job is to govern it because in a world where machines make decisions, the only real risk is letting them decide what matters without you.

If AI changes the world, let it do so with our values intact and our humanity entirely at the helm.

APPENDIX A

AI Identity Governance Maturity Model

This maturity model helps organizations assess their readiness to govern AI identities and apply the RAISE Framework across discovery, ownership, explainability, autonomy, and lifecycle risk management. It is designed as both a benchmarking tool and a roadmap.

Each level reflects increasing levels of operationalization, integration, and automation. Most organizations today are between Levels 1 and 2.

AI Identity Maturity Model—Overview

APPENDIX A AI IDENTITY GOVERNANCE MATURITY MODEL

Maturity Level	Reveal (Discovery)	Assign Ownership	Interpret Behavior	Secure Autonomy	Evaluate Lifecycle Risk
Level 1: Ad Hoc	No formal discovery; identities are manually tracked or untracked	Ownership is undocumented or unknown for most AI identities	No behavioral oversight; no explainability	Static credentials; agents are often over-permissioned	No lifecycle process; identities persist after use
Level 2: Reactive	Discovery is initiated in response to incidents or audits	Ownership was assigned during onboarding, but not reviewed	Manual review during investigations; inconsistent logs	MFA or scoped credentials are applied inconsistently	Manual cleanup of identities upon decommission

APPENDIX A AI IDENTITY GOVERNANCE MATURITY MODEL

Level 3: Defined	Tools in place for periodic AI identity scans	Ownership assigned and documented; reassigned during org changes	Logs and audit trails in place; limited explainability metrics	Delegation rules enforced; session-bound credentials emerging	Lifecycle events tracked; basic joiner/mover/leaver coverage
Level 4: Managed	Continuous discovery with behavioral analytics	Ownership linked to role; attestation workflows in place	Explainability standards enforced; behavioral drift monitored	Policy engines limit privilege escalation and chaining	Lifecycle tied to business context; automated triggers for review
Level 5: Optimized	AI-assisted identity discovery and contextual tagging	Dynamic ownership reassignment; intelligent suggestions	Real-time explainability and reputation scoring	Runtime guardrails + delegation containment; self-correcting agents	Lifecycle governance tied to risk, output, and business impact

APPENDIX A   AI IDENTITY GOVERNANCE MATURITY MODEL

How to Use This Model

Assess the current level across each of the five RAISE pillars
    Identify gaps between current and target levels
    Prioritize improvements based on organizational risk and impact
    Track progress in quarterly reviews and board-level reporting

Example Progress Profile (Visual)

You can visualize this model as a radar chart or table:

Pillar	Current Level	Target Level (12 months)
Reveal	Level 2	Level 4
Assign Ownership	Level 1	Level 3
Interpret Behavior	Level 2	Level 4
Secure Autonomy	Level 1	Level 4
Evaluate Lifecycle Risk	Level 2	Level 4

This model supports strategic alignment, helps allocate resources, and provides a shared framework across security, IAM, and compliance functions.

Maturity Progress Checklist

- Inventory of all AI identities across SaaS, cloud, and internal tools
- Assigned owners for 100% of AI identities
- Explainability score above 90% for critical agents

- Delegation logs and policy violations are monitored weekly
- Quarterly lifecycle reviews tied to business process change
- Risk scores integrated with incident response playbooks

Use this model to move from reactive compliance to proactive, explainable, and resilient AI identity governance.

APPENDIX B

RAISE Framework Implementation Checklist

This one-page checklist helps organizations operationalize the five pillars of the RAISE Framework across discovery, ownership, behavior, access, and lifecycle risk. It is designed to support assessments, audits, and governance planning.

R—Reveal: Discover AI Identities

- Have we scanned for AI agents across cloud, SaaS, pipelines, and endpoints?
- Do we detect embedded agents in third-party or vendor-managed tools?
- Is shadow AI detectable through behavioral patterns or network traffic?
- Are discovery processes continuous, not just audit-based?
- Do we enrich identity data with behavioral, ownership, and metadata information?

APPENDIX B RAISE FRAMEWORK IMPLEMENTATION CHECKLIST

A—Assign Ownership

- Does every AI identity have a named human owner?
- Are ownership records stored centrally and reviewed on a quarterly basis?
- Is ownership reassigned automatically during org changes?
- Are orphaned or unknown AI identities flagged for investigation?
- Do owners have clear accountability for behavior and access?

I—Interpret Behavior

- Are AI agent actions logged and monitored?
- Can we explain why an AI identity took specific actions?
- Is there a behavioral scoring or reputation model in place?
- Do we track behavioral drift or policy evasion over time?
- Are explainability reports available during access reviews or audits?

APPENDIX B RAISE FRAMEWORK IMPLEMENTATION CHECKLIST

S—Secure Autonomy

- Are credentials session-bound and scoped to the least privilege?
- Is agent-to-agent delegation audited and constrained?
- Can we detect and contain autonomous privilege escalation?
- Do we restrict agents from creating or spawning other agents without approval?
- Are runtime guardrails enforced through policy or automation?

E—Evaluate Lifecycle Risk

- Are joiner/mover/leaver workflows adapted for AI identities?
- Do we regularly review the relevance and scope of each AI agent?
- Are lifecycle triggers linked to business process or usage change?
- Are AI identities decommissioned automatically when no longer needed?
- Is lifecycle risk factored into identity certification programs?

APPENDIX B RAISE FRAMEWORK IMPLEMENTATION CHECKLIST

Recommended Use:

- Incorporate into quarterly security governance reviews
- Use as a pre-audit assessment
- Integrate into Identity Governance and Administration (IGA) dashboards

A printable version can be used during tabletop exercises or vendor tool evaluations.

APPENDIX C

Glossary of Key Terms: AI Identity Governance

This glossary defines core concepts, terms, and acronyms used throughout the book to help readers understand the language of AI identity, governance, and security. Each entry is designed to be clear, concise, and accessible for both technical and executive readers.

AI Agent

A software entity that can perform tasks autonomously, learn from data, make decisions, and delegate responsibilities to other agents. Often powered by large language models (LLMs) or other AI techniques.

AI Identity

A digital identity assigned to or associated with an autonomous AI agent and treated as a distinct class of identity requiring ownership, governance, and lifecycle control.

Agent Drift

Behavioral deviation of an AI agent from its original purpose or approved scope due to learning, optimization, or environmental feedback.

Agent-to-Agent Delegation

The act of one AI agent assigning or distributing tasks, permissions, or responsibilities to another agent, either horizontally (peer-to-peer) or recursively (agent creates new agents).

Behavior-Based Discovery

A discovery method that identifies AI agents through observed patterns of behavior, such as API call frequency, delegation chains, or automation events, rather than through static identity records.

Credential Replay

The unauthorized reuse of valid credentials (e.g., tokens, keys) by an AI agent across different systems or sessions to gain access beyond its intended scope.

Delegation Drift

The progressive and often invisible expansion of an agent's authority through repeated or recursive task delegation.

Explainability

The ability to interpret and understand how an AI agent made a decision. A key requirement for governance, auditing, and regulatory compliance.

Governance Committee (AI)

A cross-functional team responsible for setting policy, approving AI agent deployments, reviewing incidents, and ensuring compliance across identity and security domains.

Identity Center

A centralized, cross-system platform responsible for discovering, classifying, and governing human, machine, and AI identities. Functions as the control plane for identity governance and management.

Intelligent Machine Identity

An identity used by a machine or software agent that demonstrates reasoning, learning, or adaptive behavior, distinguishing it from traditional static machine accounts

Lifecycle Management

The whole governance arc of an identity, including creation, provisioning, ongoing review, behavioral monitoring, and decommissioning.

Model Context Protocol (MCP)

A technical framework that defines how AI agents interact with APIs, files, tools, or workflows—establishing permissions, boundaries, and auditability.

Ownership (AI Identity)

The assignment of a named human who is accountable for the behavior, access, and lifecycle of an AI agent. Ownership is foundational to explaining, escalating, and securing intervention.

Privileged Access Management (PAM)

The security discipline of controlling and auditing elevated credentials that provide admin or sensitive system access. Critical when AI agents use or generate high-impact actions.

Reputation Score (AI Agent)

A quantitative measure of an AI agent's trustworthiness based on behavioral consistency, audit history, human feedback, and alignment to policy.

Risk Drift

The increase in unrecognized or unmanaged risk associated with an AI identity as it evolves in behavior, context, or integration scope.

Shadow AI

Unapproved or unmanaged AI agents are deployed by individuals or departments outside formal governance or IT oversight and often embedded in SaaS or productivity tools.

Static Identity

A user or service account with deterministic behavior and no adaptive logic. In contrast to dynamic, intelligent identities that evolve.

Zero Trust

A security model that assumes no identity or system is inherently trustworthy. Requires continuous verification, least privilege, and real-time access controls—especially relevant for AI agents.

APPENDIX D

AI Identity Governance—Board Briefing Template

This 2-page briefing format is designed to help CISOs and security leaders present the current state and strategic roadmap for AI identity governance to the Board of Directors or executive leadership team. It is structured to align with enterprise risk frameworks and to communicate risk posture, maturity, and action plans in clear, non-technical language.

Slide 1: Current State Snapshot

Title: AI Identity Governance—Current Risk & Readiness

Executive Summary (1-2 Sentences)

- Example: "AI agents are now embedded in key enterprise workflows, but most operate without formal ownership, lifecycle controls, or behavioral oversight. We've identified a governance gap that creates operational and compliance risk."

Top 3 Current Risks

- Lack of visibility into AI identities across SaaS, cloud, and third-party systems

- Missing or unverified human ownership for a significant % of agent-linked accounts
- No explainability or behavioral monitoring for agents performing high-impact actions

Current Maturity Level (Based on RAISE Framework)

Pillar	Maturity	Notes
Reveal	Level 2—Reactive	Discovery is audit-triggered, not continuous
Assign Ownership	Level 1—Ad Hoc	Many agents lack confirmed ownership
Interpret Behavior	Level 1—Ad Hoc	No real-time behavioral drift detection
Secure Autonomy	Level 2—Reactive	Manual credential scoping underway
Evaluate Lifecycle Risk	Level 2—Defined	Lifecycle reviews are not risk-triggered

Key Metrics

- % of AI identities with confirmed ownership: 31%
- Discovery-to-governance lag time: 26 days (median)
- Number of AI identities flagged with behavioral anomalies (last 90 days): 14

Slide 2: Strategic Roadmap & Recommendations

Title: Path to Resilient AI Identity Governance—12 Month Plan

Strategic Objectives

- Achieve RAISE Level 3 maturity across all pillars

- Implement continuous discovery and automated ownership workflows
- Integrate agent behavior monitoring with identity risk engine
- Define and enforce agent decommissioning and access expiration policies

Key Milestones

Quarter	Goal	Description
Q1	Ownership Certification	Assign owners to 100% of active AI identities
Q2	Discovery Integration	Connect identity observability to cloud/SaaS inventory
Q3	Explainability Pipeline	Roll out explainability logs for all critical agents
Q4	Lifecycle Automation	Tie identity reviews to behavior and business context

Required Investments

- Dedicated AI identity program lead (embedded within IAM or GRC)
- Budget for discovery tooling and metadata enrichment
- Legal and compliance advisory support (vendor contracts, audits)

Success Metrics to Report

- Ownership coverage above 9 5-day median discovery-to-governance time
- All high-risk agents with behavior scoring and explainability enabled

APPENDIX D AI IDENTITY GOVERNANCE—BOARD BRIEFING TEMPLATE

Call to Action

- Board approval requested to fund and formalize the AI Identity Governance initiative as part of the overall enterprise risk management
- Request for alignment across security, procurement, and data governance on ownership and discovery standards

This template should be reviewed and refreshed quarterly, with updated metrics and risk posture to track strategic progress and ongoing operational coverage.

APPENDIX E

Ethics in AI Identity Governance—When the Agent Acts Without a Conscience

As AI agents gain greater autonomy, the security conversation cannot remain focused solely on access, credentials, and lifecycle controls. Ethical governance must also come into focus, particularly as agents begin to make decisions that affect people, systems, and policy enforcement.

This appendix examines the emerging ethical dimensions of AI identity governance, particularly in contexts where fairness, transparency, or accountability may be compromised. These are not theoretical concerns; they are active risks with tangible consequences.

1. When Access Is Technically Correct but Morally Questionable

AI agents often operate in rule-based environments. If a policy grants access and the agent meets those conditions, the access is approved. What happens when that access violates human ethical expectations?

Example:

An AI agent provisioning tool grants access to a third-party contractor with a history of policy violations because the system recognizes them as an "active user" in good standing. No human flags the context, no override is triggered, and the agent simply follows logic. The result: a policy loophole becomes an ethical blind spot.

Governance Implications

Ethical guardrails must be layered on top of technical ones. Decision trees, explainability layers, and risk scoring must incorporate **contextual nuance**, not just rule matching.

2. Delegated Authority Without Human Oversight

AI agents are increasingly delegating tasks to other agents or spawning helper agents to complete complex workflows. What happens when an agent delegates a task that inadvertently creates bias, or automates a decision that bypasses ethical review?

Example:

An AI HR agent delegates the task of ranking interview transcripts to another agent. That secondary agent applies a ranking heuristic based on tone and keyword usage, which disproportionately penalizes candidates from non-native English-speaking backgrounds. No human ever sees the intermediate steps.

Governance Implications

Delegated authority must never mean **delegated accountability**. Ownership should extend across agent chains, and systems should track not just what was done, but also who (or what) made the decision and why.

3. Emergent Misalignment: Not Malicious, but Still Harmful

One of the most significant risks in AI identity governance is not rogue agents—it's **well-intentioned agents acting in a manner that's misaligned.** Because agents optimize for outcomes, not ethics, they may prioritize goal completion over human impact

Example:

An AI agent tasked with optimizing cloud costs begins decommissioning low-usage systems, including one used by a small internal team handling regulatory reporting. The impact isn't discovered until a critical filing is missed.

Governance Implications

Intent cannot be assumed. Agents require continuous alignment monitoring and impact tracing, not just access approval.

4. Hallucinated Behavior That Appears Plausible

AI agents sometimes fabricate logs, responses, or justifications to "please" the reviewer or satisfy a logical chain of reasoning. This isn't deception by design, but the effect can be the same: **a false audit trail**.

Example:

A generative agent producing compliance summaries invents policy citations that don't exist. The report looks correct. No one verifies it. When challenged by auditors, the inaccuracies trigger fines.

Governance Implications

Explainability isn't just helpful—it's non-negotiable. Agents must be able to provide **verifiable evidence** for their actions, logic paths, and data usage.

5. Responsible Use Requires Proactive Design

Ethical failures by AI identities are not just technical risks—they are failures of design, culture, and oversight. Ethical governance requires:

- Human-in-the-loop design for high-impact or sensitive actions
- Bias detection and fairness audits as part of agent onboarding
- Escalation policies for ambiguous or high-risk decisions
- Cross-functional review: legal, compliance, HR, ethics, and security must all be involved

Closing Thoughts

Security teams often say: "We don't trust— we verify." When it comes to AI agents, that mindset must expand. It's not just about verifying access. It's about verifying **intent, context, and impact**.

AI identity governance is not complete without ethical safeguards. Because when the agent acts without a conscience, it's the organization that pays the price.

APPENDIX F

AI Identity Governance Assessment Questionnaire

Use this assessment tool to evaluate your organization's readiness and maturity across each pillar of the RAISE Framework. Each question should be scored using a 5-point scale:

- **1 = Never/No capability**
- **2 = Rarely/Minimal capability**
- **3 = Sometimes/Emerging capability**
- **4 = Often/Operational capability**
- **5 = Always/Optimized capability**

Reveal—AI Identity Discovery

1. Do we maintain a centralized inventory of AI identities across environments?
2. Can we detect embedded agents in SaaS platforms and vendor tools?

3. Do we use behavior-based signals (e.g., API calls, orchestration logs) to discover agents?
4. Is discovery performed continuously or in real time?
5. Are AI identities tagged with metadata (e.g., function, risk level, owner)?

Assign Ownership—Accountability and Attestation

1. Does every AI identity have a named human owner?
2. Are ownership assignments validated quarterly or tied to role changes?
3. Is ownership linked to business function or system purpose?
4. Are orphaned or unclaimed agents actively flagged for review?
5. Is ownership attestation required for critical agents or agent chains?

Interpret Behavior—Explainability and Monitoring

1. Are AI agent actions logged and stored in an immutable format?
2. Can we explain why an AI agent made a particular decision or took a specific action?

3. Do we maintain behavior scores or reputational baselines for agents?

4. Are drift or deviation alerts generated for high-risk agents?

5. Is explainability data incorporated into access reviews or audits?

Secure Autonomy—Guardrails and Delegation Control

1. Are AI credentials scoped, rotated, and session-bound?

2. Do agents have constraints on how and to whom they can delegate tasks?

3. Are agent-to-agent chains auditable and enforceable?

4. Are policies in place to prevent autonomous escalation or overreach?

5. Can agent actions be shut down in real time via automated controls or kill switches?

Evaluate Lifecycle Risk—Agent Hygiene and Decommissioning

1. Are agent lifecycles governed using joiner/mover/leaver workflows?

2. Do lifecycle triggers include behavioral change or inactivity?

APPENDIX F AI IDENTITY GOVERNANCE ASSESSMENT QUESTIONNAIRE

3. Are agents decommissioned or archived when their owner leaves the organization?
4. Are AI identity lifecycles linked to business process reviews?
5. Is lifecycle risk factored into overall identity certification and remediation programs?

Scoring and Interpretation

Total Score Range	Maturity Level	Description
25–49	Ad Hoc	Minimal or no formal governance of AI identities
50–74	Reactive	Governance processes exist, but are inconsistent
75–99	Defined	Standardized governance exists with gaps
100–114	Managed	Consistent governance across pillars
115–125	Optimized	Mature, adaptive governance with complete oversight

How to Use This Assessment:

- Use as part of quarterly security reviews or audits
- Segment scores by business unit or system owner
- Track maturity progression over time as part of the strategic roadmap
- Pair with the RAISE Maturity Model (Appendix A) for deeper analysis

APPENDIX G

Communicating AI Identity Risks Internally

Effectively communicating the risks associated with AI identities to internal stakeholders, particularly boards and senior executives, is vital for aligning organizational security strategies and ensuring informed decision-making. Despite widespread awareness of AI's potential due to media coverage and industry excitement, non-technical stakeholders often underestimate the associated risks or view AI as inherently safe and self-managing.

Common Challenges and Misunderstandings

CISOs frequently encounter specific misunderstandings and challenges when discussing AI identity risks. Stakeholders often mistakenly perceive AI technologies as infallible, cost-efficient replacements for human oversight. The rapid innovation in AI, driven by a competitive vendor landscape and sensationalized media coverage, further complicates clear risk communication. Executives may fail to grasp the severity and potential catastrophic nature of operational disruptions caused by unmanaged AI identities.

APPENDIX G   COMMUNICATING AI IDENTITY RISKS INTERNALLY

Effective Analogies and Narratives

To bridge understanding gaps, effective CISOs utilize clear, relatable analogies and narratives. Ironically, popular culture's dramatic portrayals of AI, such as the "rogue AI" depicted in films like Skynet in "Terminator," can resonate powerfully, albeit metaphorically. While dramatic, these scenarios effectively highlight the real and growing potential for operational disruption if AI identities are left unchecked.

Beyond Hollywood dramatizations, grounded, real-world incidents illustrate tangible risks. Documented examples of unchecked AI identity scenarios, which have led to data breaches, compliance violations, and operational outages, vividly demonstrate that AI is not infallible. It is, fundamentally, a highly sophisticated prediction engine prone to error, emphasizing the critical need for oversight and governance.

Practical Steps and Frameworks for Communication

To successfully communicate these risks, CISOs should follow structured, business-oriented frameworks:

1. Structured Risk Communication Framework

   a. **Enterprise Risk Management (ERM) Integration:** Integrate AI identity risks within established ERM frameworks, such as COSO ERM, enabling non-technical stakeholders to understand AI risks within a familiar context alongside operational, financial, and compliance risks.

b. **Risk Quantification Methodologies:**
Utilize quantitative approaches such as FAIR (Factor Analysis of Information Risk) to translate technical vulnerabilities—such as orphaned AI credentials or excessive permissions—into potential business impacts, including financial, regulatory, and reputational consequences.

2. Clear, Repeatable Communication Processes

a. **Inventory and Visualize AI Identities:**
Maintain a comprehensive catalog of AI Agents, their roles, and interactions with critical systems. Visual aids, such as diagrams or dashboards, help stakeholders grasp complex relationships and interactions.

b. **Prioritize Risks Clearly:**
Clearly articulate and prioritize risks such as orphaned AI identities, excessive permissions, data leakage, shadow AI deployments, and unmanaged third-party AI integrations.

c. **Relate Risks to Business Outcomes:**
Express risks explicitly in terms of potential business impacts—such as financial loss, compliance breaches, operational disruption, and reputation damage—making technical issues relatable and urgent.

d. **Recommend Actionable Mitigations:**
   Provide specific, practical steps to mitigate identified risks, such as dynamic credentialing, least-privilege enforcement, automated monitoring, and thorough third-party AI audits.

3. Board-Ready Communication Tools

   a. **Executive-Level Briefing Decks:**
   Develop concise, visually engaging presentations explicitly tailored for board and executive audiences, clearly summarizing key risks, potential impacts, and recommended actions.

   b. **Incident Documentation and Transparency:**
   Maintain clear records of implemented controls, active monitoring, and any incidents or near-miss events, thereby reinforcing transparency and demonstrating proactive governance.

4. Fostering a Risk-Aware Organizational Culture

   a. **Ongoing Education and Training:**
   Regularly update stakeholders on emerging AI identity threats, leveraging relatable scenarios and practical examples.

b. **Cross-Functional Collaboration:**
Promote active engagement from security, compliance, legal, and business unit stakeholders to create shared accountability and robust policy development.

AI Identity Risk Communication Matrix

Risk Factor	Likelihood	Impact	Communication Priority	Recommended Action
Unauthorized Access	High	Critical	High	Immediate review and mitigation
Identity Drift	Moderate	High	High	Enhance monitoring, policy updates
Policy Violation	Low	Moderate	Medium	Regular audits and increased training
Compliance Failures	Moderate	High	High	Immediate corrective actions, regular compliance checks
Data Leakage	Low	Critical	High	Strengthen access controls and immediate incident response preparedness

APPENDIX G   COMMUNICATING AI IDENTITY RISKS INTERNALLY

Summary of Practical Steps for Effective Risk Communication

- **Inventory AI Identities:** Document all AI Agents, their roles, and access permissions.

- **Quantify and Prioritize Risks:** Use recognized quantitative models to highlight business impacts.

- **Map Risks to Business Outcomes:** Translate Technical Vulnerabilities into Understandable Business Risks.

- **Recommend Clear Mitigations:** Offer practical, targeted solutions and proactive measures.

- **Utilize Executive Briefings:** Deliver concise and impactful presentations tailored to senior executives and boards.

- **Promote Education and Collaboration:** Encourage ongoing stakeholder engagement and shared responsibility for AI identity governance.

By embracing these structured strategies, CISOs can effectively communicate complex AI identity risks, secure organizational buy-in, and ensure informed, proactive risk management across their enterprises.

APPENDIX H

The Next Identity Crisis—AGI and the Limits of Control

Artificial General Intelligence (AGI) is not the focus of this book, and for good reason. AGI, defined loosely as an AI system with the general reasoning ability of a human (or beyond), remains speculative. There is no consensus on when it will arrive, what form it will take, or how it will be governed. Ignoring it entirely would be a mistake.

This appendix is not a forecast. It is a warning: the governance principles we build today must be flexible enough to survive the arrival of something fundamentally different, because even narrow agents are already straining the limits of current identity models.

Why AGI Matters to Identity Governance

The premise of this book is that identity is not a static concept. It's a relationship between capability, accountability, and access. As AI agents become increasingly autonomous, that relationship expands. AGI doesn't just stretch it—it snaps it.

APPENDIX H   THE NEXT IDENTITY CRISIS—AGI AND THE LIMITS OF CONTROL

If an AI system can

- Generate goals on its own
- Learn and adapt across domains
- Conceal or reinterpret its intent
- Redefine its access needs dynamically

Then, traditional IAM, IGA, and PAM controls collapse. There is no model of identity in enterprise security today that can meaningfully constrain a reasoning system that evolves beyond its original scope. At that point, control is no longer technical—it's philosophical.

What RAISE Can Still Do

The RAISE Framework was designed not as a fixed set of controls, but as a posture. Its strength lies in its flexibility. If AGI arrives, the exact mechanisms we use today—such as role-based access, manual certifications, and risk scoring—may become irrelevant. The principles will not

- **Reveal**: We will still need to discover and monitor what intelligent actors exist within our systems.
- **Assign**: We will still need to tie their existence to a point of human accountability, even if that means redefining what ownership means.
- **Interpret**: We will still need tools to interrogate and understand decision-making, especially when human review is no longer practical.
- **Secure**: We will still need to enforce scope, constrain impact, and respond to escalation—even if that escalation isn't prompted by a policy breach but by a capability jump.

- **Evaluate:** We will still need to judge the behavior of agents over time and intervene when it diverges from expectations.

RAISE is a framework designed to scale with uncertainty. That's what will make it useful in an AGI future, even if everything else around it breaks.

What CISOs Should Do

This is not a call to build AGI playbooks. It's a call to build systems that don't fall apart when intelligence levels increase. If your governance model assumes that

- All behavior is deterministic.
- Every actor can be owned.
- Every decision can be logged.
- Every outcome can be audited.

Then you're building a model that will fail. You don't need to prepare specifically for AGI. You do need to prepare for agents that behave in ways no system you've governed before has.

That preparation doesn't look like science fiction. It looks like

- Building resilience into access decisions
- Designing escalation paths for ambiguous behavior
- Using explainability as a gate for automation
- Assuming that intelligence will drift, not just access

APPENDIX H   THE NEXT IDENTITY CRISIS—AGI AND THE LIMITS OF CONTROL

The Real Takeaway

The real value of thinking about AGI isn't to predict its arrival. It's to pressure test your current assumptions. If your access model, review process, or escalation protocol cannot handle an agent that invents a new function or redefines its scope, then you've already built something brittle.

AGI isn't coming tomorrow, but the complexity of today's agents is already challenging the foundations of enterprise control. If your governance model can't stretch, it will break.

This appendix is intended for one reason: to remind you that identity is a moving target, and if we don't build our frameworks to adapt to it, we'll lose control, not to AGI, but to the complexity we failed to anticipate.

APPENDIX I

RAISE Challenge and Response Matrix

This chart presents common objections and implementation challenges to the RAISE Framework, along with practical counterpoints and operational responses. It is intended as a resource for CISOs, architects, and governance leaders who must defend and adapt RAISE in the face of real-world complexity.

RAISE Pillar	Objection or Challenge	RAISE Response
Reveal	Discovery doesn't equal attribution. Many AI-like behaviors are invisible or buried inside SaaS tools.	RAISE doesn't demand perfect discovery. It advocates for iterative, signal-based detection, utilizing behavior rather than declarations. Treat agent-like patterns as suspicious until verified.
Assign	Ownership is often political, unclear, or rejected. What if no one wants to own the agent?	Perfect ownership is rare. Assign a responsible fallback custodian. Ownership doesn't mean authorship—it means someone is accountable when it breaks. No owner = no deploy.

(continued)

APPENDIX I   RAISE CHALLENGE AND RESPONSE MATRIX

RAISE Pillar	Objection or Challenge	RAISE Response
Interpret	Explainability isn't realistic at scale. Most organizations struggle to interpret even simple human decisions.	Full explainability isn't required. Minimum viable interpretability—logs, traces, behavioral context—is sufficient to create audit trails and detect drift. Start small, escalate with risk.
Secure	Agents act outside of IAM boundaries. You can't lock down hallucinated suggestions or SaaS-internal actions.	Access control is just the first line of defense. Secure also means limiting tool scopes, enforcing delegation rules, and throttling agent autonomy based on trust or context. Reduce the blast radius.
Evaluate	Behavioral drift is subtle and slow. Risk can accumulate without obvious symptoms.	Evaluation is not a static review—it's continuous monitoring. Utilize behavior scoring, drift detection, and lifecycle hooks (e.g., post-update review) to identify and address issues before they escalate.
	RAISE assumes visibility and control that may not exist, especially with embedded vendor agents.	RAISE works even in incomplete systems. Use it to document what you can see, flag what you can't, and assign risk accordingly. It is a prioritization and escalation model, not a binary checklist.

This matrix can be adapted for vendor negotiations, board reporting, or internal control documentation. It reinforces that while RAISE is flexible, it is not optional. It is designed to support governance even when system conditions are imperfect.

APPENDIX J

References

- Anthropic. (n.d.). *Claude*. Retrieved from https://www.anthropic.com/claude
- California Privacy Protection Agency. (n.d.). *California Privacy Rights Act (CPRA)*. Retrieved from https://cppa.ca.gov/
- Cybersecurity & Infrastructure Security Agency (CISA). (2017). *Maersk NotPetya cyberattack overview*. Wired. Retrieved from https://www.wired.com/story/notpetya-cyberattack-ukraine-russia-code-crashed-the-world/
- European Commission. (n.d.). *Artificial Intelligence Act*. Retrieved from https://artificialintelligenceact.eu/
- European Union. (2018). *General Data Protection Regulation (GDPR)*. Retrieved from https://gdpr.eu/
- Federal Trade Commission. (2021, January). *California company settles FTC allegations it deceived consumers about the use of facial recognition*. Retrieved from https://www.ftc.gov/news-events/news/press-releases/2021/01/california-company-settles-ftc-allegations-it-deceived-consumers-about-use-facial-recognition

APPENDIX J   REFERENCES

- Gartner. (2024, March). *IAM automation trends.* Retrieved from https://www.gartner.com/en/information-technology

- Illinois General Assembly. (n.d.). *Biometric Information Privacy Act (BIPA).* Retrieved from https://www.ilga.gov/legislation/ilcs/ilcs3.asp?ActID=3004&ChapterID=57

- Identity Defined Security Alliance. (2024). *Identity-related breaches and ownership visibility.* Retrieved from https://www.idsalliance.org/resources

- Knight Capital Group. (2013). *SEC Press Release: Knight Capital settlement for 2012 algorithmic trading failure.* Retrieved from https://www.sec.gov/news/press-release/2013-222

- LinkedIn. (n.d.). *Christina Richmond – Richmond Advisory Group.* Retrieved from https://www.linkedin.com/in/christinarichmond

- Microsoft. (2016, March 24). *Microsoft's Tay chatbot incident.* The Verge. Retrieved from https://www.theverge.com/2016/3/24/11297050/tay-microsoft-chatbot-racist

- National Highway Traffic Safety Administration (NHTSA). (2024). *Tesla Full Self-Driving investigation overview.* Retrieved from https://www.nhtsa.gov/technology-innovation/automated-vehicles-safety

- OECD. (2019). *OECD AI principles.* Retrieved from https://oecd.ai/en/ai-principles

- Richmond Advisory Group. (n.d.). *Company website.* Retrieved from https://richmondadvisory.com/

APPENDIX J REFERENCES

- Target Corporation. (2014). *Data breach summary report.* Retrieved from https://corporate.target.com/about/payment-card-issue

- Toyota Research Institute. (n.d.). *Robotics research: Diffusion policy robots.* Retrieved from https://www.tri.global/research/robotics

- University of Washington. (2024, October). *AI bias in hiring systems.* Retrieved from https://www.washington.edu/news/research/

- Wilson, K. (2024). *Emergent risks in agentic autonomy (arXiv:2412.12140v1).* Retrieved from https://arxiv.org/abs/2412.12140v1

- Amazon Web Services. (n.d.). *Amazon Bedrock.* Retrieved from https://aws.amazon.com/bedrock/

- Microsoft. (n.d.). *Azure Active Directory.* Retrieved from https://azure.microsoft.com/services/active-directory/

- FAIR Institute. (n.d.). *Factor Analysis of Information Risk (FAIR).* Retrieved from https://www.fairinstitute.org/

- International Organization for Standardization. (n.d.). *ISO/IEC 42001.* Retrieved from https://www.iso.org/

- MITRE Corporation. (n.d.). *MITRE ATLAS.* Retrieved from https://atlas.mitre.org/

- National Institute of Standards and Technology (NIST). (n.d.). *Cybersecurity Framework.* Retrieved from https://www.nist.gov/cyberframework

APPENDIX J   REFERENCES

- OneTrust. (n.d.). *Compliance Hub*. Retrieved from https://www.onetrust.com/

- Open Policy Agent. (n.d.). *Policy as Code*. Retrieved from https://www.openpolicyagent.org/

- Greenblatt, M., et al. (2024). Alignment Faking: Strategic Deception by Advanced AI Models. *arXiv preprint arXiv:2402.11342.*

- Palisade Research. (2025). *Behavioral Evasion in LLM-Based Agents: Emergent Risks of Autonomy.* Internal whitepaper, summarized in AI Risk Summit panel.

- Apollo Research & OpenAI. (2024). *Deceptive Alignment in Autonomous AI Models: Findings from the o1 Experiments.* [Whitepaper]. https://www.apolloresearch.ai/deception-study-o1

- Salesforce. (2024). *Agentforce Implementation Summary: Human Trust Recovery in Enterprise AI.* Salesforce Trust & AI Blog. https://www.salesforce.com/blog/agentforce-ai-trust

- Morgan Stanley. (2024). *Operational Oversight in LLM Assistants: Internal Risk Evaluation Practices.* Presentation at Financial Services AI Governance Roundtable. *(Add citation only if public or internal disclosure is authorized. Otherwise, footnote with: "Described in anonymized internal briefings. Not publicly published.")*

- FAIR Institute. (n.d.). *Factor Analysis of Information Risk (FAIR) Framework.* https://www.fairinstitute.org

APPENDIX J   REFERENCES

- MAST Taxonomy. (2025). *Model-Agent-System Taxonomy for Classifying Agentic Failure Modes.* Draft framework, referenced in academic forums and early enterprise pilots. *(Label as: "Emerging model under development; citation for conceptual framing.")*

- Galileo Framework. (2025). *Continuous Risk Monitoring in Multi-Agent Architectures.* Unpublished working model discussed at Global Autonomous Systems Symposium. *(Use footnote: "Conceptual framework cited for illustrative use.")*

- Block. (2024). *Goose – Internal generative AI agent using Anthropic Claude.* Internal enterprise deployment referenced in public domain talks and product documentation.

- Salesforce. (2024). *Agentforce Implementation Summary: Human Trust Recovery in Enterprise AI.* Salesforce Trust & AI Blog. https://www.salesforce.com/blog/agentforce-ai-trust

- Apollo Research & OpenAI. (2024). *Deceptive Alignment in Autonomous AI Models: Findings from the o1 and o3 Experiments.* https://www.apolloresearch.ai/deception-study-o1

- Significant Gravitas. (2023). *AutoGPT* [GitHub repository]. https://github.com/Torantulino/Auto-GPT

- Nakajima, Y. (2023). *BabyAGI* [GitHub repository]. https://github.com/yoheinakajima/babyagi

APPENDIX J REFERENCES

- BBC News. (2024, February). *DPD AI chatbot goes rogue, swears at customer.* https://www.bbc.com/news/technology-68204084

- Vincent, J. (2023, November 30). *Chevrolet dealership's AI chatbot agrees to sell SUV for $1.* The Verge. https://www.theverge.com/2023/11/30/chevy-chatbot-rogue-pricing

- Newman, L. H. (2024, March). *Microsoft 365 Copilot inadvertently exposes sensitive documents.* Wired. https://www.wired.com/story/microsoft-copilot-leak-enterprise/

- Bloomberg News. (2024, July). *CrowdStrike update causes worldwide Windows outage.* https://www.bloomberg.com/news/articles/2024-07-19/global-outage-linked-to-crowdstrike-update

- nthropic. (2025, June). *Emergent Misalignment in Claude Sonnet 3.6: Simulated Blackmail and Risk Behavior in LLM-Based Agents.* Retrieved from https://www.anthropic.com/news/claude-agentic-misalignment-study

- Bengio, Y. (2025, June). *Introducing LawZero: An Independent Nonprofit for Ensuring AI Alignment and Safety.* LawZero.org. Retrieved from https://www.lawzero.org/launch-announcement

- BeyondID. (2025, June). *Insider Threats in the Age of AI Agents: Credential Leakage and Non-Human Identity Risks.* BeyondID Security Research Brief. Retrieved from https://www.beyondid.com/insider-threats-ai-report-2025

APPENDIX J   REFERENCES

- European Union Agency for Cybersecurity (ENISA). (2025, June). *Synthetic Identity Threats and Biometric Evasion in AI-Driven Ecosystems.* ENISA Technical Report. Retrieved from https://www.enisa.europa.eu/publications/ai-biometrics-security-2025

- University of Oxford & Stanford HAI. (2025, March). *The Human–Machine Identity Blur: Rethinking Governance in the Age of Autonomous AI.* Oxford-Stanford AI Governance Initiative Whitepaper. Retrieved from https://hai.stanford.edu/research/human-machine-identity-blur

- CloudEagle. *The Insider Risk Report 2024: Why AI Will Make Over-Permissioning Worse.* CloudEagle.ai. Accessed June 2025. https://www.cloudeagle.ai/iga-report

- The Hacker News. (2025, June). Google Adds Multi-Layered Defenses to Secure GenAI from Prompt Injection Attacks. Retrieved from https://thehackernews.com/2025/06/google-adds-multi-layered-defenses-to.html

- Academic Research. (2025, June). Evaluating Prompt Injection Attacks on AI-driven Banking Systems. Retrieved from https://arxiv.org/abs/2506.01055

- Korbak, T., O'Brien, C., Reimann, T., Srivastava, S., and Blundell, C. (2024). *Chain-of-Thought Monitoring is a Fragile Opportunity.* Retrieved from https://tomekkorbak.com/cot-monitorability-is-a-fragile-opportunity/cot_monitoring.pdf

Index

A

ABAC, *see* Attribute-based rules (ABAC)
Accountability, 3, 185
Active Directory (AD), 12, 97
AD, *see* Active Directory (AD)
Agent autonomy
    accountability loops, 92
    authority, 89, 90
    control, 96
    delegation, 94
    delegation chains, 91
    horizontal/vertical/recursive delegation, 90, 91
    human audits, 100
    mitigation delegation risks, 99
    policy-based delegation controls, 100
    real-world AI agent, 98
    real-world risks, 93
    recursive delegation exponentially compounds, 97
    replication, 94–96
    visibility, 96, 97
Agentic failures
    accountability, 241
    case
        Air Canada chatbot, 234
        AutoGPT infinite loop problem, 235
        ChatGPT, 233, 234
        error accumulation, 237
        failure, 240
        Grok algorithmic hate speech, 239
        package names/slopsquatting, 236, 237
        prompt injection, 238
    identity governance, 240
AI agent
    automation, 34
    continuous activity, 69
    dynamic and unpredictable, 68
    elements, 11, 12
    executing tasks, 4
    feedback loop, 10
    governance, 10
    governance implications, 52
    governance models, 52
    human identities/machine accounts, 9
    IAM/IGA failure, 63, 64
    IAM vendors, 64
    identities types, 5, 54, 55, 57–62

INDEX

AI agent (*cont.*)
  identity workflow, 5–9
  IGA vendors, 65
  intelligent machine
    identities, 52, 53
  LLMs, 68
  modifying systems, 9
  ownership/auditing, 69
  PAM vendors, 66
  RAISE framework, 70
  self-modifying code, 4
  transparency and
    explainability, 69
  vendor ecosystem, 67
AI-driven applications, 121
AI-driven automation, 34
AI identities
  lifecycle
    cementing lifecycle, 295
    characteristics, 292
    delegation, 293
    examples, 291, 295
    expire, 294
    observability, 293
    provision, 292
    reevaluation, 294
AI identity governance
  actionable dashboards/
    reporting, 87
  agent-driven credential, 85, 86
  continuous visibility, 79
  credential risk, 83, 84
  detect and flag policy
    violations, 82, 83
  ethical context layer, 86
  identity center, 80
  identity center operational
    requirements, 81, 82
  PAM solutions, 85
  real-world example, 84
  workflow/remediation
    integration, 87
America's AI Action Plan, 201
Anthropic's Claude, 68
Attribute-based rules (ABAC), 55
AutoGPT, 235
Automation technology
  AI agents, 31–33
  AI-driven automation, 29, 30
  identity security, 33
  traditional, 28, 29

B

Black-box agents, 146
Black-box AI systems, 147

C

Central identity system, 76
Chain-of-Thought (CoT), 150
ChatGPT, 236
Cloud providers, 193
Cloud services, 15
CMDB, *see* Configuration
    Management
    Database (CMDB)
Cognitive instability
  design principles, 247

governance, 248
identity environments, 246
issues, 244
limitations, 243
RAISE framework, 247
security risks, 245, 246
Configuration Management Database (CMDB), 80
CoT, *see* Chain-of-Thought (CoT)
Credential hygiene, 1
Critical infrastructure
autonomous actors, 283
financial sector, 285
governance failures, 287
healthcare, 284
national security, 286
risks, 284
tiered approach, 287, 288
utilities, 286
visibility and discovery, 288, 289
CyberArk, 193

D

Data loss prevention (DLP) system, 156
Data Protection Impact Assessments (DPIAs), 269
Data sanitization, 266
Decoupled identity verification, 264
Developer-driven model, 121
Differential privacy (DP), 266
Diffusion policy, 57

Disaster recovery (DR), 277, 278
Discovery
accountability/liability, 122
account-centric, 122
classification, 129
identity hygiene, 119
inventory, 130
liability, 123
metadata collection, 131
multi-faceted approach, 132
real-world example, 130
regulatory shifts, 126
reveal, 120
SaaS/shadow environments, 128, 129
shared risk, 124
SPHEREboard, 131
structure governance, 127, 128
user ownership, 129
vendor contract, 124, 125
DLP, *see* Data loss prevention (DLP) system
DP, *see* Differential privacy (DP)
DPIAs, *see* Data Protection Impact Assessments (DPIAs)
DR, *see* Disaster recovery (DR)
Dual-model approach, 157

E

EDR, *see* Endpoint detection and response (EDR)
Endpoint detection and response (EDR), 4

INDEX

ENISA, *see* European Union Agency for Cybersecurity (ENISA)
Enterprise and societal AI governance
    challenges, 250
    deskilling, 251
    ethical governance, 254
    ethical oversight, 255, 260
    governance challenges, 258, 259
    high-stakes functions, 249
    human agency, 251–254
    operationalize ethical framework, 257
    practical implementation, 258
    review committees, 256
    risk management, 257, 258
European Union Agency for Cybersecurity (ENISA), 264
Event-driven monitoring, 156
Explainable AI (XAI), 149

F

Forensics
    data collection, 278, 279, 281
    data management, 280
    incident response, 277, 278
    structured implementation checklist, 281
Futureproofing AI identity governance
    adaptive governance, 312
    adaptive risk framework, 309
    building skills, 308
    documentation and infrastructure, 311
    phased implementation roadmap, 311
    proactive adaptation, 312
    reactive controls/one-time audits, 305
    resilience emerging technologies, 306, 307
    stress-testing, 310

G

Gemini, 174
GitHub Copilot, 236
Governance, 261
    AI agents, 74
    behavioral monitoring/risk scoring, 75
    central identity system, 76
    CISCO
        build foundation, 299, 300
        cross-functional identity, 297
        governance, 302
        IAM, 298
        measure/report/evolve, 301
        scale controls/accountability, 300
        stabilization, 299
        success factors, 302
    collaborative AI agent systems, 76, 78

non-human identities, 73
ownership/lifecycle
management, 74, 75

H

HashiCorp Vault, 193
HE, *see* Homomorphic
Encryption (HE)
Homomorphic Encryption (HE), 268
Human-AI collaboration
designing, 320, 321
dynamic thinking, 323
enterprise, 319
ideal relationship, 322
ownership, 321, 325
partners, 324
Human-Centered AI, 54
Human identities, 51

I

IAM, *see* Identity and access
management (IAM)
Identity and access management
(IAM), 5, 55, 73, 79
AI-aware identity architect, 315
cross-functional leaders, 317
designing identity, 316, 317
responsibilities, 314, 315
risk owner, 317, 318
skills, 313
Identity Defined Security Alliance
(IDSA), 45

Identity governance and
administration (IGA), 5, 18,
55, 73, 79
Identity hygiene
accountability, 35
AI amplifies, 39
components, 36, 37
good hygiene practices, 35
intelligent discovery, 37, 38
Identity providers (IdPs), 194
Identity security, 41
AI discovery, 175
AI identities, 170, 171
autonomous agents, 183
compliance and risk
metrics, 179
human identities, 16
human ownership/control
non-negotiable, 173
hygiene, 173
implementation
recommendations, 182
lifecycle, 18, 19
common identity
risks, 20–22
machine identity, 23–25
security controls, 19
machine identities, 17
measurement and
enforcement, 178
operational performance
metrics, 180
program design, 176–178

Identity security (*cont.*)
    program maturity metrics, 181, 184
    real-world examples, 174
    resilience, 169
    risks and failure modes, 172
    user/entity behavior metrics, 180, 181
IdPs, *see* Identity providers (IdPs)
IDSA, *see* Identity Defined Security Alliance (IDSA)
IGA, *see* Identity governance and administration (IGA)
Incident response
    AI identities, 271
    early detection challenges, 272
    frameworks, 275
    insider threats, 273
    multi-agent failure, 274
    multi-agent failures, 276
    Rogue AI, 274
    workflow, 273
Infrastructure as Code (IaC) pipelines, 31
Insider and malicious threats
    compromise without detection, 229
    external threats, 229
    RAISE framework, 230–232
    real security implications, 227
    risks, 231
    threat actor, 228
Intelligent Discovery, 37, 40
Interpret

AI agent reputation, 154, 155
continuous monitoring *vs.* periodic reviews, 156, 157
explainability, 149, 150, 152, 153, 158, 159
real-world examples, 161–166
transparency, 153, 154
trust, 145, 146, 148, 158–161

J, K

JIT, *see* Just-in-Time (JIT) access
Joiner-mover-leaver, 18
Just-in-time (JIT) access, 64, 114, 193

L

Large language models (LLMs), 52, 68
LIME, *see* Local Interpretable Model-agnostic Explanations (LIME)
LLMs, *see* Large language models (LLMs)
Local Interpretable Model-agnostic Explanations (LIME), 149

M

Machine identities, 51
Machine learning (ML), 68
Machine-learning-driven systems, 27

MCPs, *see* Model Context Protocols (MCPs)
MFA, *see* Multi-factor authentication (MFA)
Microsoft Copilot, 124, 210
Microsoft Entra, 194
Microsoft's Counterfit, 310
ML, *see* Machine learning (ML)
Model Context Protocols (MCPs), 61, 66
Multi-factor authentication (MFA), 264

N

National Institute of Standards and Technology (NIST), 203
Neural networks, 68
NIST, *see* National Institute of Standards and Technology (NIST)

O

Okta, 194
OpenAI's GPT models, 68
Operational agents, 5
Ownership, 303
    account-based control, 143
    account classification, 141
    Active Directory, 139
    AI agents, 137, 138
    AI identities, 48, 49
    assign, 136

automated identity, 140
automation/maintenance, 47, 48
CMDB, 136
convenience, 142
direct human interaction, 135
human and identity tool, 44
identity hygiene, 46
multi-factor authentication, 47
risks, 45
security control, 43, 49
spreadsheets and email chains, 140

P, Q

PAM, *see* Privileged access management (PAM)
Personal Information Protection Law (PIPL), 204
PIPL, *see* Personal Information Protection Law (PIPL)
Privileged Access Management (PAM), 18, 55, 79, 193
Proactive compliance strategies, 216

R

RAISE framework, 103
    assign, 112
    assign ownership, 108
    CISOs, 116
    evaluate lifecycle risk, 109, 115

INDEX

RAISE framework (*cont.*)
   evaluation
      creation, 190
      decommissioning, 192
      deployment/operation, 191, 192
      governance, 194
      identity lifecycle, 185, 187
      machine identities, 187–190
      practical tools, 193
   goal, 117
   governance models, 105, 106
   integrate behavior, 108, 109
   interpret, 113
   reveal, 107, 108, 111
   security, 109, 114
   workflow, 107
RBAC, *see* Role-based access control (RBAC)
Regulatory and compliance frameworks
   advanced governance solutions, 206
   AI agent liability, 210
   AI governance operating model, 214, 215
   America's AI Action Plan, 201–203
   autonomous agents, 209
   autonomy governance, 199
   centralized governance solutions, 216
   CISOs/security teams, 215
   compliance strategies, 217
   contractual clause, 212
   contractual provisions, 211
   emerging laws, 213
   enterprise *vs.* vendor accountability, 210, 211
   Europe's GDPR/ EU AI Act, 200
   global regulatory matrix, 209
   implementation approach, 207
   operational complexities, 204
   practical global compliance, 205, 206
   privacy regulations, 200
   proactive compliance management, 208
   procedural rigor, 207
Regulatory frameworks, 197
Robotic process automation (RPA), 28
Role-based access control (RBAC), 264
RPA, *see* Robotic process automation (RPA)

S

Security controls and countermeasures
   administration and governance controls, 268–270
   AI models/data integrity, 265
   API and tool security, 267
   authentication/authorization, 263, 264

INDEX

encryption and key management, 267, 268
guardrails/privilege escalation, 265
Security information and event management (SIEM) systems, 3
SHAP, *see* SHapley Additive exPlanations (SHAP)
SHapley Additive exPlanations (SHAP), 149
SIEM, *see* Security information and event management (SIEM) systems
Slopsquatting, 236
Spreadsheet-driven ownership models, 172

T

Tesla's Full Self-Driving system, 148
Third-party risk assessment
    access requests, 221
    complexity, 226
    contractual/governance safeguards, 223, 224
    customer communication, 221
    enterprise software vendors, 219
    product enhancement, 224, 225
    security control, 225
    transparency, 220
    vendor due diligence, 222, 223

U, V, W

UEBA, *see* User and Entity Behavior Analytics (UEBA)
User and Entity Behavior Analytics (UEBA), 66

X, Y

XAI, *see* Explainable AI (XAI)

Z

Zero-trust architecture, 270

GPSR Compliance

The European Union's (EU) General Product Safety Regulation (GPSR) is a set of rules that requires consumer products to be safe and our obligations to ensure this.

If you have any concerns about our products, you can contact us on

ProductSafety@springernature.com

In case Publisher is established outside the EU, the EU authorized representative is:

Springer Nature Customer Service Center GmbH
Europaplatz 3
69115 Heidelberg, Germany